W9-BLK-981

HARD
LESSONS

HARD LESSONS

Senior Year at
Beverly Hills High School

MICHAEL LEAHY

Little, Brown and Company

BOSTON · TORONTO

First Edition

An excerpt originally appeared
in *Playboy* magazine.

Library of Congress Cataloging-in-Publication Data

Leahy, Michael, 1953–
    Hard lessons: senior year at Beverly Hills High School /
Michael Leahy. — 1st ed.
        p.   cm.
    ISBN 0-316-51815-8
    1. Beverly Hills High School (Beverly Hills, Calif.) — Students —
Biography.   2. High school seniors — California — Beverly Hills —
Biography.   I. Title.
LD7501.B5433L4 1988
378'.198'0979493 — dc19   88-71
                                                             CIP

10 9 8 7 6 5 4 3 2 1

RRD-VA

*Published simultaneously in Canada
by Little, Brown & Company (Canada) Limited*

PRINTED IN THE UNITED STATES OF AMERICA

For Jane Elizabeth

ACKNOWLEDGMENTS

Years before books are even the seeds of ideas, in those fallow days when a young writer lives mostly on his dreams because he has little else, there are those whose friendship, counsel, good humor, and inspiration enable him to persevere and move ahead, to remember what it was that made him want to plant the seeds in the first place. My thanks, in that regard, to Eddie Sierra, Bruce, Marcia, and Norman Burnam, Barbara and Gordon Hughes, Steve Gelman, and Dr. Russell P. Sherwin.

Most of all, my love and appreciation to Jane Elizabeth Leahy, who tirelessly scrutinized this manuscript and whose editorial efforts and keen insights throughout the two and a half years it took to research and write this book, cannot ever be adequately detailed.

Finally, a word about those students of Beverly Hills High School who gave so generously of their time so that I might understand the reality of their lives. Rarely have people of any age been confronted with such a daunting task of self-analysis. I cannot thank them enough. They were good and faithful correspondents, and even better companions. I wish them well.

Michael Leahy
Santa Monica, California

HARD LESSONS

INTRODUCTION

In the summer of 1984, I began inquiring about Beverly Hills High School, a place where the graduation rate was nearly 100 percent and the honor roll high and something was quite wrong. Within the previous year, three of the high school's students had committed suicide, and afterward I heard so many stories of excruciating academic pressure, cocaine abuse, and drifting children that I came to believe there was some news I was not getting from the local metropolitan dailies. Ultimately I decided to write a book about a year in the lives of six Beverly seniors, to follow them from the moment that they stepped onto the school's lush lawn, in September, until they departed as graduates, in June.

There are necessarily, in stories such as this one, the raw statistics and other undigested data of a city and its institutions to be understood. I kept looking for a revelatory point in these numbers, some clue to what was happening on the underside of Beverly Hills High School: student body: 2,452; 83.8 percent white; 6.2 percent Asian; 6 percent black; 3 percent Hispanic. Roughly 13 percent of the whites are classified as Persian. In recent years, a steady influx of wealthy expatriate Iranians into the city has altered the makeup of the student body until one in every eight students now speaks Farsi, which is second only to English as the most commonly spoken language at Beverly. An estimated 70 to 75 percent of the students are Jewish, a fact somewhat obscured by old TV series and other pieces of American pop mythology that would have outsiders believing the mostly blond Protestant offspring of actors roamed the campus. A small percentage of the student body has parents in the entertainment industry, but, as has been the case for the last half century, a substantially larger contingent of Beverly students comes from the homes of attorneys, doctors, bankers, financiers, and business executives. Over the years, parental scrutiny of school operations has remained consistently intense.

It is difficult to imagine a public high school boasting of a more impressive academic record. In the 1983–1984 school year, slightly more than 20 percent of the students received a grade point average of 3.6 or higher, on a scale where 4.0 represents straight A's and 3.0 straight B's. Of the 586 graduates from the senior class, 90 percent went on to college, 35 percent to some branch of the prestigious University of California system, while, among the most illustrious achievers, four students went to Harvard, two to Yale, one to Princeton, four each to Brown and Stanford, three to M.I.T., and one to Cal Tech. The latest mean SAT score of Beverly Hills seniors — 982 on a 1600 point scale — runs 76 points higher than the national mean and 138 points above that of Los Angeles public high schools. While the annual per capita expenditure for American pupils is $3,449 nationally (Los Angeles can afford but a paltry $2,554), Beverly Hills spends a whopping $5,505 per student. Students' scores on tests given by California education officials routinely place Beverly in the top 1 percent, statewide, with its graduation rate of more than 98 percent dwarfing Los Angeles' (58 percent) and the national average (70.6 percent).

Everything about Beverly Hills High School encourages its young inhabitants to believe that theirs is a world without limits. All the departments, from the sciences to the humanities, offer numerous Advanced Placement courses for accelerated learning and college credit. There are computer classes equipped with state-of-the-art technology and instruction, and professional internships available for students in areas ranging from business and public relations firms to hospitals and suicide hotlines. Organized programs, in fashion merchandising and accounting, rival those offered by small colleges. The school's media department, arguably its most glamorous and envied, offers classes fielding two teams of reporters and on-air anchorpersons for a regular thirty-minute cable news show that reaches more than twenty-five thousand cable television subscribers. Limited enrollment means a student must audition in order to have a chance at winning one of the fifteen or so broadcasting slots. Sixteen-year-olds somberly discuss what will happen to their "careers" if they don't make it. The schedule of programs for the school year of 1985–1986 included "How Hollywood Works," a discussion, hosted by a student moderator, with film and television producers, writers, and actors discussing the realities of their business; "Face to Face," an interview program with political and social leaders answering a student reporter's queries; "Careers," a largely informational program designed to satisfy the many questions of Beverly students about professional and entrepreneurial opportunities; and "After Prime Time," a series of comedic skits by students about life at Beverly. Every year the high school's radio station, KBEV, fields disc jockeys to play rock and roll on their own shows, each weekday afternoon during the school year from 3:30 to 6:30 P.M. Nothing is denied the ambitious and talented. "Sometimes the place feels like a little college," one of the students says. "The competition is *unreal*. But, if you can make it here, you can take nearly any class you'd ever want. There are bucks here. It's not like there's a gold mine around — I mean, you even see the binding cracking on some old books — but, still, the school always finds a way to get the big bucks. You're never *without anything*, you know?"

In that respect, the school resembles those of many in highly affluent communities of the United States, dynamic institutions designed as spawning grounds for success, made golden by the good fortunes of the local citizenry. Beverly Hills bears striking similarities to big-city suburbs such as Grosse Pointe, Michigan, and Glencoe, Illinois, both of which possess renowned area high schools with national reputations for excellence; the lesson being that no great school can exist in the absence of generous public or philanthropic outlays. Without its city's advantages, Beverly would be a considerably different place, with strikingly fewer resources. Educational funds come, in part, from a lucrative property tax base, but these funds must be shared, according to state law, with poorer school districts in the area. Over the years, revenues have been supplemented by earnings from seventeen oil wells that stand on the high school's property and which the Beverly Hills School District leases to an oil company in exchange for royalties based on the company's profits. In the 1970s, when petroleum prices skyrocketed, the school district's annual earnings exceeded $1.5 million, helping Beverly Hills to pay its highly regarded faculty some of the most handsome teacher salaries in the country. But, in 1986, with the oil market slumping, the school's royalties dropped to $300,000 for the year, and mild concern arose. In the summer of 1987, the Beverly Hills Board of Education, searching for new sources of revenue, struck what may ultimately prove to be a lucrative deal with Twentieth Century Fox Film Corporation, which reportedly has considered plans to license out a new Beverly Hills High School logo — a hot-pink palm tree with books for leaves — to manufacturers of clothing, cosmetics, and notebooks. A joint announcement added that a television series based on life at the high school may be developed. The hunt for revenue seldom slows, with significant contributions coming from a wide variety of sources in the community. One week children arrive at their elementary school bearing the California state tax-rebate checks of their parents, who have signed the checks over to the school.

"This school system always knows how to tap the dough," says a Beverly teacher. "You exist in Beverly Hills, around Hollywood and all the other big hitters — well, you learn how to play the financial game, too. You learn where the money is, and how to go about getting it. There's a lot around. Parent groups and private educational associations provide some, too. The bottom line remains, we're never hurting."

Yet Beverly Hills is not Kuwait, not a land of limitless riches and profligacy, and, like other affluent American suburbs, must regularly refute the notion that it is a paradise of sybaritic millionaires. According to a revised 1980 census, only 28.8 percent of Beverly Hills households had an annual income of more than $50,000, with median family income standing at $40,300. Professionals made up only about a quarter of the city's population. Of Beverly Hills' 32,646 residents, 94.18 percent were white, 4.6 percent Hispanic, 2.76 percent Asian, and 1.29 percent black. High-profile political activists, especially those from the motion picture community, may leave the impression of a community more liberal and Democratic than the rest of affluent America, but, in 1980, Beverly Hills supported Ronald Reagan over Jimmy Carter along with nearly everyone else. "This is a place that doesn't want to see their boat rocked, just like most other places," says the teacher. "They have this fierce determination to have control over their lives. They don't want any nasty surprises. They want to make sure that they're going to stay financially comfortable and socially acceptable, and that their kids are going to sail along, just as they have. They don't want any social problems — drugs, sexual complications, you name it — interfering with their kids' drive for success. If they think something is getting in the way, they'll try to cut it out or be all over somebody. That is, if they know about it."

For teenagers, Beverly Hills is no more a den of hedonism than any other major American city. Social attitudes and mores appear to be nearly identical to those found in the middle-class high schools of the Los Angeles Basin and the San Fernando Valley — the evidence of drug and alcohol use no more or less high, the discussion of sex and birth control equally as obsessive. If Beverly has had its share of troubling teenage problems, so, too, have less privileged American communities like Omaha, Nebraska, and Bergenfield, New Jersey, been forced to confront the social traumas of teenage suicides, drug addiction, and ennui. If there is any meaningful difference between high school students in a community such as Beverly Hills and teenagers from predominantly middle-class or blue-collar areas, it may be that wealth simply affords the Beverly teenager greater access to what other teens cannot readily obtain — cars, clothes, tutors, credit cards, alcohol, drugs, and resources for dating and partying. This does not suggest that all Beverly students come from upper-income families, a point that the census data make clear. The locations and demographics of the four grammar schools in the Beverly Hills School District through which students are eventually funneled into the high school — El Rodeo, Hawthorne, Beverly Vista, and Horace Mann — reflect the contrasting economic strata of the city. Included among the parents of Beverly students are a barber, gardener, and store clerk. "But most kids have families with quite a bit of money," says a girl whose father sells hardware. "You can *feel* it. It's like in how their hair looks, or their jewelry. There's pressure. Because you want to be noticed. That's natural. You want to be up there with the hottest people."

The progeny of the divergent groups come together at fourteen or fifteen as high school freshmen, all equals in the pursuit of success, or so the story goes. We tend to see teenagers like the seniors at Beverly Hills High School nearly always in this rosy egalitarian context, to believe that, irrespective of their families' incomes, stability, or emotional histories, the students are similarly gilded inhabitants of the same privileged school class. Indeed, we generally view students from largely middle-income area high schools in the same manner, proclaiming them the beneficiaries of America's limitless opportunities and promise, when the opportunities, in fact, may have dimmed and the promise replaced by a grim competitive struggle among the young to gain footholds for survival. It has always been the curse of youth to be labeled as privileged and indulged by their elders, of course; but what was once merely a difference in generational values now has become a disturbing blindness to the reality of teenage lives.

Revealingly, few Beverly students feel comfortable discussing their families' monetary or social positions, viewing such things as ephemeral. Talk of money and homes is perceived as tacky, a taboo. On the other hand, a wardrobe sufficiently attuned to the season's trendiest styles and a late model imported automobile appear to go a long way toward imbuing their owner with a stylish reputation. The wealthy and upper-class students seem keenly aware of their vast affluence, knowing a few middle-class kids well enough to realize that their own material status is unique, enviable, the product of their parents' brains, effort, and, in some cases, luck. Some admit to seeing their life's great task as simply holding on. They have come to embody the flip side of the classic American vision — teenagers aware that an economic climb may not be in the cards for them, that they may be the first in their families to feel the slide of downward mobility. A troublingly large segment wonders whether they have the ability to achieve the immense success necessary to remain in Beverly Hills, most openly fearing a life without great advantages or opulence. Professional ambitions, therefore, generally tend to be higher among the young here.

With such urgent goals and expectations comes heightened academic pressure. Some seniors worry that they might not possess the hunger to make it, that growing up, say, with a housekeeper, large allowance, personal automobile, and tutor has left them a little soft, placed them at a disadvantage against those middle- and lower-class denizens, in patched jeans, who next year doubtlessly will be studying twelve hours a day, in college libraries, to beat them. A few seniors have already resigned themselves to futures of scaled-down existences, far outside Beverly Hills and the rest of upper-income West Los Angeles. A certain anomie has settled over them. "If it's going to happen when I get older — like not being able to live here and having to live like some geek in the Valley — then it's going to happen," says one girl. "Meantime, I'm going to party all I can. I'm going to go wild while I have something to do it with. Party, party, party. Then the world can collapse."

In the summer of 1984, these sentiments numbed me with the kind of profound disillusionment that strikes only when one's fundamental assumptions about life have been thrown into serious question. I realized that, behind the high school's gates, lurked a subculture I no longer knew anything about. My own sheltered and staid high school career, a generally tolerable, breezy, and productive exercise in making the climb that ended with my graduation in 1971, could scarcely have been less instructive or relevant. There were no dance clubs open to teenagers on weekends then, in Los Angeles' San Fernando Valley, where I lived. Most students considered drugs, aside from marijuana, to be dangerous, and resisted temptation in favor of six-packs. I cannot recall ever hearing of cocaine. A big Friday night would consist of a football game, followed by a ritual convoy ride to Shakey's Pizza for a large pepperoni and root beers. If all had gone well to that point, a couple might then have driven into the surrounding hills to stare at smog-covered skies, in search of passion. It was, on the whole, notwithstanding the Vietnam war and the social cataclysms of the era, a relatively innocent time. Most of us knew how to enjoy the moment. *The moment* meant everything then; we were not much for looking ahead. We were allowed to be kids for a long while.

But that was another era, long gone, never to return, I have realized, listening to the voices of Beverly reveal the present. "They just do the best they can to make it here," said a teacher during the summer of 1985. "They are good kids. They are just facing things a high school kid of the early 'seventies and before that knew nothing about. Plus, the standards are different at Beverly today. The admired kid here is not necessarily the good-looking athlete. The possibility of success in the future is important to someone's overall attractiveness. Kids are already planning their law practices or where they might set up their businesses. Sometimes you can't see their problems through that act of maturity they put on for you. If they're not well adjusted, then that illusion can be a real problem, because some of them are facing pressures that they don't know how to cope with. Your whole worth here, in these kids' eyes, is determined by how well you're doing academically and socially. A C is a horrible grade to them, a failing grade. Sometimes a B is, too. There's been a lot of cheating. The anxiety is only growing worse."

By then, I had committed myself to the writing of this book, to presenting a narrative of events in the 1985–1986 school year, with a minimum of commentary, so as to afford readers the opportunity to arrive at their own insights and judgments about the quality of students' lives, to formulate their own solutions to the myriad of problems that must ultimately be addressed. I am personally wary of offering social prescriptions. I am a writer, not a psychologist or sociologist, and perhaps the most meaningful observation I can offer, as the reader begins this book, is the simple admonition that we seem to be confusing personal perceptions, culled from the briefest of glimpses of teenagers, with the not so visible truth. It did not take long during my conversations with Beverly students before I understood that their world was nothing like the one I had imagined from casually observing teenage behavior in malls and at rock concerts. After that initial shock, the task became to listen to students long and carefully enough until I adequately understood the panorama of life at Beverly.

It would take an entire year. I talked to more than eighty Beverly students during the course of my research. In the beginning, I had anticipated tracking the lives of a small group of Beverly seniors, merely giving them pseudonyms while dissecting their individual existences, without otherwise disguising their appearances, pursuits, conversations, or private thoughts. It soon became apparent that even with pseudonyms, however, a student's anonymity might be compromised in a relatively small Beverly senior class (just over six hundred students) where the mere disclosure of a small physical or sartorial detail about a person (a particularly aberrant hairstyle, say, or a rock cult T-shirt) would possibly leave him identifiable to scores of his classmates. Also troublesome was the possible discomfort and embarrassment families might suffer from reading a candid account of their teenagers' activities and feelings. I decided at that point to construct some of the student lives with composites. During my research, I spoke at varying lengths with teachers, administrators, and counselors at the high school, as well as with a highly regarded private tutor in the area. I relied principally, however, upon firsthand information gathered from the lives of twenty-five or so Beverly seniors with whom I conducted long interviews that probed the intimate details of their own lives and those of their friends, covering such areas as daily routines, academic pressure, professional ambitions, family relationships, sexual activity, and alcohol and drug use. An initial interview generally spanned two to three hours, followed by subsequent contacts that included additional in-person interviews, telephone updates, and brief meetings after school hours at the school's athletic field or other areas open to the general public. Before settling upon any "type" of character, "fact," or "feeling," I would seek a thematic corroboration from a number of interviewees. Each of the composites, therefore, is based upon the lives and thoughts of many Beverly seniors, generally more than a half-dozen students. For example, the life of a lonely girl resentful, among other reasons, over the constant attention that a friend receives from boys might be fused with the lives of other girls whose particular anxieties differ but who feel similarly isolated and neglected; who may be suffering, say, from parental indifference or the scorn of peers. One girl may seek to alleviate her problem by listening to music for hours through headphones. Another may ingest hallucinogens. A third may drive for hours on a freeway. The fusion of such different personalities represents a composite.

Everything in this book, whether disguised in nonessential details or not, derives from the real-life experiences of Beverly students. Dialogue and private thoughts of the characters were reconstructed from interviewees' statements relating to how they felt about the things happening to them, as well as conversations they had with classmates, parents, siblings, relatives, boyfriends and girlfriends, teachers, and school officials. Since the credibility of interviewees was critical, I would regularly compare their versions or interpretations of events at the high school against those of other sources. With few exceptions, their accounts proved to be amazingly free of embellishments or biases. They became trusted and reliable sources, the result, I believe, of their excitement over the book and their regard for interviews that they viewed as pleasurably cathartic experiences. They had few, if any, axes to grind, realizing that, in any event, I would be shrouding such things as identities, places, and dates. If their feelings, opinions, and behavior were subject to occasional inconsistencies, these were usually the result of emotional changes, paradoxical and inconsistent behavior hardly being unusual for teenagers, or any of the rest of us. In the end, their recollections were to capture the thematic accuracy and spirit of Beverly students' conversations, as well as their temperaments, styles, and characters. What finally emerges is a faithful effort to illuminate the truth while protecting the privacy of the teenagers who provided it.

Truth of course is the most important — and elusive — thing. For the rest of this book you will be following the existences of six students throughout their senior year. I do not pretend that they constitute the entire spectrum of interests, abilities, accomplishments, philosophies, and vices, for I could not begin to tell you exactly what the spectrum looks like; and, besides, I have tried hard not to pigeonhole any of the students I met. I saw C and D students as well as those on honor rolls, loners as well as social butterflies, but I am not writing the definitive study of Beverly's 2,452 students or thirty million American teenagers, simply observing lives which sometimes have receded for me, just as they have for their parents, friends, and teachers; six disparate existences, each with a unique set of idiosyncrasies and anxieties, that nonetheless may convey some sense of what it is like to grow up as an American teenager in the last half of the 1980s.

SUMMER'S END

Summer has come to an end. The calendar next to his Apple computer poster says summer actually lasts for a few more days, but Steven knows better. Summer is fucking dead. He's realized it since early this afternoon, when he walked into a drugstore on Cañon Drive in search of a candy bar, only to hear a shrill, unseen voice over on the next aisle moaning, "AP calculus is going to be a bitch." Pleasantly tired after a morning of surfing, he suddenly felt a jolt of adrenaline run through him. Frozen in his tracks, as if stunned by an electric cattle prod, he momentarily experienced a heightened awareness of all the store's sights and sounds, could hear the unseen voice mumbling, "You *know* that if you get a B in the class, it screws you at Cal Tech and the *big* schools." A salesclerk, standing against the Back-to-School Specials rack, yelled at him because he had entered the store in bare feet. "Shoes on, *please*, or you'll have to leave immediately," she huffed. He raised his hands like a captured criminal. He spread his legs just as the jive-ass pimps and drug dealers did on "Hill Street Blues" before they got frisked. He stood there, grinning wanly, in his still-damp OP swim trunks and the Coors T-shirt that smelled of sweat and salt water, and he did not move. The cold linoleum floor beneath his burned feet felt good. His soles had blistered in places from standing too long on scorching sand, and the linoleum was the first relief that he had felt all day. He had a touch of sunburn, too, on a part of his shoulder that had long been resistant to tanning and upon which he never quite put enough sunscreen. His stomach suddenly felt funny; he had eaten three stale bologna sandwiches that his housekeeper packed for him, along with some greasy potato chips. Still, even with this clerk barking, he could not complain: He had met a girl at the beach, and he had been in the water for five hours, during which the sun had made even blonder the streaks in his otherwise light brown hair and darkened the tan on his chest and legs. He had never looked better. It had been, all things considered, an excellent day, until the faceless voice on the next aisle had mentioned calculus. His stomach muscles tightened then, and he sensed that the stale bologna had nothing to do with his queasiness. The old tension had simply returned; school had unofficially arrived.

The clerk was still glowering. He slipped on some deck shoes he had been carrying and, head down, hurried toward the candy section for his Hershey bar with nuts. A squeaky voice shouted his name. He turned around to see a stumpy, bespectacled kid standing against the Back-to-School rack waving at him. Just seeing that earnest little face made him think of all those nerds getting ready to study six hours a night to beat him. He rushed home, took his surfboard off the racks of his car roof for the first time all summer, placed it against the garage wall, bounded upstairs, and sat limply on his bed.

Pressure did that to him, he thinks now, lying down, closing his eyes. During finals in his junior year, the tension left him so wracked by fatigue that, at five P.M., he would need to take a short nap. Deep-breathing exercises had been prescribed by his good friend, Laura, to help relax him. He hasn't seen her for a week. Where is she now when he needs her? Probably getting laid by what's his name . . . Adrian, Abel? Sometimes his own annoyance leaves him wondering: Is he jealous? No, no, she can have sex with whomever she's hot on, but you'd think she'd want to return his calls, see how her good friend is doing. God, he hates the way his pulse pounds at the base of his throat. It has all happened in the last two hours. C'mon, don't let it get the best of you, he tells himself. *Psych up, psych up.* What classes can he take this semester without jeopardizing his class standing? *No, no: wrong approach. Think aggressively.* The kids who burrowed themselves in their books, like that study-until-you-drop geek in the drugstore, beat you out of the best colleges otherwise, with all of their Honors and Advanced Placement courses. He tells himself he has to start awakening earlier to condition his brain to school's 7:30 A.M. start. No more watching his tapes of "Wheel of Fortune" and Vanna White. He'll need to resume his lucky school routine, abide by his superstitions: Only when finished reading the *L.A. Times* does he allow himself to step into the shower. Only after shampooing and blow-drying his hair will he turn on his stereo. Only after putting on his Talking Heads tape will he, in sequence, rub on his underarm deodorant, brush his teeth, dab a few drops of cologne on his face, neck, and chest, and apply a little Clearasil to a chronic spot of acne, like a small brush burn, that lies on the underside of his jaw. His shirt goes on after his pants, socks, and shoes, and when he drives to school it is always the same way — south down Rodeo Drive, past Sunset Boulevard, past Santa Monica Boulevard, past Van Cleef & Arpels, where his mom buys her jewelry, past Giorgio's, where, fifteen years ago, their old and departed housekeeper would hold his hand and pull up his drooping toddler's shorts while his mom put berets on him just so the salesgirls would coo.

From his Volkswagen Rabbit, he can look at nearly any store in Beverly Hills and tell a visitor about its status: which shops, according to his mom, are "musts." The Bistro is a "must" for its capellini, and Gucci an "ultra-must" for luggage and handbags. Marvin Mitchelson is the "must" divorce and palimony attorney; Michael Ovitz the "must" agent; and some former beautician named Susie the "must" astrologer. There is the "must" doctor for men at the start of a new marriage, in sudden need of reversing their vasectomies, and the exercise man for overweight and recently divorced women unwilling to leave the sanctuaries of their manors. There is the plastic surgeon who will come anywhere for a secret consultation, and the hairpiece man who keeps his prestigious and confidential client list in a small vault, and the skin specialist who will, after administering a rubdown and mudpack, proceed to close oversized pores. Steven has culled much of the information from his parents' gossip and the many shop and department store catalogs they leave strewn upon the big-screen TV in the den, perusing the advertisements as he imagines an anthropologist studying the hieroglyphics of an ancient hedonistic culture might, looking in wide-eyed disbelief for any depraved excesses that might illuminate the sybarites for him. He has a wry enough sense of himself and his own contradictions to confess to people that he has his own set of "must" places and specialists — shops like MGA, Camp Beverly Hills, Saks, and Benetton; The Grill when he wants a good steak; Carney's on the Sunset Strip for hamburgers and shakes; the martial-arts instructor in Brentwood when he wants a karate lesson; and Max the Chiropractor when the leg he hurt in a minor automobile accident begins to throb again.

Come to think of it, the leg has not hurt for a long time; the rehabilitation must be virtually complete. He thinks less these days about his health than about his appearance — clothes, hair, skin, weight, teeth — all these body parts merging into one package for him, which should be flawless if he wants to continue his ascent among the popular partying studs who count most. He reaches for the long-handled lacquered pink mirror on the night table alongside his bed, a gift given as a joke on his birthday, a year before, by Laura, who had immediately assured him that she was only teasing him because he seemed so *totally into* his looks. The guys around him had laughed. Steven jocularly gave his pretty blonde friend a soft pal's punch to the arm and mockingly tossed her gift onto the couch, but, when the party broke up, he quietly stuffed it into a bag along with the rest of his birthday stash, and brought it to his bedroom. You never knew, he thought, when you might need to get a close look at your pores. These days he monitors that little spot of acne on his jaw's underside, and scrutinizes his hair, which has reached the perfect length, he thinks; the girl at the beach whom he met today gigglingly confessed that she found it sexy, the way it curled in the back and just over his ears. He can't get over how many new babes have come up to him this summer and said hi, obviously interested in him — it was in their body language, one leg positioned advancingly forward, the other tentatively back, hands on their tiny tanned waists, mouths in that girlish pout he has come to recognize as at once smug and inviting. He wants them all. And they want him, one of the Golden Boys, he's become convinced, nothing short of a miracle when you think of how they all but ignored him three years ago when he was skinny and his hair had no sunstreaks or sexy curls, was cropped severely above his ears, military school style, the way he had worn it as a Cub Scout and Momma's boy. With his small Top-Siders and well-pressed Lacoste shirts, he had passed for an 'eighties version of Little Lord Fauntleroy, the perfect fourteen-year-old preppie, an appearance that endeared him to his parents' friends but made him bland, and something of a geek to Beverly's cutest girls, who dreamed of mavericks with golden tans, nice eyes, and hot buns. During freshman year, Laura had gently illuminated the facts of life at Beverly for him, then passed along gossip about a couple of guys who were rumored to have gone to fat farms and changed their eye color with contact lenses.

He himself grew three inches and gained thirty pounds, let his hair grow out, and started surfing. These days he wears stylishly oversized cotton pants or flattering narrow jeans with baggy shirts and sweaters, the conventional fashion this year. Sometimes on Friday nights, aiming to be different, though not radically so, this possibility as worrisome to him as the stigma of blandness, he'll step out in a tight-fitting T-shirt emblazoned with a rock logo, beneath a leather jacket that he picked up on Melrose. Hip enough, without making him look like one of those burnouts who supplement their outfits with leopard shoes or a couple of diamond-studded earrings. Maybe he *is* too conservative, though you can't be expected to step entirely out of your old skin. He thinks that he has found the right balance between geekdom and outrageousness, between an advantageous social life and his burdensome studies geared toward preparing him for the Ivies, between a frenetic life and the tranquillity of his afternoons at the beach with a couple of surfing buddies and a few six-packs. Which makes him think: Did he take the empties out of the back seat at the beach? Shit, he hopes no dregs have spilled and left a telltale stench in the car's carpet. Must check before the arrival home of his parents, who have spent a couple days down in Newport Beach at the "must" tennis ranch, with some guy whom his mother described as a guru of the two-handed backhand. *Jesus:* He has turned the vanity mirror over and gotten a frightfully close look at his skin's pores, huge under this magnification, and greasy looking, a reminder that he needs to buy some skin-care products when he heads to the mall. He'll pick up a couple pairs of khakis and sweatpants while he's there, too, these part of this year's hip attire — absolute musts. He chuckles, softly mocking himself for having bought into the same standards and myths as everyone else.

He is a seventeen-year-old at once secure enough to laugh at the ironies of his world and malleable enough to become a success within them. The only thing worth losing sleep over, in the end, he philoso- phizes, is your grade point average. His near straight-A average of 3.85 has not come easily, not with so much competition in his Honors classes, and since sophomore year, he has studied diligently until about twelve thirty A.M. on Sunday through Thursday nights. He has always been superstitious, the first kid to arrive in a classroom on exam day, the last one, if at all possible, to turn in his exam, the kind of kid careful not to step on a sidewalk's cracks. During sophomore year at the start of a biology exam for which he felt doomed — doom being anything less than an exam grade of B-plus or a course grade of A — his black fountain pen ran out of ink. He turned to a classmate, borrowed one of her blue Bic pens, and ended up getting an A. Thereafter, he could not take a test without a blue Bic pen identical to the one he had borrowed. He bought the Bic pens by the gross. It was about the time he came upon the Rodeo Drive route. Reciting geometry postulates to himself, he had missed a turn on the way to school one day and suddenly found his car snarled in Rodeo's slow tourist traffic, Steven cursing at the top of his lungs, furious at having allowed exam pressure to put his brain in a fog. He had to drive four blocks out of his way before he finally got to the school's gate, ten minutes tardy to his first class. He received a 96 on his geometry test that morning, his highest mathematics mark ever at Beverly, and a sure sign to him that his new route was fated. He has kept the route a secret from everyone, even Laura, who might decide he's a geek, if she knew. Hell, everybody has something to hide, he's discovering. A friend from seventh grade whom he had never seen do anything more hedonistic than swim naked in his pool checked into Coke-Enders this summer, Laura told him. Most of the time, Steven keeps his nose clean, so to speak. Notwithstanding his own eccentricities and superstitions, he has been, on the whole, a model teenager, heavily involved in local charitable and political organizations, doing three months of volunteer work with Live Aid the past summer, mostly soliciting contributions over the telephone. He generally obeys his parents' wishes, helps his friends, and thinks ill thoughts of no one with the possible exception of the nerds in his Honors science courses who, he thinks, are trying to beat his brains in. "Things could not be much better," he says one day to a visitor, "but if people knew how whacked-out I was, well . . . ."

A boy who watches "Wheel of Fortune" nearly every summer day and likes skits in which he dons a wig and plays the show's blonde letter-turner cannot take himself too seriously. He good-naturedly ridicules his never-ending search for a paradise where less work would mean higher marks. During junior year, he became convinced his history teacher did nothing more than scan students' essays to decide whether they seemed to understand the topic at hand. On his term paper, Steven wrote a short personal request on page twelve, nestling it in the middle of a paragraph, convinced that it would go unread, along with most of his paper. "If you're still reading this, Richie," he wrote, "please circle here." Richie was the teacher's first name, but no student dared call him this to his face. When Steven received the term paper back, it had a red circle around his probing sentence, along with a scribbled message in the margin: "*Minus 25 points* — do this again and I'll be giving you a D at best. Even think of trying anything this deceitful in the future and I'll make your life in this classroom a living hell. Have a nice day — Richie." His otherwise outstanding paper had been marked down to a C. "Served me right," Steven says. "I'd been an asshole, I guess."

He has acquired a normal complement of teenage contradictions, neuroses, and outrageousness, which, he guesses, is what has come to make him so likable among his peers. His best friend, Laura, a luminary herself in the senior class, may be more polished, but, in private, she worries aloud to Steven that she may be falling out of favor with a powerful clique, wonders whether other girls' envy has festered into absolute contempt. She's too perfect for her own good, thinks Steven, who realizes then that it goes beyond this, that perhaps she is a touch too remote for others. His surfing buddies say she seems a bit stuck-up, though this might be the sniping of horny guys jealous that some dude in his twenties has been nailing her. He finds himself defending her these days, not knowing quite why, for he's secretly miffed, too, wants her to start being a better, more attentive friend. Still, he doesn't need to see her ostracized; he's already lost one buddy in the last year, a kid who got angry at a party and hasn't called Steven since. Sometimes that happens: Good friends just sort of disappear, like they never really knew you at all. You need to accept it.

He is, at his core, a happy, ingenuous boy, gifted with curiosity about the way the world works and a memory for details, especially numbers. "Six hundred and seven are escaping in June," he says, which is to say that he has counted 607 classmates' names in last year's yearbook. He guesses that he has never spoken to four hundred of them. "It blows me away thinking about people trying to protect themselves: six hundred and seven people with all their skeletons and freaky things that they won't tell anybody," he says. "I wish I *really* knew, like, *ten* people in my class. That would be a freak — to know what they are feeling and things. But it won't happen; that's for sure."

The Beverly Pursuit is the path to success. . . . One wrong move, and the student could be traveling in endless circles. Sure, he will have a chance to roll again, but he will have to take advantage of every opportunity. Sometimes a student will land in the wrong square, but he must be patient. Someday he will be able to cash in all his chips and reach the center of attention. Of course, everyone wants a piece of the pie. If a student does not have the right moves, he will go hungry. . . .

— *Watchtower*
(the Beverly Hills High School Yearbook),
1985 Edition

When Hillary feels scared or trapped, she walks. At registration for classes, someone says that her ex-boyfriend has been spotted French-kissing a girl on the school's front lawn, and Hillary walks out of the building to the far end of the campus, toward an athletic field, adjoining the oil wells, to be alone. Curiosity-seekers from outside Beverly Hills sometimes drop by to stare at the wells, as if they were totems of the city's vast fortune. Hillary just comes here to escape, to drink Diet Pepsi, to draw sometimes.

A tall, shapely, raven-haired beauty, she reigns as one of the

Beverly queens whom other girls most envy, a perfectly tanned fashion plate who has modeled part-time for local department stores and been pursued by several of the school's most attractive boys for the last two years. Yet the girl has never believed in her charms, a conviction solidified last spring, in junior year, when her boyfriend of four months dumped her with a parting shot that she should lighten up, stop being "such a quiet, unsocial geek." Actually, she had never been unfriendly with the boy or his friends, merely shy and diffident, Yesterday's gawky child whose beauty had not arrived until the spring of eighth grade, and who had not known thereafter how to cope with the attentions showered upon her. As hard as she tried, there were moments when she could not see herself as anyone besides "The Straw," the nickname bestowed upon her, years before, by fifth-grade classmates poking fun at her skinniness and pasty complexion, first a barb, later a semiaffectionate moniker that became more indelible with each half-inch she grew. In sixth and seventh grades, while her female classmates sprouted perky breasts, she simply grew more angular, a misshapen giant placed at the net in volleyball games and in the back row of class pictures with boys who were the school's biggest basketball players. Five-foot-nine at thirteen. *The Straw.* . . . So painful had the name and her own sense of freakishness become that she blinded herself to her body's subtle and periodic changes. She didn't know exactly when things changed, but, in her freshman year at Beverly, a boy who had once called her a giraffe began talking with her for no reason that she could fathom, shuffling his feet and stammering until she realized that he was flirting, flirting with *her.* She went with him a few days later to a party, and ended up dancing with one of his older friends, a high school junior who introduced her to necking in the front seat of a 280ZX, Hillary yanking his hands off her breasts.

"My brothers are saying you've got the hot bod," her friend Karen told her the next week at lunch. Hillary could not speak. At the end of her P.E. class that afternoon, she stood in front of the mirror that hung against a bank of scarred lockers, removed the towel that covered her body, and quickly surveyed herself through eyes that had taken on new filters: Her breasts had become ample; her legs, once like stilts, were full and shapely about the thighs; her waist had a woman's curve. The scarecrow had given way to a striking fourteen-year-old beauty. What had once been her genetic curse — her height and innate thinness — was now her charm; she didn't need to struggle to stay slim, as other girls did. Nor, as she discovered, would she ever again have to struggle for boys' attentions. She spent the first half of the following summer with a sophomore surfer, and the last half with a senior football player who took her on dates to the beach in his older brother's silver Porsche. She tried mimicking the behavior of older female cousins while in the company of boys, becoming an avid listener to male boasts as well as their heated discussions of cars and sports, not trusting herself to talk, for she had never learned, as a grammar school pariah, how to banter with cute boys, untutored in the art of making cute, flippant jokes or the right moves under the pressure of a high school mating dance. She smiled to compensate. Smiled when the sophomore surfer asked about how she would feel about skinny-dipping at night. Smiled when the senior football player asked if she wanted to do a couple of lines before they parked on Mulholland. Smiled as she did one line and received her initiation to sex in a black leather bucket seat that reclined to the floor — a custom-designed seat, said the football player, that his brother had installed for nights just like these. His words had the disconcerting effect of making her feel like an extension of the car seat and its grooved black headrest, another custom-designed extra. Horizontal on the leather, her clothes in various states of disarray, she considered it all in a microsecond — and told herself to smile. Her silences only added to her allure, she discovered, some boys mistaking it for wry amusement or an aloofness that could be penetrated only by a boy with consummate looks and style. There were dates, in the next year, with another football player, a swimmer, a musician, and a baseball player. She had become, in that most flattering of high school locker-room descriptions, a challenge.

By her junior year, she had heard so much gossip about her body from Karen that she had come to regard it as her greatest asset, the sole reason for her new social prowess, the only thing standing between her and a return trip to the land where she would be The Straw again. She began taking special care of her treasure, hanging expensive skirts on it, joining aerobics so it wouldn't lose its curves, sitting in a sauna after her workout to burn off what she imagined to be a pound, perhaps a pound and a half, of body fat. It was about the time that Dan, on whom she had had a crush since the fifth grade, asked her out for the first time. She went with him to a party in Bel Air, succeeded in looking cool while saying almost nothing, and made love with him in the back of his father's Seville.

She would do anything to keep the body gorgeous after that. Like a geologist whose life's obsession lies in studying shifting physical formations, she kept constant watch over her body's curves, rigorously inspecting herself, naked, in front of her bedroom mirror each night, wondering if there might be any extra fleshiness about her butt. She began taking an appetite-depressant, Dexedrine — two pills, three times daily. Dan gave her a pendant, and asked whether she might want to go on a vacation to Mexico with his family later that spring. She got her first modeling assignment, a "sweater deal," as her mom called it, for a small boutique.

Nothing could possibly go wrong, she thought, and then it did. Just as she had been unable, years earlier, to detect the early signs of her blossoming, so, in junior year, did she fail to notice her decline in Dan's eyes, his sudden doubts and irritations, the way he increasingly turned toward other girls at parties. She neither danced well nor found it easy to talk with Dan's friends, who generally opened conversations by asking, "What's happening?" She didn't know how to deal with girls discussing in breathless whispers who was sleeping with whom, or debating over what boy might offer them the wildest time, if only they could get away from their own boyfriends long enough. Dan endured her silences for three and a half months, then said disgustedly, "When everybody is talking, why are you in the kitchen talking with some geek about bullshit? Why can't you party like everybody else? Get into it a little."

She never learned how to cope successfully with the battlegrounds of their parties, where girls were to come dressed in sexual combat fatigues — the tightest jeans, the loosest-fitting blouses, three or four buttons always left undone to reveal whatever cleavage they possessed, preferably ample and without tan lines. Once, when she steered Dan away from a drunken sophomore girl wearing a sheer lace bodice, who had been rubbing his shoulder, he snapped, "Hey, you gotta learn how to party a little. Have a margarita. Do you know you're looking pale? You need your tan back." In another week, he cut her loose. "You might have a face and a body," he told her, "but you're such a quiet, unsociable geek."

When a school counselor to whom she had gone for scheduling assistance asked how she would describe herself, she replied without hesitation: "Kind of pretty but intimidated." She had arrived at that self-image weeks before, in an English class, where one of her classmates had described the heroine of a novel as "beautiful but intimidated."

"You might have a face and a body, but you're such a quiet, unsociable geek."

Pretty but intimidated, then.

Her self-image has extended to her notion of where she fits on the Beverly academic ladder. "You go to the best high school in Los Angeles," Hillary's mother has told her. "You'll be cheating yourself if you don't take some of these classes. What do the kids say? *Go for it.* You could spend ten years taking classes at your school and you still wouldn't get all the way through the course schedule."

Hillary feels overwhelmed by the competition at Beverly. Nothing in the vast array of course offerings and resources excites her as much as the television broadcast classes; yet, despite the urgings of friends who tell her that she has a pleasant voice to go with her great looks, Hillary doubts that she would fare well in one of the school's TV or radio auditions. She has been disappointed a couple of times in Beverly theater department tryouts already. So many talented people here, she thinks, sitting on the ground by the oil wells. She looks in the direction of the school's radio station. "The greatest thing about Beverly is that it's all there for you if only you can make it," her mom said during freshman year. Hillary dreamed about making it in those days. Some of the school's most popular kids then were deejays who carried radio nicknames like "Madame X" and "Farmer John," and Hillary wanted a taste of their mini-celebrity. Her dreams have ended now. "It'd be so excellent to be one," she says. "And I'd go for it if I thought I had a chance. But I don't. I *know* I don't. It's pretty hard to get picked here for anything. But if you do — my mom is right — you can be hot. Only, like, here can you be 'Madame X.' "

Only at Beverly can you be, like, Madame X. Only at Beverly can you be, like, a television anchorwoman on cable or do a video show with your own Duran Duran clips. Only at Beverly can you take eight classes in the same semester, or be an intern for CNN. Not everyone makes it, however — which is the whole point, as Hillary sees it. She decides to spare herself the agony of a TV audition, and makes a mental note to ask a friend what teachers in the less-popular elective courses are the easiest graders. Her 3.1 g.p.a. on a scale of 4.0 is "just average" around Beverly, her mom keeps reminding her, adding that she could use a couple of A's by the term's end, in January, before the college admissions offices make their decisions. Her prospects don't look that hot — a few rinky-dink private colleges and a bunch of ivyless, pavement-covered state colleges that, with their uniformly sterile, boxlike structures, look like franchises — the Golden Arches of Education. She may be stuck next fall at a congested, smoggy campus in East Los Angeles, or in the

numbing flatlands of Northridge, out in the Valley of all places, surrounded by gas stations and a Taco Bell. She'll retake her SATs. Her
mother has already enrolled her in a preparatory course for the test, and
bought her three workbooks. This morning, Hillary wanted to talk about
the possibility of retaking her English Achievement Test, too, but it will
have to wait: Mom is out for the day and night. Three dates this week
now, all with the same guy. Hillary found a note from her this morning,
saying that there was leftover lobster bisque in the refrigerator, along with
sandwiches from Jurgensen's. The housekeeper has gone home for a
couple of days. Her brother has already left for his college to meet some
guys for four days of drinking on river rafts. She needs something to do;
she's been bored too often these days. A date would be nice. She's over
Dan, she knows, though she could have done without the news that he's
making out with somebody. What a jerk.

     She walks away from the wells and drives home, thinking that she
could give her father a call at his apartment, but, then again, the last few
times she has asked him to a movie, he mumbled drowsily that he had
been using his Friday nights to catch up on his sleep after a succession of
sixty-hour weeks at his law firm. She felt a pang whenever he said it,
pictured the faded brown papered walls of his apartment, the spartan
living room, the thin carpet riddled with cigarette burns, nothing to grace
his monastic quarters — no imported rugs, no stereo, no VCR or cable,
just a musty white couch, a couple of chairs, a small dining table in the
kitchenette, and a modest bedroom, filled with his filing cabinets and
books. When she gets home, she leaves a message on his answering
machine — "Hope you're having a nice weekend" — then calls a friend
in search of a party. No one home. She calls a second friend, leaves a
message on a machine, lies back on her bed, and stares at the hunks on
her wall, cut-outs of male models from GQ, some in formal wear, a
couple in jockey briefs, assets bulging. Just once she'd like to see everything. She's heard that guys' things look different, some narrow, others
fat, some with less hair than others. She didn't think of paying much
attention when she was flat on her back and groping in the dark with
those guys, wishes she did; though, having had only four things to
glimpse, it's not like she would have seen a sampling of the world's
greatest dicks anyway. She hates feeling sexually naïve. On her door is a
taped magazine advertisement for male strippers from a Westside night-
club. She went to the club one night to watch them, got a seat so close to
the stage that she could see the tongues of middle-aged wives wagging
inside dancers' mouths, the hunks coolly skirting away and grinning,

teasingly waving admonishing fingers at the women, who would stick dollar bills and little notes in their G-strings, gasping, telling their friends when the dancers moved on that if they could just get *fifteen minutes with one of these guys, God, that would be heaven.* . . . After the show, she hung around, and two of the dancers emerged from their dressing rooms, in polo shirts and jeans, asking if they could buy her a drink. They talked about their agents, their weight-lifting regimens, and what kind of suntan lotions they used under the afternoon sun so as to look tan but not leathery by the time their shows rolled around. Their mystique faded by her second vodka tonic, and she left with a skinny real estate man from the Marina who looked like Kenny Loggins to her until the next morning. Which was long enough. Her fantasies have always been hard to hang on to. She never gets tired of looking at her cut-out magazine hunks, however, having decided that her dream man would look like the fair-haired English hunk donning the tuxedo on her wall and sound like Mickey Rourke. Eighteen-year-old boys bore the shit out of her, even her ex when she thinks about it, though he had at least done her the favor of getting Alexander Godunov to shake her hand at a studio party. *God, she'd thought she'd die.*

———

Paul's in trouble again. His older sister would have beaten the rap — that much he knows. His father caught him smoking a pinch of sinsemilla in a water pipe last night — but it might just as well have been a kilo, because the old man will certainly want to hand out a punishment and tell him again that he is *thisclose* to falling into Depravity's Abyss and becoming one of Life's drooling, brain-fried Mutants. Sometimes he wishes he attended one of those fancy prep schools thousands of miles away in the East where you get to live in a dorm and need to see your California parents only during the holidays, after they've missed you so long they feel obliged to let you perpetrate whatever insanities you feel like for the two or three weeks you're with them, outside of maybe fucking up their Gold Card credit lines. His older sister, who used to run wild in high school and college and drive his folks crazy, stealing his father's vodka and banging up his mom's car with her low-life boyfriends, goes to an art history graduate school year-round in England now and comes home only at Christmas, when his parents treat her like she's a cross between Rembrandt and Princess Di, instead of the plump brat that she is: making her special dinners, buying her theater tickets, and asking for her opinions on everything from Gauguin and Monet to the English

Michael Leahy

pound and Margaret Thatcher. Like she even knows something about that crap. Get real. Last year, his father, kissing her hand like she was that Van Gogh dude, presented her with an easel and paints when she stepped through the door. She used the paints to color some popcorn necklaces in between downing wine spritzers. She had always been good at reading his parents' signals, knew she had free rein to go bananas. When he would complain to his parents, they'd frown and tell him that his sister was in need of a well-deserved rest after her *taxing studies in England*, dragging out the words as if she were studying sixteen hours a day in dimly lit catacombs, part of the implication being, of course, that it wouldn't do him any harm to learn what real academic labor felt like. He'd shut his mouth, go to bed, and be awakened, in the middle of the night, by low ecstatic orgasmic moans coming from the living room and the scent of Colombian wafting up the stairs. She'd go back to England with a contented lioness's smile, partied-out.

Screw it, Paul thinks, glumly eating his Rice Krispies and watching early-morning cartoons on the small Sony in the kitchen. He hears heavy footsteps on the stairs. In the next instant, his father pushes through the swinging door that leads into their kitchen and pads toward the refrigerator in his socks, brushing his golf shoes and happily humming the same tune that he hums every morning. Paul never recognizes it.

"Hi, pal," his father says to him and pats him on the back. Not a bad sign, maybe. The older man scratches the overnight shadow of his beard, opens the refrigerator, and grabs his customary can of grapefruit juice, the humming getting louder; he must *really* be looking forward to this golf game.

Thinking he sees an opening, Paul says, "God, I really got to hurry. I got to get down to the store to get some things for my English class."

The humming stops. "You aren't going anywhere."

"I told Tony and Randy I'd go to the beach with them later."

"Not today you're not."

"Why?"

"You know very well *why*."

"Oh, shit, Dad. Give me a break. What did I do?"

"We've been over this."

"You heard *one* thing that I said and you freak, you totally mis . . . misconstructed."

"*Misconstrued.*"

"Whatever."

"And, very clearly, I didn't misconstrue anything. I heard you say it to your friends: '*Deal me a load.*' Even your *mom* heard it."

Why had he shouted the incriminating words so loudly? "*Deal me a load.*" How could he have known his father would be listening? If the guy was home at all in the evenings and not six thousand miles away on business, he stayed on his ass in the den, making phone calls, checking on deals for the international import-export business and oil companies that he represented as legal counsel and financial adviser, and always keeping an eye on the TV's twenty-four-hour cable sports channel. Sometimes, wakening in the middle of the night to go to the bathroom, Paul would take a few surreptitious steps downstairs to catch a glimpse of the old man sitting in the dark, his face illuminated only by television's Great White Glare, watching something like wrist-wrestling or Irish curling. What an addict. The dude has a satellite dish now, so he can get stations and shows from almost anywhere. Late-night kick-boxing in Phoenix. Basketball from Denver. Soccer in Dallas. So what the hell had prompted his father to walk away from it to check up on him? Bad luck, that was all. He always has had bad luck. No use making excuses. Bottom line, he could have avoided the fucking hassle had he only told Tony and Randy to lighten up. They had been giggling so loudly after doing a bong-load that he'd had to raise his voice to let them know he had run out of smoke. They still hadn't heard him. "*Hey, deal me a load, Tony,*" he shouted finally.

Tony loaded a bowl to the rim with sinsemilla they had bought that morning. All the while, Randy was bitching that, with his parents on vacation, his housekeeper had become lazy. "She's just taking frozen dinners and sticking them in the microwave, pisses me off," he moaned. "I told her not to even bother, and she got pissed off, like I was being a prick. Dumb fucking-ass Mexican. Fuck her. I can make my own dinner. Hey, you guys know how to make some shit. What can I do with Chicken-of-the-Sea tuna?"

"Put it on a muffin with cheese," said Paul.

"Myself, I like having it between a girl's legs," Tony said.

Only when they had finally stopped laughing did they hear the soft knock on the bedroom door. Tony pushed the pipe and paraphernalia under Paul's bed, and Randy sprang to his feet to open a window. Paul took his time opening the locked door. It was his father.

An early sign of trouble had come after Tony and Randy left. His father sat him down and told him that he had heard the entire conversation. The Depravity lecture followed. Then, for the rest of the evening, his old man paced furiously around the house repeating the incriminating words to Paul's mother: "Then he said, Joanne, *'Deal me a load.'* " His father paused once to tell him how disappointing his performance had been at Beverly during his junior year: "I never hear from your mother of you doing homework, I never hear of you participating in extracurriculars, I never hear of you getting any A's." Actually, he had bagged one A, in ceramics, but that had been more than canceled out by his C's in both terms of chemistry. He received unspectacular B's in everything else, a record that his mom never fails to remind him won't be good enough. "You've got friends and you're a charming, funny guy," his father said, eyes on the tube, where a vested man was telling viewers how to catch big trout. "But that isn't carrying you very far. Now I learn you're doing *drugs*. In your bedroom. *Marijuana*. Well, that's going to stop, immediately, pal. Were you on drugs when you had the accident in your mother's Cadillac?"

"No. Jesus Christ, I just brushed some hedges. That was her *thrasher* Caddy. It had dents all over it already. It just sits there in the garage."

"You were on drugs, though, weren't you?"

"Right. I mainline, Dad. Give me a break."

"*Look* at you. *Look* at that gut of yours. Doesn't that bother you? Why don't you get yourself in some kind of shape?" His father has always known how to sting him. It's true: His weight problem is getting worse. Once, in grammar school, he had been one of the cool, funny little boys with whom the cute girls liked to hang out. The reputation has endured even if his tyke's body hasn't: Some of the hot girls from the old grammar school days still invite him places. But reputation could carry you only so far. Sometimes he feels his own hanging precariously over a ledge. His bulk threatens to turn him into a *cartoon*, not his description but his dad's, a word that he has not forgotten though it was uttered over a year ago. At five-eleven and well over two hundred twenty pounds the last time he dared step on a scale, he has no opportunity to wear tight jeans or form-fitting cotton slacks or shirts, keeps himself in baggy clothes that help to disguise his weight and wears Air Jordans in the hope of looking more athletic. He has tried other things to affect an outdoor image, sitting under sun lamps and putting lemon juice on his sandy brown hair in an effort to turn it blond, though the effect so far has only been to make his hair stiff. Even if it worked, it'd be an illusion, he tells himself. At some point, he knows he has to face the matter of his obesity. He doesn't need his father telling him, however. "I don't care if you hassle me about the other shit, Dad, but not my weight; that's fucked."

"Don't ever talk like that."

"Then drop that shit, okay?"

"Well, we are going to have new rules for you this year. And I'm calling Tony's folks about this, too."

"Jesus Christ. *You're freaking, Dad.*"

"I'm calling now."

"Fine. Go ahead and humiliate me and ruin Tony's last month of vacation. What are you doing? *Dad, don't pick up the phone. Shit.*"

But his father wouldn't be able to put a dent in Tony's life. "My father was pretty cool about it," Tony told him later. "He told me that he doesn't want me smoking grass or doing anything else again. But he wasn't totally *harsh* about it. It was just a warning."

Paul couldn't believe it. "You weren't grounded?"

"Not even."

"No lecture?"

"Not really, dude. We spent most of the time talking about whether I'd be better off next year at Berkeley or San Diego or some college back East."

Fuck him. It isn't the impunity with which Tony does things that disturbs him so much as that smiling assurance with which he moves through the world, the assumption that it is his destiny never to be punished, hampered, slowed, denied; that he is golden. At Beverly, Tony studies no more than he, maybe even less at times, yet carries the superior g.p.a., 3.7 to Paul's 3.0. Handsome and charming, Tony regularly mistreats the girls he dates, ignoring or altogether dumping them in the end, but this doesn't stop new babes from flocking around him. Paul, the model of kindness and good humor, goes months without a date. Parents, especially mothers, who love Tony's grace, will ask Paul, "How is your friend doing — that very handsome boy, what's-his-name, *Tony?* Is that his name? *Tony?*" Sometimes he can't stand his best friend. Still, Tony has never done anything to court all the praise, besides breathing; some people are just born into the world as princes; he heard somebody say that once in a TV movie of the week. *Fate.* Yeah. And it has just been his fate to be born into the world as a dead-ringer for a Twinkie-binging sumo wrestler. If he gets any bigger, the world can start calling him Orca. What's fair? He has done his best to compensate, he thinks, developing a sense of humor that seems to please and entertain other kids, a brazenness they find hilarious for its shock value. Insult humor, Tony calls it. Paul is never quite certain how the barbs are going over, careful not to turn his humor upon the soshes, the social stars with the power, looking instead for anonymous or weaker foils who can't hurt him. He thinks Tony senses his insecurity, has always been grateful that his best friend doesn't use it against him. Instead, the guy is always offering to help him out of things. "Hey, give me a call if your father hassles you too hard," he said after the bedroom bust. "Maybe I could say it was my idea and take the blame. We could think of something."

Too late for any help now, Paul thinks, in the kitchen, staring at his cereal, hearing his father lug his golf bag toward the door. But he appreciated Tony's offer. Tony never ran away from a friend in trouble. During their sophomore year, when Paul had been temporarily on the outs with some of the soshes because he had gotten terribly drunk at a party and accidentally busted some kid's tape deck, Tony intervened and dragged him to parties until he managed to get back into the soshes' good graces. Tony has been there to help him across the abyss if he needed a little assistance, say, a hand out of a party and a drive home if he became too wasted, or a gentle warning if one of the soshes found his jokes a little hard to handle. Sometimes he wishes he didn't need to go to their parties, that he wasn't so concerned with winning acceptance. Pete Rose has drawn close to Ty Cobb's all-time record for hits, and Paul would like to do nothing more than sit in front of the television for a few days and watch baseball, but he should be getting out more, with school and senior activities about to begin. He has a hard time dragging himself away from the TV. He can't get enough of those old black-and-white reruns from the 'fifties and 'sixties, like "Dennis the Menace," "Father Knows Best," and "Leave It to Beaver," where everybody looks so happy and successful, and life turns on family hijinks. His father angrily told him at the end of his junior year that his grades might have been better if he hadn't made himself "a prisoner of the boob tube," a statement that made Paul laugh considering his father was watching Australian-rules football at the time. Besides, Paul doesn't see the problem: Television has simply been his escape from boredom and pressures. He knows better than anyone what he must do, academically. His 3.0 won't cut it at the admission offices of any prestigious colleges, so the semester ahead represents his final opportunity to raise his grade point average before colleges make admission decisions. Last Chance City. He has already plotted what he must do to save himself. For starters, he needs a new tutor. The college kid he used during his sophomore and junior years might have been a good instructor, but only a mediocre motivator. Before anything else, he needs a change of attitude. Taking at least one class he enjoyed couldn't hurt. He has tentatively decided upon enrolling in Ultimate Frisbee, where he can get a P.E. credit for doing nothing more than playing a football-like game with a Frisbee. It might make the drudgery of his other classes tolerable. *Burn, burn,* he tells himself. Goals take shape in his mind: work hard, party hard, get laid.

His father shouts at him from the front door. Unable to make out the words, the boy walks out of the kitchen to see his father, arms folded across his chest, frowning and staring at some dirt on his putter. "Maybe you need to see someone," his father says gently.

Someone means a retired local therapist, an old family friend who once gave Paul a cheap-ass bowie knife as a Christmas present. Paul used the knife to separate unusable seeds from his marijuana. "I use the knife a lot," Paul's thank-you note to the therapist read. "It was very thoughtful of you, all of my friends think." Shit, the therapist never has had a clue about anything; the dude is older than his grandparents. "Dad, I don't need any of that," he says. "Why don't you give me a chance once in a while?"

"We'll see," his father says, heading for his golf game.

"He was kind of threatening me," he tells Tony that night on his bedroom phone, door closed, cable television and stereo both on at maximum volume so that no one who may be outside can hear. "I didn't lie. I told him what we were doing. I can't use the car, but just for two nights. That's not bad."

Tony snorts. *"Dumbo."*

On the television screen Wally is telling Beaver to take a bath or he'll punch him in the arm. The Beav's parents have gone out for the evening and left Wally in charge. Paul likes how older and younger brother sit down to dinner together, Wally inspecting the little boy to make sure his ears and shirt are clean, Beaver displaying his freshly scrubbed hands and looking up in admiration at big brother, who says, "C'mon, eat up, Beav." His own father eats his dinner on a tray surrounded by his papers and briefcase, sitting in front of the cable sports channel. Sometimes Paul's mother joins him; sometimes not. Paul is free to eat whenever he chooses, which tonight comes early, when he grabs three tacos that the housekeeper made and heads up with a tray to his bedroom. He phones Tony to ask if he'd like to come over and bring a couple of brews. "The Beav is intensely funny with a buzz on," he says. "Get over here."

"No, I'm just going to hang," Tony sighs. "Listen to a tape or something, I don't know."

"You going out tomorrow night?"

"I don't know."

"That chick we saw at Cutter's was so excellent."

"Which one?"

"The one all over you."

"I don't know."

"God, I don't know how you can rest with all those babes around. If I had your chances I'd be scamming all over, bud. You don't always know if they'll be around."

"School's starting, they'll be around."

"I've got to lose some weight. Chicks don't want blimps, right?"

"I think you should take it easy."

"Well, you don't have my problems. Let me tell you: You can't argue with a hard-on."

"You act like you're the only one with them sometimes."

Does he? He looks up. Beaver and Wally are on all fours trying to clean up a bathroom they've flooded with tub water. "There just isn't that much to do around here," he says. "It would be cool if we could double-date or something. I want to meet just one babe. They're all over. There's so many. I should be able to do it. *Just one*."

"You should slow down," Tony says.

———

Andy goes very slowly, which has always been his problem at Beverly, he thinks, sitting at his bedroom desk, trying vainly to remember the meanings of twenty-eight vocabulary words from an SAT preparatory workbook he thought he had memorized. *Garrulous . . . Plaintive . . . Maelstrom . . . Rebuke . . . Ineluctable . . . Ditheism . . . Avuncular . . . Prodigious . . . Wistful . . . Tumescent . . . Lurid . . .* The list mocks him: no more than a couple of words come back to him now. He feels like crying, tells himself to stop being such a wimp, to tough it out. For forty minutes, he works at rememorizing the list, then, in need of a break, puts on an album. School isn't a place for anyone, he's decided, with the possible exception of those dweebs who study with Zen-like concentration for five or six hours at a stretch. He has problems focusing for more than a half-hour, forty-five minutes tops, before he starts daydreaming. All the while, he feels himself falling farther behind, cursing himself for being such a failure, asking what quirk of genetics left him without the innate discipline or brilliance of the academic studs. He has been nervous for the last year or so, thinking about it; believes his nerves explain why he can't put any weight onto his emaciated frame. Even wearing a jeans jacket and one of his bulky sweaters, he looks like a toothpick. Over the summer, he actually lost five pounds. It didn't help in August when he heard that a couple of old friends from his elementary school days had scored in the high 1300s on their SATs, designating them as among the top 10 percent of all test-takers and, with their g.p.a.s of roughly 3.8, virtual shoe-ins at schools like Berkeley and Stanford. Having failed to hit even 1100, he remembered when he had regularly outperformed his little friends in fifth and sixth grade, and took half a Valium. The year ahead looms as a death march to him, a nine-month nightmare of dawn study sessions, humiliating parental inquisitions, and perilous exams that could break him. The bad dreams and thoughts are back. He has become obsessed with stories of teenage suicide, particularly that of a Beverly girl, an honor student and avid writer, who shot herself in the head the year before, after writing a poem about the pressure of grades and the prospect of death. Andy got a copy of the poem and had been unnerved, reading its numerous allusions to Beverly's intense competition, feeling as if the dead girl had written about his own existence. He has worried a great deal about his state of mind lately. He tells himself that he has to get more positive. He needs to register for the SAT again, and search for some extracurricular activities at school that will give heft to his college applications. He's accepted a volunteer job at a local hospital, believing a reference to this on his applications couldn't hurt with those liberal Eastern colleges; though then again, said a young doctor at the hospital, it might not count for shit. A buddy told him that not even the University of California campuses at Santa Barbara and Riverside, viewed as the least selective of the state university system, were offering admission to white applicants with g.p.a.s under 3.3, the news followed by his buddy's relieved sigh, for *his* g.p.a. was 3.32 *exactly*, not nearly high enough for UCLA, Berkeley, or San Diego, he complained, but, still, *solid* Santa

Barbara material, provided he did decently in his final year. Straight A's, he had figured, would increase his g.p.a. to 3.53. *Amherst* might even take him with a 3.53. Andy finally had had to cut him off, telling him he didn't want to hear any more of his shit. *Another* former elementary classmate who has soared beyond him, he thinks now, recalling how the kid could never quite grasp addition and subtraction of uncommon fractions in fifth grade and sometimes stole answers from Andy, who caught on to everything then. Where had his buddy passed him? How? Then again, was it any surprise, really? The kid studies from six to eleven every school night whether he has homework or not, using whatever extra time he has to reread and review; maybe the surprise, thinks Andy, is that his buddy didn't leave him in the dust sooner. Wherever you go at Beverly, even in the technical arts, there is some genius just waiting to wipe you out. And some of these Asian and Iranian kids, studying even while eating their lunches — they scare him.

God, he wishes that he were gone from Beverly. He wouldn't mind being a roadie for a rock and roll band, or perhaps playing guitar or piano for some garage band just starting; he loves music more than anything, with the possible exception of making money. He has been practicing on the Fender Stratocaster guitar that his father bought him during sophomore year for his sixteenth birthday, but, as with everything else, Andy has never been able to apply himself to the instrument for more than a half-hour at a stretch. Even so, he has made rapid progress, jamming to tunes blasting on his bedroom stereo, until, with a minimum of work, he has become proficient at mimicking the leads and accompaniments to nearly every rock and roll classic. The cute thirteen-year-old who lives next door heard him playing one afternoon, last month, and came over to say how much she enjoyed it.

Chicks like rock and roll. He'd like to get good enough so that he could join a band and meet something with long legs in black pantyhose, like those blondes he sees on the ZZ Top video who all but rape the guy they rescue from a shitty job in some bad-ass redneck diner or at a parking lot. Andy can't remember which; he mixes up the hundreds of videos he's watched; all that counts is that the guy ended up on some hot dance floor in a tuxedo, with the chicks. You need to be either a fabulous rocker or some rich dude like his dad to get the hottest chicks. If rock and roll doesn't work out, he'd like to be an entrepreneur, less a job title to him than a glamorous fantasy in which he will be calling his own shots, gambling and winning, acquiring a reputation, charming the babes.

Rural real estate appears an attractive gamble as well as space laboratories and highly advanced computer video games, both risky ventures, said his dad, who then added wisely that you had to gamble big to enjoy the good things in life.

And he should know. A graying forty-five-year-old, his dad isn't the world's handsomest dude, but he has a tan and a Maserati, and a condo on which a decorator has spent nearly a quarter of a million. The success of the package was visible in the prodigious physical assets of his female companions, every one of whom has been blonde and under thirty, since his divorce from Andy's mom. The latest, a twenty-six-year-old UCLA coed named Joyce, for whom Andy's initial sullen contempt had been transformed over six months into a reverence generally reserved for a beloved older sister or fantasy girl, took him to a concert this summer and confided that she could see herself married to his father someday. Andy didn't mind hearing that. Yet his father's view of Joyce always has been considerably more casual. There had been a barbecue at his father's condo, and Andy overheard his father talking about how having your own small computer software corporation with overseas offices meant, among other things, that you could do a couple of exotic tax-deductible business trips a year. Babes always enjoyed a topless two weeks at Cannes, his father then said to a buddy. The two men guffawed, exchanged back slaps, and then the other man said, "What some guys will do to ball a broad." His father didn't argue, merely replied, "Well, yeah, Joyce has her moments." His father can be a prick. But no one can argue that the old man doesn't know how to wield his style and bucks in order to get the most out of life — and women. Not a bad role model if you want to be completely honest. Andy hasn't had much luck at Beverly with girls, remembers junior year, when he walked across the school's front lawn and passed groups of excited babes pointing at other guys, bigger guys, more handsome guys. With a small mouth, a longish face, and otherwise ordinary features to go with his thick blond mane and blue eyes, he has never had the kind of physical presence, the sheer size, charisma, and sexiness to be a high school star. Desperate to stand out, he has periodically altered his wardrobe, switching in junior year from his narrow James Dean–like jeans garb, with collar up, to a British punk-rock look, with black stirrup pants and pointy-toed boots. In March, he donned leather pants; in April, leopardskin. Nothing changed, however, it proving virtually impossible to stand out from the scores of anonymous Beverly souls anxious to make fashion statements for themselves, to carve out identities, to escape the nagging feeling that they were somehow serfs to the school's golden lords. Andy has given up and gone back to his jeans garb, all but junking the idea of trying to meet a hot Beverly girl, settling for going to teen clubs and picking up less fussy Valley girls, who are easily awed, he suspects, by signs of money. Shit, you need too much of everything with a Beverly babe.

At five-foot-eight, he feels insubstantial, if not utterly invisible, a ghost whose steps will not leave so much as the imprint of his shoes on Beverly's lush, deep grass. He spends more time than ever these days at home. His mother bugs him about it. "These are the best times of your life," she says, her harangue having lasted all summer. "You should be getting out and meeting people, doing things with your friends, experiencing, Andy, *experiencing*." He could tell her to follow her own advice, but doesn't: His mom has problems enough. Besides, she's probably right. He needs to meet some people in his senior year. He has vowed to try.

She never knows when to quit. "Meet some of the *top* kids," she'll advise.

"Mom, it's such a full-on competitive place," he'll say. "You can't look at it that way."

"Life is the same way," she says.

"Beverly better not be like life," he shoots back.

He hears the front door open. She's home. He turns off his stereo, returns to his desk. She's at the door to his room before he realizes it. "Better get cracking," she admonishes. He looks down glumly at his list. *Sallow . . . Turgid . . . Rakish . . . Expiation . . .* He's in trouble.

———

Maybe it's her weight, Kelly tells herself. The seventeen-year-old guy with the long surfer blond hair whom she met at a teen club and who had promised to call her a week ago still hasn't, and so she has given up on the idea of having a date with him or any of her other high school heartthrobs this weekend. Maybe she can baby-sit the little kid down the street. Or get into Gazzarri's on the Sunset Strip with her fake ID and find that old guy who flirted with her the last time she was there. She can't quite get a fix on his name — Donald? Darren? — a tall and tipster-thin guy with a nice smile and sandy hair, though she noticed a couple of strands of gray in it. An old guy. Maybe as old as thirty.

Older men were much less fussy than high school boys, and

considerably sweeter, willing to listen to your problems and worries, and so she regularly found herself at Gazzarri's or the Roxy early this summer, confiding in guys whom she had known only a few hours and spending the night with a few of them when her mom was out of town on business, which was often these days. She confessed how insecure she felt wearing tight clothes to Doug — that was his name, *Doug* — who simply shook his head, leaned over, and kissed her on the cheek. They took a ride into the Hollywood Hills to look at houses, she awaiting his suggestion that they go back to his place, he telling her about his job as a country band's manager, pointing out stars' homes and producers' mansions, finally dropping her off in front of Gazzarri's with a pat on her arm and an invitation to hear his band play, the following month, in Long Beach. "This has been a lot of fun," he said. "Hope we see each other soon." Then he was gone. She has since sworn off older men, who might be kind but don't take you seriously enough. Besides, she needs to come to grips, she tells herself, with this failing she has with high school boys, most of whom have been repelled not only by her weight but her attitude, she's certain.

She'll never be statuesque, she's always moaning to her mom, who tells her that elegant stature is in the *body carriage*, whatever the hell that means. All that Kelly knows is that five-foot-one girls with big hips, short chunky legs, and large breasts get described in her fashion and romance magazines as "robust" and "stout" — the generic adjectives — or "dowdy" and "dumpy" — the descriptions reserved for the boring, unlikable, or altogether disgusting. In grammar school and even through her freshman year at Beverly, she managed to keep her weight in check, slightly pudgy but content at one hundred ten pounds, bicycling, swimming, and jogging to stay there, jumping on the scale three times a day to make sure. Ultimately, the regimen became too taxing and boring, and, besides, she hadn't been getting many offers for dates from decent-looking guys. Within a couple of months of her inactivity, ten new pounds clung to her hips. She has a closet full of chic clothes — cashmere V-neck sweaters, miniskirts, leather pants, and two designer dresses her mom gave her as birthday gifts — but she prefers wearing skirts, dresses, and baggy sweatpants that conceal, by her own estimate, twenty pounds of excess flesh. Dressing has become a paradoxical effort to hide her body in veritable tents while trying to draw attention to her best features — her large, luminous brown eyes and silky long brown hair. These days she wears heavy bluish-green mascara and puts Day-Glo pink plastic pincher clips in her hair, but none of the cutest, nicest boys at school has yet been moved to compliment her like the older guys at Gazzarri's.

She can't escape her body, she's become convinced. A few short-lived diets, late in junior year, trimmed only two or three pounds from the frame. This past summer, in quiet desperation, she turned to laxatives and diuretics for the first time, hiding the packages under her mattress, careful never to remove them unless her mom and housekeeper were occupied downstairs, ingesting the tablets behind her locked door and finding excuses when her mom asked why she spent so much time in the bathroom. Recently, she increased the dosage, and swears these days whenever another report about eating disorders finds its way onto the television screen. *Over 10 percent of adolescents have eating disorders,* one report says. *Over 10 percent use diuretics or laxatives. . . .* What hypocrites, she thinks. One set of commercials tells you that you're being cheated unless you treat yourself to Shakey's Pizza, Dove Bars, Winchell's donuts, and a never-ending smorgasbord of corporate-boxed hamburgers, tacos, fried chicken, fish fillets, and caramel chewies. No sooner have your taste buds been activated, then you're confronted by some nubile bitch in a TV commercial asking if you want to get rid of those "extra pounds around the legs and thighs," "that tire around the middle," "that dreaded cellulite." She remembers a TV reporter falling into chitchat with the anchorwoman, then bemoaning teenagers' "evident ignorance of the medical implications of all this." As if the chick had never had a cosmetic overhaul. A week can't pass without one of her friends gossiping about how another Beverly Hills matron has rushed into a plastic surgeon's office to get a tummy tuck or a thigh and ass job. You lose weight if you want to compete and survive. You take your chances. If the laxatives and diuretics don't do the job, she has already decided to move on to something stronger.

To an outsider it is hard to understand why. She looks not pudgy but merely robust — that hated word again — perhaps ten pounds at most over the ideal weight for her height and build. But the girl who judges her figure against those of fashion models, whose magazine pictures she scrutinizes for hours, sees a blimp when she undresses. Staring in a full-length mirror is an exercise in masochism. "Sometimes I feel so bad about myself," she confided to her mom, early in the summer. "Not *myself*, really, just, I guess, my *appearance* — but maybe that's the same thing, right? I look in that mirror and, I swear, *I swear* I look like one of those Russian women who weigh about three hundred pounds. I don't look that bad, do I?"

Her mom hugged her. "Of course not," she said. "Everybody has little handles at your age. It's baby fat. Did the taxi come yet?"

"Mom, *nobody* has baby fat at seventeen."

"You're fine, dear. Help me with one of these bags."

"Don't keep making it sound like I should ignore it, Mom. I won't. I have to do something."

"Well, you could concentrate more on books and less on V*ogue*, for starters."

Advice from a mother on the run. "One thing you gotta understand about your mom and the real estate business," Kelly's father said to her, at a restaurant earlier in the week, "is that she worked very hard to get to this point in her career where she has a real shot at the big commercial deals — the malls and the office buildings. It takes a lot of time. There are both business and legal parts of the transaction to worry about. It's as demanding as an attorney's work, sweetheart, and so if you understand that I have to spend a lot of time in court and with clients, you should understand the demands upon your mom when she goes out of town on her business trips, too. It is not easy for anybody, I know that."

"God, I wish each of you would stop defending the other. It's too weird."

"I know that since the divorce, it hasn't always been fun for you, but you know that you can always reach me when you need to. Right? Your mom is doing the best she can. We all are, under the circumstances. And you're looking *terrific*. Looking forward to school? I think you should really pledge to rise to the top this year. I know you can do it. All it takes is determination. Maybe you should start by reading a book a week."

Advice, then.

In very bad moments, if she needs to talk to her mother, such a conversation will generally occur over the phone and last five to ten minutes, during a break in negotiating sessions from a hotel suite in Portland, Salt Lake City, or Denver. The conversation will immediately address Kelly's problem or complaint at hand — a lack of allowance money for the movies in Westwood; a shortage of low-cal frozen foods in the refrigerator; the absence of the Saks credit card from its customary position in the foyer drawer; her depression over having nothing to do; demands for money so she can go somewhere, *do anything*. They will generally be interrupted by one, maybe two calls coming in on Call-Waiting. Her mom will hastily conclude with a short pep talk and a request that Kelly give her phone messages and news of important mail.

In the big house, on a Friday night, she will sometimes be joined by a couple of friends, if they are dateless and without a party to attend. On nights when everyone is busy, she usually baby-sits for Timmy, the four-year-old down the street whose parents are gone more often than not and toward whom she has come to feel a kinship of sorts, a bond cemented by their mutual loneliness. She could go alone to one of the open Beverly parties, but she has never felt comfortable at them, wasn't amused at the last one, in junior year, when some guy, trying to be funny for his friends, asked whether she'd like to get naked. The guy then made some cutting remark about the shawl she was wearing, which hurt her, because she liked to imagine the shawl resembled the one worn by Wendy, no last name as far as she knew, just Wendy, the young woman who played guitar and sang back-up for Prince. No one caught the resemblance. She simply looked weird. "C'mon, you shouldn't get down on yourself," Tina, her best friend at Beverly, tells her. "You're the one I always make sure is around, because you're the only honest one. Everyone else is always playing games. You don't let people get away with bullshit. You've got a good personality because you say what you're thinking. It cracks me up. It's funny. Don't think you're not special."

Even with the pep talks, it is hard for Kelly to feel anything but mediocre. She has an open and friendly face, but not a beautiful one, and since spotting an advertisement in last year's yearbook for facial surgery, she has considered having her nose done and her breasts reduced. Looks count for so much; you can't pinch pennies. And it's not as though she can make up for her physical dorkiness with brains or a sterling personality. Unless a miracle happens, she is destined for a crummy junior college. Her g.p.a. has fallen somewhere between 2.3 and 2.5. No stud electives for her. She wouldn't mind becoming a TV producer, and could get very excited about being an artist. But how do you succeed in those things in L.A., where everybody looks like a superstar? Deep down, the teenager wishes her parents had never left Connecticut. She can remember the slightly rancid smell of mittens on the classroom radiators and the tiny puddles of dirty water that formed around the legs of her second-grade desk when she removed her snow boots each morning — but not much else. She went back to Connecticut for her twelfth birthday. It snowed heavily and she no longer liked it. Still, maybe she would have had a better chance there. The weather would have been tolerable because, after all, she would have known no other kind. In any event, the atmosphere at an Eastern school couldn't be more tense than her current environment. "It's like some kids here are just superbrains right from first grade," Tina complained to her once. "You just have no fucking chance. If you're not hot, it doesn't matter how hard you work, you're going to have a hard time."

Kelly thinks that makes sense. Too many beautiful people with thin thighs and big brains here. Let the others make their school-year vows. She just wants to get out. She wishes there were something to do. She calls Gazzarri's and asks if Doug, the country rock manager, has stopped in. The voice on the other end says gruffly, "Doug's with his old lady somewhere."

———

Melinda is the pretty and savvy exception on this campus of plenty, the slim embodiment of what most here aspire to be, the one in control, the honor student whose schedule includes time for parties and concerts, the lone wolf beholden to no cliques and dependent upon few people's affections, a winner, an object of curiosity, the girl who by shaving study-time and discovering shortcuts to higher grades, has beaten the Beverly system and made it play by her rules, proof perhaps that there is something to be gained from flouting the system, some balance that comes to you, a certain sanity. She carries a 3.9 grade point average but generally studies only after having lunch at home with one of her two close friends and watching her favorite soap operas. She has the respect of her teachers but, armed with a plethora of forged absence excuses, cuts school when the mood strikes. She moves easily among the popular girls in her class and, with her shoulder-length blondish-brown hair, brown eyes, and winsome smile, has drawn the interested scrutiny of some of the school's most sought-after boys. Yet she has never courted the social stars, spurning their school dances, barbecues, and games. Deep down, she has never liked or trusted them — all these pretty people stabbing each other in the back while sacrificing their self-respect. Better to be alone with a couple of people whom you can trust. She leaves the campus as soon as her school day concludes for the sanctity of her television and lunch on a tray. After the soaps, there is usually time to exercise or go to the beach and work on her tan. Just having a life that has nothing to do with school feels good, especially considering how many of her classmates act as if nothing other than their existences and images within the school matter; that if they fail there, they've failed everywhere. Forever. You had to laugh about the place, as if it were some black comedy, and the perspective of distance has helped; she always has fun. There will be a party next week at Pepperdine University, in Malibu, to which she and her close friend Pam have been invited by a college freshman. Pam will drive, so Melinda can have all the rum and Cokes she wants. You have to allow yourself to get wild every once in a while, she reasons, to have some balance in your life. She trusts her instincts to warn her when she's about to step over some dangerous edge, doesn't mind edges, sees them as part of life's natural thrills. You just had to know how to navigate — and when to stop. Some people are cursed with no capacity for direction or self-control, she thinks, just keep *blowing it*. Losers. She knows how to keep her balance.

There was a time, a few years earlier, when she had run around with girls with whom she shared a streak of rebelliousness, provoking some parental questions. But dissipation was never in the cards for Melinda, who believed that unless her grades remained stellar, she'd one day be exiled to a mediocre California state college. In her second semester of freshman year, she received straight A's, the first of many flawless report cards. "I just did it on my own," Melinda said later. "I didn't need any *help*."

The lesson through Melinda's eyes: She could accomplish virtually anything, if she remained on track. Never has she wanted anything in life so much as to be a success, preferably a rich businesswoman in a tailored navy Evan-Picone suit, with a degree from Harvard Business School, and so she has decided that nothing less than a 3.8 or 3.9 grade point average will be personally acceptable to her. During the summer, while driving with her mom through a neighborhood of middle-class and lower-middle-class homes in Los Angeles, she blurted, "Where do you think the people around here went to college?"

Her mother understood the point of the question. "I don't know, it's hard to tell. Maybe junior college. Maybe a state college."

Later, passing through an affluent section, Melinda asked the same question.

"Maybe Berkeley or an Ivy League school," her mom answered. "Something in that category."

Melinda has filed the information away in the part of her brain that fuels soaring goals. A girl with standards so high does not associate with just anyone. She has a close male friend who attends college in San Diego; yet, though she suspects he has a crush on her, she likes him only platonically. No high school or college boy has yet to compare with her favorite television soap opera hunks, and though she had a picnic with a Pepperdine senior majoring in business, her interest waned after he started telling her about his dream of opening untapped Asian markets and selling blenders in mainland China. She had been talking about Charles Manson, telling the boy how, this past summer, she had driven over to the house on Cielo Drive where Sharon Tate and her guests had been murdered. To Melinda, that was *bizarre*, that was right out there on the edge, especially when a coyote ran into her car's path and she heard a sickening thud, the car coming to a wrenching halt, the coyote trapped under the front wheels, unable to move until Melinda put the car into reverse and the animal was finally free to limp off. That had been *intense*.

The boy, munching on a sandwich, responded that he was for capital punishment. He said that he thought he'd enter the University of Southern California Business School. He told her that one day he'd go to China on a summer vacation and get his blender operation started. "He was sweet and smart but a little too boring," she says later. "He just wasn't real interesting; like all his feelings and values were set. I think you have to keep an open mind. I guess I don't like people to be ordinary. I don't like Middle America and Ronald Reagan and all that stuff. That might sound snobbish, but I don't. I need to be excited — and I guess I need to have a challenge sometimes with guys, except with Roger, my friend in San Diego, because he's only a good *friend*. I like things more when I can't have them. I know that sounds bad. I'm just thinking of where I'm going to college right now. That's everything. Relationships can come later. The college interviews, I hear, are pretty important. Everybody is saying that you should make a good impression and look nice when you go to them."

She will be able to do that. With her demure bearing, pretty eyes, and endearing smile, the maverick looks All-American, especially in a tailored gabardine skirt and silk blouse. "I think it will be a good school year," she says. "I'd just like to find a couple of activities so I have something to put down on my college applications." She has thought about volunteering at a community center where she would assist with day-care as well as visiting children in need of an older friend. "That might be fun," she says. "Classes by themselves are too boring."

She sighs. It's 3:30 on a Thursday afternoon in September, the school year bearing down on her. "Summer seemed to last about five minutes," she says, thinking about that, shrugging. "Who cares? Like I'm glad I'm getting school over with." She laughs, steady, as always. "I still have my soaps."

———

So you have six Beverly lives there. Four are ambitious, while two are relatively indifferent about their studies. Two are A students, three have decent to mediocre records, and one seldom works at all. Three come from homes where parents have divorced. Three have, by their own estimates, used drugs on a regular recreational basis for the last two years. All six have had sex. Three of the six consider themselves at least mildly religious, attending services periodically and nearly always on religious holidays, deriving some small sense of identity from religion, just as they do from their ethnicity, socioeconomic status, and high school. However, none regards religion as an integral part of his or her life, seeing philosophical value systems of any kind as somewhat beside the point in a world where money and power predominate. Only one of the six students has any serious interest in the political world, the other five's thoughts about politics and government ranging from casual disinterest to outright contempt. However, all of their existences continually remind you, like it or not, that there is more to them than you might wish to see; that to *classify* them is to miss the real story. Paul confesses: "Sometimes you think you understand yourself pretty good, and then you do something real stupid, and you don't know if you're any better than a worm, if that makes sense. Like you get spacey and you go into a wading pool at some amusement park with your clothes on. Shit, I don't know why I do everything. I kind of think I'm pretty strange."

When asked by strangers where they live, nearly all Beverly kids say, "West Los Angeles." To say "Beverly Hills" makes them distinctly uncomfortable. They simply call their high school *Beverly*. "No one would be caught dead saying, like some geek, 'I go to Beverly Hills High,' " says Paul. "It's kind of tacky to just blab 'Beverly Hills' like that. People who don't live here totally think you're rich and your parents drive a Mercedes and your mom has a doggie outfit on her manicured poodle and all that stuff. It's better to say, 'West L.A.' Some people think you've gotta be snobby if you're from Beverly Hills, even if you're not. And they think about you, like, 'Oh, he's gotta be hot; like he must drive a Porsche and wear the most happening clothes, party insanely, and is going to Harvard or somewhere.' So, it puts a lot of pressure on you, too, which I've got enough of. Look at me. Like I'm sure. My clothes are kind of geeky to start with, right? I don't like to hang around Beverly if I don't have to. I get out of there as soon as school is over. Sometimes I wouldn't mind listening to the radio all day and just watching cartoons — cooling out a little."

He is, you realize in such moments, an adult-child, as they all are. They are in the midst of a volatile physiological and psychological change that they can't fully grasp at times. They grope along with resolve, raw intelligence, and good humor. They will need it all, in September of 1985.

School begins tomorrow.

SEPTEMBER

On the third day of school, Kelly goes to Zuma Beach. She was dressed for school and had even done a short homework assignment, but then a part-time bartender with nice eyes, named John, whom she had met at the Hard Rock Cafe, called. He asked if she wanted to go to the beach, and she said okay, if he didn't mind her bringing her Walkman. First, before they hit the beach, he said, he had to stop by the post office to mail his alimony and child-support check. His ex-wife lived with a biker from a motorcycle gang in Ventura. A couple of months before he had mailed the check a little late, and the biker had threatened to kill him. "Maybe a check on time will mellow the guy out," said John. He was thirty-three, the father of two children, ages ten and six, whom he never saw, and his burdens made him only more forbiddingly attractive to Kelly.

The trip to the post office in his old Chevy Impala takes fifty minutes, because John forgot his checkbook and has to stand in line for a money order. Then he takes her to the home of a friend, where he exchanges the Impala for a pickup truck, so he'll have more room for his surfboard and a coolerful of Coors. They finally make it to the beach and a patch of sand near a Zuma lifeguard tower, at twelve thirty. John asks her to rub suntan lotion all over him. She does, and he returns the favor. She drinks three beers, and falls asleep in the sun. It is three o'clock before she wakes up. She puts on her headphones and listens to a Duran Duran tape while John takes the opportunity to rub suntan lotion over her legs. He gives her the rest of a joint he has smoked down to a saliva-glistening nub. He puts seven M&Ms on her stomach and bites them off. He has a nice body, but he doesn't talk about much of anything except for a '79 GTO that he says, "I'm making *cherry*." She's never heard the expression before. She has two more beers, and listens to a Go-Go's tape on her headphones. John rolls a second joint for himself and looks at pictures in his *Soldier of Fortune* magazine. It is another day for Kelly at the beach. Three days later, she will be unable to remember John's last name.

———

In school throughout that first week, the other five sit in their hot class-rooms, Steven and Melinda listening to teachers and taking notes, Hillary and Andy daydreaming, Paul looking anxiously at his classmates, hoping for a joke, a laugh, a cussword, any diversion from the days' numbing rote. The hours sometimes become intolerable even for the disciplined Steven, who alternately listens to lectures in his Advanced Placement classes and surreptitiously reads material that has nothing to do with school — sports sections, James Bond novels, political biographies, *The Catcher in the Rye*, rock interviews in *Rolling Stone*, anything that can transport him to an asylum of the mind where life is dynamic and ther-mostat-cool at seventy-two degrees. A classmate, next to him in history, hides a rolled-up *Playboy* in the center of his textbook. He turns to see one of the class's 4.0s scrawling "Dead Head" on the back of his hand. "What are you doing?" Steven asks the kid, who turns his hand over to reveal a sketch of a guitar on his palm.

"I'm burnt on this shit," the kid whispers, shrugging. Steven wishes he hadn't heard that. Something about having your conceptions of successful people shattered: It doesn't do you any good. He always imag-ined the kid doing nothing but happily turning out reams of notes. "Dead Head," the kid scribbles on the top of his desk.

On Fridays, "just for the hell of it," Andy sticks a wad of gum on a bottom corner of his desk to see if a janitor will remove it over the weekend. Three times already he has placed the gum in the same bottom corner, and three times it has been removed. "It probably makes the dude's day, seeing it," Andy says. "I know I should be paying a little more attention and working a little harder. Some people just take notes, notes, notes, like robots. No wonder they get great grades. You have to be a robot to do well here."

In English, a nervous Hillary copies the paper of the girl sitting next to her during a surprise multiple-choice quiz. Her nerves begin betraying her: She feels sweat running down her sundress. "Fuck," she murmurs. Someone looks over, snickers cattily. *Just finish*, she tells herself. She glances over at the girl's paper and gets three more answers. "Okay, let's wrap it up," says the teacher. Hillary, who is four answers short, starts to look over at the girl's paper a last time, but the kid has already passed her quiz up the aisle.

Paul has his own problems. His government teacher has assigned him to a desk too small for his massive frame, and when Paul complains, the teacher tells him, bitingly, that, unfortunately, all the desks are the same dimensions. The class laughs. Paul smiles to show that he has not been hurt. Through the rest of the hour, listening to another class discussion on the death penalty, he grows increasingly restless, tries to pass the time by staring across the room at Leslie Paul, whom he would love to ask out, if only he could lose fifty pounds and if Gregg Silver, her boyfriend, disappeared from the picture. He sees her turn and whisper to another girl. The girl laughs. What did Leslie say? He wishes people would talk loudly and joke in class the way those kid actors did in "Welcome Back, Kotter." As it is, the only irreverent classroom line he has heard since school started came when the government teacher asked what happened on Black Thursday and a kid answered, "A Neil Diamond concert." The teacher frowned, continued his discussion of the stock market crash. The kid didn't dare try another joke. You never knew whether a teacher might hold it against you if you were on the borderline between a B and an A, or a B and a C. He takes out a pad and doodles a name — LESLIE, LESLIE, LESLIE. The girl in front of him, he notices, likes to sketch oceans and sea gulls. Fifteen minutes to go in the class. He doodles other names, other words: PRINCE, DIRE STRAITS, BEER-BONG, TOKE HEAVILY, ELVIS COSTELLO, RONNIE RAYGUN.

On Friday night, Steven takes Laura to a party in a neighborhood of the Palisades nestled above cliffs along the ocean, where his beach buddies live. "I'm surprised you could get away," he says on the drive over. "I mean, from your boyfriend and all. And just to see some people from Pali High."

"Why did you say that?" she sighs. She is applying lipstick while using his rearview mirror. "*He* has to work. Besides, *he's* not a jealous little teenager, thank God, like these football infants I went out with last year. He's not another wimpy immature Beverly geek."

Steven chooses to ignore this.

"There's going to be a film," he says.

"Another stag?" she demands.

"No."

"Promise me. Because I can't look at another schlong."

"*Schlong?!*"

"That's what my dad calls them."

"Your dad's bizarre."

"Like yours *isn't?*" she hisses. "He's always looking me up and down at your house. I think it pisses your mom off."

Could this be true? His father has always been, in his eyes, just another successful and staid commercial developer lustful of nothing more than making the next deal, a good provider, caring father, and faithful if somewhat distracted husband to Steven's dutiful housewife mother. "Like what does he do?" Steven asks.

"He just *looks*. And your mom gets full-on quiet like she's pissed at him."

Laura's head is getting too big. "He's just being friendly. My mom's doing her needlepoint. I think you're suspicious of any guy who doesn't drive a fucking beat-up motorcycle. You need a film with a few laughs. It'll probably be funny."

"But it's nothing perv?"

"*Shit*. He just said a *movie*, okay? If it makes you feel better, there're *no* schlongs in it."

"There better not be."

"I think you could actually use a schlong, is what I think."

"*Sorry* I don't like stag films. Shit, excuse me for living. Why do you get so disgusting and intense?"

"Okay, okay. I was just *joking*."

"It's so lame, after a while. Like all these sixteen-year-old boys who can't get laid are there, with nothing better to do. But I could get into a good film tonight. Maybe it's an Eddie Murphy."

It is the next worse thing to a stag flick, she decides, when they get there — an old surfing movie, *Big Wednesday*. A bunch of Steven's friends are crowded around the television, watching old 'seventies surfers, while their girlfriends sit behind them, massaging their necks.

"This isn't exactly what I thought we'd be doing," she whispers to Steven on the way in.

"Just have a good time," he whispers. "Maybe the world will end and you'll meet somebody you like."

Inside the party, they go their separate ways, Laura heading toward some girls in the kitchen, Steven saying hi to some guys on the living room floor. Some kid is snorting coke off a coffee table through the stub of a McDonald's straw. A couple of boys lob french fries at a parrot sitting in a cage. "*Hello, hello, hello,*" screams the parrot.

"Do you know they have these old people working at McDonald's now?" asks a boy, firing a fry at the parrot. "At the counter. Like you can ask Gramps to bring you a fish fillet."

"I don't think it's very cool to talk that way about them," says a girl.

"Like you really care," snarls the boy.

Steven turns up the volume on the television so that he can hear a wave breaking. "Must be a fifteen- or twenty-footer," he says loudly, hoping that this will get his Pali friend to shut up. Laura, having reappeared at the edge of the living room, already looks bored.

"I love to surf," says one of the girls. "Todd and I go out all the time together, don't we, Todd?"

Her boyfriend mumbles something Steven can't understand.

"I think it's, you know, kind of neat, kind of like spiritual when we're together," says the girl. "It's so great to do it, like on an empty beach especially, around sundown. We get this incredible *sync* or whatever you call it when we're doing it."

"Not *always*, but most of the time," says the boy.

"I meant surfing."

"Oh."

Steven sees a little index finger waving in his peripheral vision, and turns to notice a smirking Laura, who has been cornered on the end of a couch by two kids with wispy blond mustaches, sixteen, maybe seventeen. They're talking excitedly about "some great tubes at Manhattan." She catches Steven's attention and rolls her eyes. He ignores her. Let her work her way out of this one. Sometimes he thinks she's getting a little snobby, always telling him how high school guys bore her, how she's loved meeting someone older, someone "worldly," someone, in any event, who isn't talking constantly about clothes, cars, surfing, grades, or getting laid. It annoys him, this suggestion that neither he nor his buddies are mature enough for her to hang out with. On the screen, a blond surfer is putting his arm around a brunette in an old-fashioned bikini, the bottom part of which covers her ass completely, not like a good bikini, where you can check out a girl's cheeks. The 'seventies must have been a little repressed. Laura is squirming slightly. One of the boys is tickling her and asking if she works out at a gym. "Feels like you got some firm abs working there," the kid laughs, his finger moving up just a tad. Steven turns toward his buddies on the rug, who are doing the last lines of coke and staring at the television. More surfers are toppling off boards.

"They're twenty-footers," says his Pali friend. "At least."

An exasperated sigh from one of the girls. "Are you guys going to watch surfing all night? I don't think I want to stay if you are."

The Pali kid pounds the coffee table. "*Shit.* Why can't we watch one fucking movie without you screaming in my fucking ear, Cindy. You can be such a bitch sometimes. Stop hassling us. Goddammit. Fucking shit."

"Shit-shit-shit-shit-shit," screeches the parrot.

"That bird is so stupid," the Pali kid says softly, looking at no one, grabbing the television's remote control and making the sound higher.

"Shit-shit-shit-shit-shit."

On the way home, Laura says to Steven, "I don't want to hang anymore with your surfing buddies."

"Well, you have to do what's best for you," he says, in a tone so flat she raises an eyebrow.

"Are you mad?" she demands. "What's this, 'Well, *you have to do what's best.*' You *are* pissed."

He says nothing.

"Would you mind giving Darlene a ride to school on Monday? Her car has to go in the shop and I can't drive her because I have a doctor's appointment."

"I don't think so. I'm going to be in a rush that morning. Plus I have to do some things."

"Are you still taking your weird little way to school?"

She knows? No, no, she couldn't. Must be bluffing. "That's not why I can't drive her," he says.

"You never drive anybody to school. You don't have to fool me. So you got your weird little way, so what?"

"Who's getting *intense* now?" he asks her.

"Not me."

"I just like driving alone Monday mornings," he says weakly.

———

Few students car-pool. Car-pooling is to be resisted at all costs. Seldom did they walk to grammar school as young children, usually being driven by parents or housekeepers, and so they have come to regard transportation as a solitary experience. They view cars as their private dominion, do not want their space invaded. Each afternoon's end brings a stampede of students to the parking lot, purses flapping in the rush, hair flat against their ears, keys jangling, each teenager climbing, safe and alone, into his chrome asylum, and roaring away in a cacophony of blaring engines, U2, and Michael Jackson. The school usually becomes a ghost town by 3:30 P.M. Only a meager, though loyal, contingent comes to football games. "There is not much excitement or school spirit or whatever they call it, here," one athlete says. "Athletics at Beverly are not *happening*, if you know what I mean. I don't think I'd even go to the games if I wasn't on the team. I want to be out of there each day and moving, doing something else, anything, I don't care. I don't want to just be around, that's for sure."

There are no hubs at the high school or in the surrounding community, around which they come together. In such an atmosphere, friendships have parameters. There is companionship but fewer confidences shared, for confidences carry risks of betrayal and stature lost, and so they have become a group disinclined to bare their souls. Paul and his friends walk together wearing their stereo headphones, each kid bobbing his head to and fro in time to his own headphone's beat, not exchanging a word. "Walking from school with friends," Paul says, "is weird, because you have to spend all that time thinking about what you can bullshit about. In your car, you got a tape player at least, if you have to drive people."

It is his way of defending a routine: Get off the school grounds as quickly as possible, get home to a TV or tape player, invite a friend or two over, and "kick back and enjoy some tunes or a hot cable movie without having a lot of people bullshitting." He thinks of something else: "But if a story is real intense, I'll want to hear it, like some bizarre party story or school shit."

Most of the gossip turns on stories about pressure. At his house, Paul asks a family friend who has come over for lunch whether he heard the story that one of the kids who killed himself in 1984 drove a black Volkswagen Rabbit off a cliff. The friend says he didn't. "A nice car," Paul says. "A pretty hot car, really. A lot of kids think it was a brown Rabbit, but it was really black." Paul stares at the television, upon which a car roars around a mountain turn. A commercial for BMWs. Paul murmurs approval. "I can't see totaling a good car *full-on* like that," he says, still thinking of the suicide. "A *black Volkswagen Rabbit.* That's a *hot car.* That was dumb."

The teenager and older man talk on different planes, look at each other in mutual bewilderment. They are watching the news, the anchorman mentioning something about the Vietnam War Memorial in Washington, D.C., and Paul mumbles how sad it all seems. "They would've won the war, if they'd had atomic bombs then," he says.

They *did* have atomic weapons, the friend tells him.

Paul's eyes narrow. "So they didn't drop 'em because it was too close to Japan or something?"

Paul's father enters the room. Paul excuses himself by saying he has to go to work. He has a part-time messenger's job with an independent film production company, picking up and delivering reels, cassettes, scripts, and, on special occasions, black trunks filled with technical equipment, for which he is permitted to use the company's truck. He got the job, he thinks, because the president of the company owed his dad a favor. The job pays $9.56 an hour. It is money he doesn't need, really, considering the exorbitant allowance his parents give him — anywhere from forty to sixty dollars a week, or more, depending on his needs and desires, the truth being he generally gets whatever he wants. Still, the extra bucks from the job can be funneled toward the purchase of things his parents needn't know about. And if nothing else, the job has convinced him that he'd better get his act together in school, that he doesn't want to spend his life being a fucking delivery boy. Inside that crummy company truck without a tape deck or carpet on the floor, riding high above the rest of traffic, he gets a different view of the world, noticing things in other vehicles that he wouldn't see in the sunken seat of his red Celica — a girl, leaning over an automatic transmission in a blue Mercedes, one hand holding onto her leather bucket seat for balance, the other stroking a boy's crotch; an old man in a rusty Buick, two half-eaten donuts lying alongside him on torn upholstery, its white stuffing and springs sticking out like dead guts; a black woman in an old Fairlane, radio gutted and steering wheel stripped of its plastic casing; a man in a navy blue blazer sitting behind the wheel of an immaculate gray Seville, a woman in red by his side and three little blond boys, brothers doubtless, sitting in back, all in tiny navy blue blazers, hands folded upon laps, perfect clones of the man in front. Winners and losers sharing roads, though not much else.

Today, he gets stuck in traffic during rush hour at the corner of Wilshire and Santa Monica. A bus stops at the corner, automatic doors open, and a ragtag band of humanity is jettisoned. The destitute always seem to be at the front of bus exits, he's noticed, as if years of packed bodies and unwelcome scents on these hot rides have made them so claustrophobically despondent that they cannot bear to spend a second more aboard the moving corral than absolutely necessary, scurrying from the rest of the herd as soon as their feet hit pavement, dashing across Wilshire, putting more distance between themselves and the other sweating cattle with every second, finally reaching the solitude of their dark, private space, once more in control. Paul isn't supposed to, but, once in a while, he picks up hitchhikers in the company truck. The bums are the safest because you can tell they are carrying nothing. Paul watches a bearded man with a torn windbreaker wobble across Wilshire. The light changes, traffic moves. The bus pulls away. Paul puts his truck into gear, stares down. A man in a shiny new silver Corvette is French-kissing a woman, hands cupping her tits. Winners and losers. He has to get his act together. Buses have begun to scare him.

When he arrives home, his father is in the den, tinkering with the stereo.

"Mind if I put on the television?" Paul asks.

His father shakes his head. "Very softly, though. Why don't you turn on the Dodgers. Valenzuela is pitching."

Their basset hound trudges into the room, panting hard, drool gathering around the corners of his mouth. Paul pets his dog, feels burrs under the old, dry, thinning coat in which he used to love to bury his head, but which, more often than not, smells funny these days. Twelve years old, Bones doesn't have much time left. He occasionally pees without warning on the carpet now, which, his vet says, is a sure sign his body has begun failing him. Paul has never had anybody die in his family, not even one of his relatives back East. His parents bought Bones as a puppy for Paul, but the housekeeper feeds the dog and takes him on most of his walks. A kennel service grooms him. Paul likes to play with him in front of the TV.

"Well, Bones, you're in luck," he says to the dog, who cuddles at his feet, head on his shoe, staring drowsily at the screen. "Dad doesn't know that your favorite show is on — 'The Twilight Zone.' We can't watch the Dodgers. Dad doesn't know how disappointed you'll be. Bones just loves science fiction, don't you, Bones?"

Bones farts.

Rod Serling says something about a rocket mission. Bones licks Paul's shoe. His father stares up from the stereo, frowning. "How can you be sure that Bones even *sees* a picture on the television?"

"Look at how excited he is."

The dog stares somewhere off in the direction of the screen, licking Paul's socks.

"I have some calls to make," his father sighs. "Lower it."

The next morning, a Thursday during the second week of school, he's angry. He arrives early at school and takes his place on the steps outside the Beverly Swim-Gym, the old swimming arena that is also used for basketball and gymnastics competition. The gym fronts the school at one end, and so it is among the ideal places for checking out the action, for seeing who is driving a new car this semester and who has broken up with whom and which girls have undergone metamorphoses over the summer, either from good to bad, or the reverse, which is a hell of a lot more interesting.

He might have been in a great mood, if his father hadn't begun hassling him last night. Nights always seemed to be his father's time for giving advice. Last night's piece of advice was, "Struggle," which is his dad's way of saying, "Work hard." His father likes to use his old 'sixties buzzwords. *Struggle* is one of the old man's favorites, especially in discussions with dinner guests about politics. "I have some advice for those moderate antiapartheid business forces in South Africa," his father told a group of friends at a dinner party. "Lie down on the streets, and the government will collapse." Everyone nodded, and then his mother rang the little dinner bell and asked the housekeeper to bring out the pâté de fois gras. Paul had some advice for his father: Struggle, and eat some Spam. He usually kept such sentiments to himself, but, last night, with his father railing at him about the need to *struggle* in order to find "his own place in society," he finally exploded: "Dad, I hate this 'struggle' shit. I don't know exactly what I think, maybe, but all this that you're saying doesn't help either. Just give me my room and let me work on my computer and leave me the hell alone. I *like* my life."

"What worries me, Paul, quite seriously, is that, at seventeen, you have no idea who you are. And you are relying upon other people to tell you. They can't."

"Hey, Dad, that's intense."

"You're a man who isn't going to have a rudder."

"You can keep the rudder."

He tries to put his father out of his mind and focus upon the reason he came to school so early. Sitting on the Swim-Gym steps, he resolves to check out some of the unattached sophomore and junior girls. Kids drag past Paul, a few rubbing sleep from their eyes, others swearing about how humid it is already. Tony comes by, drinking a quart bottle of 7 Up. "God, I wish I was swimming," he says.

"People are bummed," says Paul. "Nine months of this shit to think about. Look for some chicks, will you?"

No stunning metamorphoses on this day. If anything, the changes are a little depressing to him. One of the cute girls in the junior class looks like she burned out during the summer, deep circles under her eyes, her skin ravaged by too much sun. A sophomore blonde, whom they remember as being slim, waddles by them, having gained twenty pounds at least, looking even worse because she has streaked her hair orange like Cyndi Lauper and taken to wearing a bare midriff *à la* Madonna. Three distinct rolls of flesh are visible around her midsection. As she walks, the rolls undulate, like waves.

"If you had a board," says Paul, "you could ride her."

"Another fucking Wanna-Be," says Tony. "I think I'm gonna take a workout at the gym this afternoon. Want to come?"

"No, I'm going to bail early today and get a pizza."

"Okay."

Paul hears a nagging voice in his head. *Struggle.* "Shit, maybe I better do an hour of aerobics."

On Friday, Andy's mother is out on a date with a small-time producer who calls her up every six months or so and with whom she always ends up spending the night. Actually, he's glad she's out of the house tonight. With some quiet, maybe he can get a little studying done. Two hours later, having been able to digest only a few pages from his history book, he decides he must get out. He gets a beer. The kitchen clock says 11:12.

It's too late to call anyone, so he drives a half-hour to a teen club in the Valley. A tap on the shoulder. A peroxide blonde with a bare midriff stares unabashedly at him. "I met you at Jill's party, remember?" the girl says.

"Sure, at Jill's," he lies.

The girl nods and giggles. "*Riggghht.*" The languid word seems to have three, four syllables. "I'm Angie. You're . . . ?"

Because there is nothing else to do, because he feels, staring at this girl's eager face, that he *must*, he dances with her as a Duran Duran song segues into "Dancing in the Dark." She sways from side to side, opening her eyes exaggeratedly wide and looking at him hungrily, just like the brunette in Springsteen's video does for Bruce, even swinging her arms with the same rocking motion. He doesn't even realize the song has ended, when the girl grabs hold of his arm. They are moving, out the front door, toward the parking lot, where her friends are sitting in a guy's Porsche, some girl with her head on the guy's lap.

"Where are *you* going?" one of her friends shouts at Angie. She waves and says she'll see them later. Andy wonders where she is dragging him. They stand against the wall and she chats: She is a tenth-grader at Cleveland High School, in the Valley. She wants to be a beautician or maybe a computer salesperson. Her family moved here from Nebraska, five years ago. She didn't hate Nebraska, she says, but Los Angeles is better because there are more people with tans and better movies and music, things that interest her, not like in Omaha, where people mostly talked about *futures*.

"What's that?"

"Farm stuff."

"Oh."

They listen to Mötley Crüe all the way to her house, and, once inside, she turns on the television in a tiny living room, sits on the couch, taps her hand against a pillow to indicate Andy should sit next to her. She says that her parents are out of town. Andy instinctively reaches for the television control box on the top of the set. It isn't there. She's got no remote control. He finds a video program — not MTV, because this house doesn't have cable — but some program on a network where a British guy runs down the hits and talks to the bands. Sting's face appears on the screen. "He's so gorgeous," says Angie. She looks enraptured as she says it, which is fine, thinks Andy, who is content to just sit and relax with this girl for a half-hour before something happens. Angie stands up, leaves the room, and when she returns, she has two Carta Blancas in her hands. "Can I ask you something?" she asks.

"Sure."

"Do you like me at all?"

"Yeah, I think you're cute." Just don't tell somebody that you're interested in getting serious with them, he thinks. "I have to tell you," says Angie, "I think you're real cool. I don't know if you can get a full-on crush on somebody in one night, but I'm getting one. I hope that doesn't freak you."

Lust is something he'll accommodate. Sublimating biological needs is plain unhealthy, not to mention boring. He bends down and kisses her slowly, sticking his tongue in her mouth to see how she'll respond. She opens her mouth even wider. When the time comes, she takes off her jeans and panties, and puts them neatly over a chair with her halter-top and everything else, pausing to fold and smooth the jeans. She studies them, he notices, to make sure the crease is straight. Calvin Kleins, fifty bucks a pop. This Valley girl wouldn't likely be able to afford many pairs. Taking a brush out of her purse, she takes a few swipes at her hair and then knocks some pillows off a couch. Making love there isn't as difficult as he would have imagined; once in position, you don't need much space. He comes easily, maybe too quickly, because Angie is still writhing, her heat coming off in little pools of sweat on her shoulders and stomach, eyes closed, chin tilted toward the ceiling, pushing, pushing, heaving her body toward the stucco. He does not even know when it happens for her, but suddenly she is still, breathing slowly, a frown on her face. "There's a draft in here, could you find me a blanket?" she asks softly. He puts his sweater over her and runs into a bathroom, takes a towel, and lays it over her legs. He sits on the couch, smiling at her. She stretches and purrs, pulls down his face, and kisses him. "I feel like I could sleep a whole day."

"I have to get going soon," he says.

"Why?"

"Well, your parents . . ."

"My parents don't get home until noon."

"I have to help my father clean out some office files tomorrow morning," he lies. He stands and reaches for his pants.

Smiling, she tries to pull him back onto the couch. He yanks free. "Hey, I *have* to," he snaps. He puts his pants on. She sits up, scans his face, looks a little helpless. He bends down again and kisses her mouth, hard and reassuring. "My father really gets pissed off if I'm not up early to help him."

"That's cool. I understand." She puts his sweater on him, and begins unfolding her Calvin Kleins.

"I'll call you," he says. "I had a great time."

She has no choice but to accept this. She slips the Calvin Kleins back on. "Call me soon, okay? You can call me anytime you want. Here's my number." The number is on a piece of notepad paper that has a picture of a pink elephant and a caption reading, "I NEVER FORGET."

He smiles. "Okay, I'll call you this week. Maybe I'll come by your high school and pick you up. Where is Cleveland?"

"Well, I don't go to Cleveland exactly. I go there in two years. I'm kind of in junior high."

"*Junior high?*"

"But I'm in eighth grade. It's only two grades away."

On the way home, he takes Mulholland Drive's turns at sixty-five, the car's backside spinning precariously, the boy trying to purge all of the bad things he is feeling, swearing at himself for having gone to the club at all, for wasting his time, for being with some Valley girl whom he'll never see again. He feels exhausted. It will be at least four thirty by the time he gets to bed. He has statistics homework, his essay, and an SAT preparation book to work on over the weekend. At this rate, he won't get started until noon, maybe two in the afternoon. The car is going over the center line. He steps it up to seventy. And what if Angie gets his phone number? Why hadn't he left her alone? Each time he does something like this, he always insists on leaving the girl right in the middle of the night, so as not to lead her into believing there is any chance in hell that he might be interested in a relationship. Surprisingly, only a few ever get angry. He passes a sign on some rocks that says, "Go faster," and then a road sign on which someone has taken spray paint to change the thirty-mile-per-hour speed limit to eighty. He presses his foot to the floor and does ninety, screaming in the turn, the car hitting a bump and rising into the air a couple of inches, his adrenaline pumping like hell, sweat beading on his neck, his mind making decisions in microseconds over the precipice, feeling like he has been miraculously delivered when he pulls into the eerie calm of his driveway at four fifteen.

It is not until the middle of the afternoon that he finally awakens and sits down to look at his SAT booklet. Turning to the mathematics section, his weak area, he finds a few basic algebra problems. A question: "Two cars are 680 miles apart, traveling toward each other. Car A, traveling at 60 miles per hour, has left three hours earlier than car B, which is traveling at 40 miles per hour. How long will car A travel before the two cars meet?

"(a) 12 hours (b) 5 hours (c) 8 hours (d) 6 hours"

Andy has no idea. He anxiously thumbs through the book to see whether he needs to study this kind of problem at all. Maybe it's not on either the SAT or the Achievement Tests. He finds an explanation in the book. All the problems come from either the SATs or Achievement Tests, Levels I and II, says the book.

The answer is: (c) 8 hours. He has no clue how the book arrived at it. He walks downstairs, takes a Budweiser out of the refrigerator, and drinks it at the kitchen table. He eats a sandwich. He watches a Tom Cruise movie. He looks at a little plaque on his den wall, a surprise from his father after third grade when he received the highest marks in his class. It reads, "To a terrific son — straight A boy — June, 1977." At the bottom of the plaque there is a salutation, "Love, Mom and Dad." His parents had had an IQ test administered to him that year, and he had scored exceptionally high, off the board, said his dad proudly, the test results seemingly validated by Andy's sterling marks in fourth and fifth grade. Where did he spin off the road? What is the point? There is no point. Bad way to think, bad way to think. Tom Cruise is making out with a hooker on a subway train. He'll look at his SAT booklet tomorrow.

With Hillary's friends busy on Saturday night, she decides to get an early start on the weekend's mountain of homework, doing physiology and English assignments, not even bothering to watch "Saturday Night Live" when it comes on at eleven thirty, determined to get ahead in her classes. She falls asleep on the living room floor at two thirty, and awakens at noon on Sunday only because she hears the front door open and slam. It is her mom and her latest boyfriend, a doctor. Hillary doesn't move. The two adults mumble hello.

"Why are you sleeping on the floor?" her mother asks.

"I was studying late. Fell off, I guess."

"Studying on a Saturday night?"

One of her English texts lies on the coffee table. She gestures at it, removes the glass that has left a water stain on the pages. "I'm trying not to fall behind." Something occurs to her. "Why didn't you wake me up this morning?"

"I wasn't here. Harry and I . . ." — she rubs the arm of her doctor, who is already looking away, inspecting an antique cigarette box — ". . . well, we got into some car troubles over near Palm Springs and we had to get the car fixed. A radiator, I think." She laughs uneasily and looks at this man Harry, who is studying an abstract on the wall. Her mom, Hillary has noticed, keeps a constant monitor on her boyfriends' movements and reactions. Running scared.

"Yes, I think it was a radiator — wasn't that it, Harry?"

The doctor's eyes do not leave the abstract. "She's seventeen, there's no need for that now," he says, in a tone he must use on supercilious young residents. "No purpose in that. She can handle the truth. Do you have something to wet my lips with?"

Hillary lies back on the living room floor, closes her eyes.

Her mom opens the antique cigarette box, lights a Winston.

The doctor makes himself a scotch and soda.

"You all right?" her mother asks Hillary.

"Fine."

"The soda water is kind of flat," says the doctor.

———

Monday. In front of an administrative office at Beverly, a list of honor students from the previous semester hangs taped to a window. The list is so long that there seems to be nothing special in being acknowledged. Not to be on the list, however, is often to feel stigmatized. "Everybody knows who's a star and who's not," says Andy. "If you feel average, you feel like a loser. Everybody knows that. That's the way it's always been. It's a pretty old thing."

It is a new thing to Beth Cann, thirty-seven, Beverly's newest counselor. She has come here from Glendale High School, twenty miles and a galaxy away, where over 25 percent of the seniors do not go on to college and 50 percent speak a language other than English in their homes. "I had Hispanic kids, Korean kids, Vietnamese kids, and other Asian immigrants in my caseload who were ESL," she says, educational jargon for students who are learning English as a second language. "The kids were from families struggling to make it, working very hard to get ahead, to learn the language, fit in. It was very rewarding and moving." At Beverly, the ESL kids, constituting about 17 percent of the student body, come largely from the families of Iranian expatriates. It is not the same for Beth Cann. "You admittedly have to adjust to some new sets of expectations," she will say, months later. "Most here succeed academically, and that is nice. It's especially nice when you see some kid in your caseload who is doing well. But I think I still get the most pleasure, like I did at Glendale, helping out the kid with a problem, who then manages to do a lot better."

She looks the way you'd like a counselor to look if you were sixteen years old again — friendly and attractive, with the kind of short brown hair that is in style this term, and a humor which suggests that two visits a term to discuss your academic future with her would not be torture. She has put her inspirational posters and bumper stickers on the walls of her new office: "You Have Failed When You Have Failed To Try"; "There Is No One Else In The World Like You"; and "CANN CAN." She has come here ready to inspire and motivate, only there does not seem to be much motivating needed. "There are so many self-starters here," she says in amazement, "so many who want to know if they can take more courses, do more things; want to know what they'll need to get into the Ivies. They just want information from you and then they are out the door."

She graduated from UCLA in 1970, a period when ambition was regarded with suspicion. "Now the whole 'fifties pragmatism has come home to roost again, I think," she says. "I've talked to a lot of kids who know what their parents make. Quite a few of them know what their parents' mortgage payments are, car payments, taxes, and expenses. They know the bottom lines, because their parents give them that kind of information more often, especially single parents who treat them more as friends or companions than they do as kids. The kids are regarded, at an early age, as little adults, and they learn that it is a very competitive world out there. Academic success is greatly admired and expected in this community. At Glendale, kids would cluster to discuss the basketball team. Here, they cluster to find out where so-and-so is applying to college. . . ."

There have been years when as many as sixty Beverly students have applied to Stanford, with fifteen being accepted during one particularly bountiful spring. "It matters so much to get into the right school," she says, "the big school, Harvard or Yale or some other Ivy League, or some public Ivy, as a lot of people are calling them, like the University of Michigan or Berkeley. . . . The feeling that they *must* get into such a school, that it is their only ticket to success, *that's* new. Before, the attitude was, 'Well, I hope I get into Ivy, but if I don't, I'll work hard and be fine.' Now, for a lot of them, it's 'I must make it or else.' A Cal State becomes embarrassing, a disgrace, for these kids. These kids are already thinking fifteen years ahead. I have a kid who asked me what medical specialty makes the most money. He's worried about his *subspecialty*. The kids only see a few professions. Unless it's part of the Magic Twenty — lawyer, doctor, psychologist, television, business, computers, engineering, and all of the rest of the predictable ones — they're not interested. Teaching? Forget it. . . .

"I don't think that it has everything to do with being materialistic. I just think, unfortunately, that these kids have been told that if they don't make it big now, they'll somehow fail forever."

She glances at her bumper stickers. "What can I say to them? Sometimes I'll tell them that, twenty years from now, no one is going to be reminiscing about trigonometry or Spanish V. I'll say, 'This is your one chance to be kids. Have fun. Let your hair down.' I'll tell them all of that, but a lot of kids don't want to hear it."

———

Steven has been an educational star from the time, two years ago, when he took a speed-reading course and a study plan class from a private educational company that immediately enabled him to categorize and memorize facts with an ease he hadn't imagined possible. Since then, he has received an A in every class but chemistry, raising his g.p.a. to 3.8. His only regret is that he didn't take the course a year earlier. Still, it hasn't been bad, he thinks, looking at the A on his first history test of the year. At the top of the test's short essay answer, the teacher has printed in big red letters, "Well-organized essay," and, in the margins, there are scattered scribblings: "Nice transition"; "Good topic sentence"; "Fine use of supporting materials"; and a comment that Steven doesn't understand, "Steve, is this *polemical,* perhaps?" Steven doesn't know what the word means. He doesn't care. He has been concentrating upon learning facts, in his English and history courses — dates, places, names, famous figures and eras, particular passages from famous plays and historical speeches, and brief, preferably one- or two-sentence descriptions of watershed events — because this material will probably serve as the foundation for his big exams. Understanding unifying themes, knowing what light "the facts" shed upon a particular historical period, concerns him only to the extent that he may be asked to summarize the material in a paragraph or so. No detailed knowledge is essential, because the teachers never expect the essay answers to run more than a page or so. Forty- and fifty-minute classes simply don't offer the luxury of long essay tests. Because time is precious and facts are the province of his existence, he has taken to reading only what he must. He has had a recurring dream in which he arrives for an English exam exhausted and hopelessly underprepared because he labored until five A.M. on a government paper and ran out of time. You have to cut corners. Novels for his English class are best read in Cliff Notes that provide you with brief descriptions of plot and character. History is best read with the sweeping-eye technique that he learned in his speed-reading course. Books are a dying art form, he thinks, to be largely replaced at some point in his lifetime by compact discs from which he'll be able to get stories and reports at his leisure, when not watching TV or tapes on his VCR. The compact discs will be largely informational, he imagines — detailed forecasts of stocks and metal markets; stories about social trends and hot personalities; essays on shifting foreign political alliances that spell problems for American interests. Novels, the dream world of literature, will be supplanted by spectacular video fantasies. He sees all this as an inevitable and welcome change, for art will then become accessible to the millions who do not care to read now. Intellectuals whose work went previously unnoticed will find themselves forced to turn to media that will give them respectable audiences for the first time. Everybody will profit.

The leaders, he believes, will be the ones who will be able to put all of these futuristic networks together, while making sure no new competition cuts in on their gold mines. That's where he can see himself, making the right connections, carving a niche atop the crest of change, studying trends, using television in a new way to mold public opinion. Music might be the next great tool in political and social campaigns, he's beginning to think. He can see a candidate being marketed largely around music videos, like those Chrysler commercials where you see an Americana landscape and then hear a swell of music boasting that Industrial America's pride is back. The commercial ends with the shining curmudgeon face of Lee Iacocca and an American flag. Very hot. Yeah, Iacocca could be a winner in politics. He thinks the first video candidate might be only a few years away. Something to think about there, something, perhaps, that he could get into as a college kid, while the field is still relatively uncharted. He can see some surfing shots in such a film. He doesn't yet know what their significance would be to a candidate's campaign: maybe a message that you needed to dare to ride your dream, something inspirational like that. He tries to imagine the music playing over the waves, the candidate sitting on the beach looking reflective. Yeah, that might work. And *he* could do it. Getting off to a good start in school has made him feel omnipotent. After his last class, he decides to go surfing, and drinks a couple of Michelobs on the drive to the beach.

———

Kelly likes the Go-Go's. She has every album they've ever made, and she likes to sing and dance to them anywhere, anytime, but especially when her mother and the housekeeper are out of the house and she can turn the stereo on as loud as she wants. In the empty house, she can have a few glasses of wine, go a little crazy, dance around in just her bra and panties, and fantasize she is on a giant outdoor concert stage. She can pretend she's the lead singer, Belinda Carlisle, and jump around on the couches as if they were giant amplifiers. But, tonight, she has to be quiet. She can only listen to her tape through headphones. It is two A.M. She went dancing on a school night at Gazzarri's again, and by the time she drove home, pressed the coded buttons disengaging the alarm, and stepped inside her house, it was 1:45 A.M. Her mother had left a note: "I am very upset with you. There is some fish in the microwave. I want to talk with you tomorrow night at eight. Tell Ismelda if you won't be here and tell her where you will be. *This must stop.*"

Shoeless, a glass of wine in her hand, she sways back and forth in front of the den's tape player, eyes closed, humming softly in tune with Belinda Carlisle, imagining herself on the big stage. She feels a little lightheaded from the wine, wishes she'd eaten dinner earlier. Ismelda, their housekeeper, has left her some brownies on the kitchen table, along with a note. "Goode things," it reads in the same black crayon she sometimes uses for her grocery lists. Sweet Ismelda. Ismelda has been making things for her as long as Kelly can remember — chocolate chip cookies, Mexican cookies, popcorn balls with little ribbons, rock candy. The twenty or forty dollars a week that Kelly gets from her mom feels like an impersonal welfare check by comparison. A selfless woman, even saintly, her father said about Ismelda before he moved out of the house. Last year, Ismelda gave her the stereo headphones as a surprise gift, and Kelly had been touched until her mother suggested that this might be Ismelda's kindhearted way of hinting that she couldn't bear listening to the blasting stereo any longer. Since then, Kelly has stuck to the headphones when anyone else has been in the house. Belinda Carlisle is wailing. Kelly points at the crowd in her mind, wiggles her bottom. She sees little green numbers on the VCR: 2:36 A.M. She feels a headache coming on. She has to get up in four hours so she can do her hair. Her two-page essay on capital punishment will have to go unfinished.

On Monday afternoon, while baby-sitting little Timmy from down the block, she gets a call from Tina, who asks if she'd like to meet at Power Burger. "Sure," says Kelly. "I'll take Timmy with me. We'll be there in five minutes." A half-hour later, with Tina already waiting at a table, she pulls into Power Burger in her Porsche, parking the car across two spaces, so that no other vehicle can get close. She nudges a pouting Timmy out of the car, and Tina immediately asks if she got into trouble last night for coming home so late.

"My mom just told me I had to keep better hours," Kelly says. "I've had that conversation with her about a million times in my life. I could do it in my sleep."

She strokes Timmy's hair. The boy takes off stereo headphones he's been wearing. "I want *hamburguesa* and *papas fritas*," he says. "And *agua*."

"Stop talking Spanish," Kelly says. "Your mom keeps telling you that."

"And *lechuga* on the *hamburguesa*."

"Give me a break, Timmy."

The boy puts his headphones back on. "I'd totally not let my housekeeper talk Spanish all the time," Tina says.

"His housekeeper's real nice," Kelly says. "She gives him presents and sleeps with him when he's sick. Ismelda was like that for me."

The girls eat their hamburgers and compare cosmetics. An hour and a half passes. Tina says she has to go.

"*Timmy*." Kelly picks up the little boy's headphones and shouts into his right ear. "Tina has to leave. Where do you want to go?" Timmy puts his thumb with ketchup on it into his mouth. "The Wherehouse," he finally mumbles. "Okay? We can get a Prince tape."

━━━━━━

That week, Melinda's four-day trip to the East to look at colleges begins with a walking tour of Harvard. She's disappointed; the guys look wimpy and the girls dumpy. Something tells her that she might have to readjust her expectations of Ivy League schools; not everybody looks like Rob Lowe.

On a Friday night, she meets two of her Boston cousins and goes to a party in Cambridge. One of her cousins and her boyfriend are wearing matching overcoats. Melinda thinks they look weird. She can't relate to these people. The girls are wearing full makeup and long formal skirts, and no one seems willing to make conversation with a California visitor whom they've never met before. There are twenty people or so in the small house, watching videos on TV, the stereo on, a couple of people off dancing by themselves. Melinda sits down next to a fat boy eating clams from a can and wearing a frayed T-shirt. She says hello, to which the boy nods and murmurs, "Hey." He turns away, stares at the TV. Melinda asks him where he goes to school, hears a mumble that sounds like "B.U." Some people are talking about South Africa. Too boring. She goes upstairs in the strange house, finds a bedroom, closes the door, and phones her good friend Cecilia in Beverly Hills. "I'm at this party with all these rude geeks," she says. She wonders whether she should tell the owners of the house that she has made a long-distance call, and is still thinking about it as she gets aboard the jet to fly home, two days later.

The next week, at a meeting of community center volunteers for the day-care and Adopt-a-Friend program, a coordinator asks newcomers to sketch something that reflects their feelings about life. Melinda sketches a sun and an overcast sky. Somebody else draws a mushroom cloud with a skeletal hand. The most interesting picture, Melinda thinks, is one of a man walking backwards toward a coffin, sketched by a boy who has always struck Melinda as carefree and gregarious. Prodded by the coordinator, the boy says he just has this feeling of stumbling blindly through life, unable to see the misery and death that lies out there somewhere, waiting for him. Melinda leans forward, on the edge of her seat, listening to the boy and others confess to dreams, anxieties, paranoia. Melinda won't dare discuss anything about her personal life, not with kids whom she barely knows. "I can't believe sometimes what people say to complete strangers," she says later. "I just totally wouldn't want to say something that somebody might use to think you're weird. I don't trust people that much. You have to be careful what you say at those meetings or at a place like Beverly. But I love to go to the meetings. I can't wait to hear what people are going to say each week. It's like I'm watching 'Santa Barbara' or something."

———

On a foggy Saturday morning in late September, Andy goes to a converted art studio in West Los Angeles for the first session of an SAT course, his dad's words from last night still ringing in his head: "It's costing me four hundred, so make it worth the investment, okay?" Andy didn't want to spend his Saturday mornings locked up in a room for three hours, but he figured he had no choice: He just couldn't discipline himself enough to sit down with his SAT books and take the dozens of reading comprehension tests, learn the hundreds of vocabulary words, and do the algebra and geometry problems that he never bothered to study in high school. He feels like a loser. Most of these kids don't look as if they fall into the category of superstars trying to boost their scores into the 1400s or 1500s, more likely defectives, headed toward junior colleges, simply praying for a mediocre score. The blonde girl next to him is peering intently into a tiny makeup mirror and humming some song under her breath. On his other side, a kid in red tennis shoes and a jean jacket, smaller than himself, with two, maybe three days' growth of beard, spills sunflower seeds on his desk and begins arranging them in a semicircle. Andy observes him warily out of the corner of his eye, sees him take a dull pencil and begin swatting the sunflower seeds across the room. "Direct hit, direct hit," says the kid. He turns to Andy. "You got a pencil I can borrow?" he asks. "I wasted this one. Come on, man, just give me one from your load." Andy has brought four sharpened No. 2 pencils to the class and placed them on the corner of his desk. His surplus looks stupid. He gives one of the pencils to the kid, who sends a seed flying into the back of the blonde girl's teased hairdo. "Have destroyed friendly craft," the kid says.

An instructor suddenly enters the room, and, in a single deft motion, the boy has put the pencil into his shirt pocket and swept the sunflower seeds into his hands. He begins eating them. *Crack, crack, crack, crack.*

"Hey, man, could you eat those things a little more quietly?" Andy asks him.

"Sorry, man," says the kid.

"The SAT doesn't reward real knowledge and insight," says the instructor. "Look at it as a game. We're going to bust the game. But that requires . . ."

Crack, crack, crack, crack.

"Could you get rid of those seeds, *now*, man?" Andy demands. "I can't concentrate."

The kid pauses in mid-chew, arranges two seeds between his bottom teeth and incisors, surveys Andy, and grins. CRACK, CRACK, CRACK. Andy feels goose bumps on his shoulders. He hears only fragments of the instructor's words: ". . . will require your complete commitment. . . . This course can be fun, but more important than it being fun, is how important it is to your future, to what college will accept you."

CRACK, CRACK, CRACK.

". . . Accomplish all of this and I think we can raise your score anywhere from fifty to two hundred points. Let's begin right now by learning how to discern thesis phrases and how not to get bogged down in technical terms in the scientific sections. Let's examine this thesis phrase where you can see that . . ."

CRACK.

Andy's body twitches involuntarily. "Do that again," he says, doing his best to sound sinister, "and I'll fucking stomp your face when we get out of here, jerk-off."

The kid scrutinizes him, smiles. "All you had to do was *ask*."

Ninety minutes later, the instructor calls for a ten-minute break. Andy stays in his seat a few minutes, looking over his notes, feeling good; the class has already opened his eyes, he thinks, to techniques that will increase his speed in the comprehension sections. That alone could be worth fifty to one hundred points and a possible score in the high 1100s. Why limit himself? A score in the 1200s or 1300s might send him to a hotshot school. He is smiling, flush with the glow of his fantasy, when he hears a small voice behind him say, "Do you have a quarter I can borrow for the phone?"

Andy wheels around, glimpses a packet of seeds sticking out of a shirt pocket. "Maybe next time you shouldn't spend all your money on those shitty sunflower droppings," he tells the kid.

"Hey, I'll give you a dollar for two quarters," the kid says. "I have to call home. Just give me a little change and I'll give you a buck."

"Oh, shit." He hands the kid the quarter, and says, "Forget it," when the kid extends a dollar bill. Andy shakes his head, wishes the dude would just go away.

He walks back into the class, the kid following a couple of paces behind. An hour and a half later, employing some of the instructor's new pointers, Andy surprises himself by doing moderately well on a mock math section. Walking out, he feels elated.

Twelve thirty, his watch says. He's due at the hospital by one fifteen for his volunteer shift. After it ends, he'll look at his SAT booklet some more. He sees four kids pile into a GTO with a dent in the rear. A sticker on the bumper says "University High." They aren't Beverly kids, he realizes, wondering why his mother hadn't found this out and enrolled him in some course closer to home. He climbs into her Jaguar, turns the key, hears nothing. He gives it one more try. Dead. "*Shit!*" he screams so loudly that he can see the other kids glancing back, snickering.

He walks toward a phone booth. "That phone is dead," announces a voice familiar by now. *Crack, crack, crack.* "You gotta go to the gas station at Barrington if you want a phone."

Andy nods and, without looking at the boy, begins walking away. "Your car flooded?" the kid asks.

Andy turns around. "I think I left the inside lights on," he admits.

The kid offers Andy a ride to the gas station in his Volkswagen Bug. Must be one of those people, Andy thinks, who won't let you alone once they think they've touched your life for either better or worse. "I think I'm going to leave my car here," he says. "What'd be cool is if you could drive me to the hospital where I work. It's only ten minutes from here. I can pay you."

"Okay," says the kid. "You don't have to pay me. You gave me that quarter."

They cruise down Olympic Boulevard, David Bowie doing "China Girl" on the radio, the kid singing along. Andy usually dislikes it when people sing along so loudly that they nearly drown out a song, though, in this case, it isn't so bad because the kid sings pretty good, does a better than passable imitation of Bowie warning the China Girl to keep him out of her life; that he'll bring her television, blue eyes, and weapons to control the world if she lets him in. For months, Andy had thought the song meant that Bowie would give the China Girl a lot of cool Western things, like a hot stereo and TV, but then he read a review and found out what the song really meant. He doesn't quite understand why Bowie would get so bummed out about the China Girl watching television or getting blue eyes; hell, all these Asian kids ever want are our blue jeans and sweatshirts — he's read it in *Time*. The kid is still singing, his voice rising to falsetto to imitate Bowie imitating the China Girl, who's trying to ease her lover's torment by telling him to cool out and shut up. The kid does it well, sounding just the way Andy imagines a real China girl would, one part submissive love-servant, the other hard-core fuck-you revolutionary ready to slay the imperialistic dog. "You sing a lot better than you chew seeds," he says to the kid.

"I'm going to try to put together a band," the kid says. "I want to play parties. Shit like that."

"That sounds cool. I wanted to play in a band, but it was, you know, too hard to find one. I play a little guitar."

"Listen to this." The kid puts a tape into his cassette player. A group, not Led Zeppelin, is singing, "Stairway to Heaven." The singer could be a sound-alike for Robert Plant. "Me," says the kid.

"No shit?"

The kid shakes his head, turns into a driveway as Andy points at the hospital.

"Hey, my band is practicing tonight if you want to come by," the kid says.

"What's your name?"

"Jason."

"Mine's Andy."

"We'll probably start around eight thirty or nine if you want to come."

Jason's band practices in his family's garage in Culver City. The kid looks surprised when Andy shows up, but he immediately gives him a beer and introduces him to the other guys, who are tuning instruments and talking about amps and synthesizers and mixing consoles, a technical language foreign to Andy, who tries to stick close to Jason. The phone rings. Jason's father shouts out that one of the kids is wanted home by his mother. "Goddammit," says the kid, who gently puts his rhythm guitar down, and, running to the phone, tries to persuade his mother to let him stay another hour. He slams the phone down. "My mom needs me to drive my little brother somewhere," he says. "I have to go. Sorry."

The boy begins to leave. "Hey, could you just let us hang on to your guitar?" asks Jason. "Maybe Andy could try to play, just for tonight, since we're all here anyway. I'll bring it back as soon as we're all done. Promise."

The boy hesitates, looks at Andy, then Jason, as if trying to figure out whether there is some special, unspoken reason for inviting the new kid here tonight. He manages to smile. "Sure," he says agreeably. "Take it. I'll be home late tonight."

"I haven't played with a band ever," Andy interrupts. "I'll probably suck."

"Yeah, you probably will," Jason says. "But if you want to stay, you play."

"Yeah, dude," says another guy. They set the equipment up, and Andy plays. It isn't as hard as he imagined. Fingers remember, even under the pressure of a tiny audience of four guys. He likes them. Between songs, they have a couple of beers. When they finish playing at eleven thirty, they all pile into Jason's Bug to get chili cheeseburgers at an all-night stand. Andy has to stick his feet out the window so that everyone can fit. "Man, you play all right," Jason says to him, between his Bowie impersonations. It's the best Andy can remember feeling in a long while.

OCTOBER

Monday morning brings him crashing back to reality. Tests in physics are returned, and Andy has received a C. "I'm fucked," he snaps that night. "It means it might be over for me in physics. Means I probably won't get anything above a B even if I bust my balls. It's like I don't know how to do it anymore, like knowing how to study. It used to be so easy for me when I worked, and you kind of wonder why it isn't now." By the evening, having been offered help in physics from his mathematics tutor, Andy feels better. Tutors are regarded as learning tools of the elite. Each of them, except Kelly, has taken advantage of at least one tutor or SAT preparatory course. Andy and Paul have tutors for English and mathematics whom they see, on the average, twice a week. Last spring, when it looked to Steven that he was on his way to receiving a mediocre B in trigonometry and a disastrous C in chemistry, he hired a math-science tutor who helped him get the A in trig and B in chemistry necessary to remain in contention for Ivy League admission. Hillary had tutors periodically during her sophomore year for French and geometry. Hillary, Melinda, Paul, and Steven took special SAT courses, during their junior year, for which they paid private companies over two hundred dollars apiece. Andy is taking his second preparatory course within six months.

No exam they take in high school will be as important as the Scholastic Aptitude Test. The national norm is a score of about 900. A score of 1000–1100 will generally land the otherwise qualified applicant in a state school, and 1200 will provide him with a good chance at winning admission to a competitive private college. Anything above 1300 means that the accomplished student will receive serious consideration from the Ivies. A poor showing on the SAT, conversely, more often than not consigns applicants to undistinguished schools. Andy has heard about the criticisms of the test, the claims that it doesn't gauge learning aptitude as much as it tests what applicants already know, but he hasn't noticed that the controversy has lessened colleges' reliance on the test. Just a casual look at the median SAT scores of the nation's top private universities and state schools makes clear that, with few exceptions, a score below 1150 is tantamount to rejection.

Students at Beverly know this, even if the colleges will not admit it. As early as the spring term of their sophomore years, they begin preparing for the SAT, in hopes of conquering the three-hour, one hundred forty-five question format — trying to do its slightly unconventional algebra and geometry problems that don't permit test-takers simply to plug in learned formulae and theorems the way most textbook problems do, and confronting the test's formidable verbal section, consisting of antonyms, analogies, sentence completions, and reading-comprehension questions. Unlike the mathematics section, the verbal section does not lend itself to easy improvement in test scores, since it is largely a test of a student's reading habits from elementary school, a vocabulary exam, in short. Steven spent the hot summer before his junior year trying to build his vocabulary by memorizing the meanings of more than a thousand words employed on past SATs, in addition to taking two SAT review courses at a combined cost of six hundred dollars. In the end, he doesn't believe he gained more than twenty to forty points on the verbal section when he finally took the test. However, he believes that the preparatory courses paid big dividends on the math section, perhaps giving him an additional fifty to one hundred points.

He scored in the high 1300s, putting him in the running for the Ivies. Melinda, who took the test during the spring of her junior year, scored in the mid-1200s, giving her a reasonable-to-outside chance at the Ivies, depending upon the particular school, more likely destining her for admission at a second-echelon school — Wesleyan, Amherst, or Williams. Paul and Andy, who scored in the low 1000s and mid-1000s, respectively, on the spring SAT, will be retaking it this month, having finished SAT prep courses that purport to improve students' performances by one hundred points on the average. Having scored in the low 1000s, Hillary doesn't figure that she can get any higher. Kelly, who received a dismal score in the low 900s, says in a flat, defiant tone that she wouldn't have minded an 800. Steven admits that any score under 1350 would have forced him to retake the test. "That would have meant going through hell again," he admits. Paul and Andy are dealing with the anxiety for the second and last time.

"This is my last shot forever," says Andy.

On Thursday, he gets another essay back, this one on the Equal Rights Amendment, Andy having done his best to give the teacher what he demanded — "thoughtful analysis and cogent arguments." He's received a C-minus, can't believe it, has to fight the urge to go up to the teacher at his desk during the middle of class and say that he spent two hours reading *Newsweek* articles on women's rights in preparation for writing the goddamn two pages. *Two fucking hours* . . . and having to settle for a cold dinner because he hadn't wanted to take a break and risk losing his weak concentration on the material. In the paper's margins, the teacher has written, "You haven't at all developed these positions to which you refer. There isn't enough of your viewpoint here or any factual substantiation cited." At the bottom of the page, another comment: "Andy, these sentences don't have transitions or any logical link between them. You've strung eight different arguments together with no cogent theme. Try harder for lucidity. Lucidity is key."

Lucidity: Another of those words he should damn well know but doesn't. He can get its message, though: He can't write worth shit. He folds up the paper quickly, slips it in the pocket of his three-ring notebook to prevent the competitive geeks on each side of him from getting a look at it, and slowly lowers his head on his desk, closing his eyes. For a moment. Just a moment. He needs it. Cheek to wood, he feels perspiration dampening his desk, his heart pounding. This was supposed to be the class that offered his best shot at an A. The future looks blacker than an attendance clerk's heart. He wonders: Do junior colleges have dorms or do you just party by vending machines? A class discussion has begun on somebody's economy. It takes him a while to realize it. His head ringing in a hot daze, he stares in the direction of his teacher, actually through him, glazed eyes locking upon a map of the world, his mind barely turning over, unable to think of anything but *Lucidity* and that C which, with its minus sign, so big and red and indifferently scrawled, kind of says it all, he thinks. *Minus*: It doesn't mark him as a moron so much, only as someone not nearly special enough. An average guy. A loser in a very competitive world, maybe; but someone who would eventually learn to get by, along with all of the other average guys, and be content with less. This is the blackest thought of all. He tells himself to take it easy; tries, as his father is always urging him, to think of great possibilities: With a high enough score on the SATs or Achievement Tests, a C in this class won't matter.

"*Andy? Earth to Andy!*" Words about the Federal Reserve Something fly by him. The teacher is staring at him, waiting. Andy says, instinctively, that he doesn't know, isn't sure. About the answer. And such. Fortuitously, bells ring, the discussion ends, class is over. Forty minutes seem to have passed in a surreal two. His head still feels heavy. The teacher reminds kids sprinting for a door about a reading assignment, then waves a big index finger at Andy to come forward.

Shit. In one motion, he grabs his sweater, flips his big three-ring notebook shut, and trudges up his row, bumping into kids rushing the opposite way toward the rear door, one bruiser swearing at him when Andy's blue felt pen goes sailing out of the spiral notebook and bounces off the kid's natty corduroy pants, leaving a conspicuous mark. "*Jesus Christ*," moans the kid.

"Don't be a dick," Andy mumbles, keeps moving. The teacher shakes his head, wearily motions for him to take a seat alongside his desk.

"You mad at the world, Andy?"

"No."

"You're swearing at people, you're falling asleep in my class, you won't participate. You want to tell me what's going on?"

"Nothing. I'm sorry. I'm just not feeling real good today." He stares at his watch. He still has practice tests in his SAT booklets to do. How long is this guy gonna keep him? His teacher rifles through his class book, looking at test and quiz scores. "Andy, you can't exactly afford not to pay attention in here, you know."

"I know. I'm feeling really bad, that's all. Really."

His teacher rolls his eyes back in his head and coughs theatrically. "*I'm dying, Andy, I'm dying*. Hey, not that I don't believe *you*! Listen, whatever this illness is, don't let it go on too long, if you understand what I'm saying. We don't want a repeat of sophomore year. I'm sure you don't want to go through that again."

Andy says nothing. During sophomore year, he had failed so many early quizzes and tests in history that one day he had had to beg this teacher to assign him enough extra credit to raise his grade to a C. "Hey, *I* don't need a repeat of that," says the teacher, grinning. "I had to spend one of my weekends reading those extra-credit papers that you probably copied right out of some book. Am I close? Maybe an encyclopedia? Just maybe?"

Andy shrugs, the thinnest of smiles working at the corners of his mouth.

The teacher laughs. "Am I clairvoyant or what?"

Andy likes the guy. They've been together, off and on, for three years in this classroom, bickering over late assignments, borderline grades, and the legitimacy and frequency of Andy's absences. "The only way you could be absent more often," the guy once said to him, "is if you were blindfolded and being held for ransom by wild and crazy guys in robes who forced you to listen every day to the Ayatollah's Top Forty. And then they'd still have to add another day to the week."

For no reason at all, the guy breaks into his impression of Elmer Fudd having a serious conversation with Ronald Reagan. "Get that Wussian Wabbit, Mister Pwesident. Let's woast him." Andy laughs.

"You ought to smile like that a little more often, buddy," the teacher says. "Nothing could be as bad as you look sometimes."

"God, that's *harsh*. Totally. I don't look bad."

"I didn't say you *look* bad. But you don't look like you're enjoying yourself very often. Are you *that* bored in here?"

He doesn't want to embarrass himself or this guy by mentioning the essay. "No."

"Start proving it."

"I've just felt run down lately. I've been kind of studying late. I've got this SAT thing on Saturday."

"I imagine you are working harder. I'll accept the excuse this time. *Only* this time. Don't be putting your head on your desk anymore while I'm talking. One last thing before you're out of here: *My God*, don't be swearing at your classmates right in front of me. You put me in the position where I *have* to say something if you keep doing that. Either that, or else they'll know I'm as crazy as you."

Andy nods, stands, turns away, and then wheels back, unable to help himself, needing to know the answer to the question so bothering him. "Can I just ask you one thing? If you know I'm working harder, how could you give me a grade like C-minus? It's senior year. If I was a teacher, I'd think about that. I didn't see how, after all that reading I did, you could do that to me."

The teacher shrugs.

"You don't really care anything about the pressure, do you? You have no idea."

"Andy, you know that's not true." The teacher motions for him to sit down again, then spends the next twenty minutes going over his essay, pointing out to him major lapses in reasoning and grammar, offering suggestions for improvement, and rewriting a few of Andy's sentences to present a model of a cogent argument. "Now don't go copying this for another class's extra credit," the teacher admonishes, grinning.

Andy wishes he could hang out with the guy a little. Does the dude party ever? Does he have a home? What would they talk about anyway? It'd probably be too weird. He used to talk a lot with a P.E.

teacher in his freshman year, but the teacher was so swamped by other kids wanting to talk and play ball with him that Andy gave up. God, he's blown a half-hour here already. He's got a hundred or so vocabulary words to study in the SAT booklets. He's gotta get going.

"Andy? *Andy?!* You paying attention here or back on Venus?"

"Uh-huh."

"Uh-huh what?"

"Uh-huh, yes."

"Do me a favor, willya? Every once in a while, show me you're not brain-dead by shaking a finger or something."

"Sorry."

"I'm trying to get across some points here."

"I know. Okay. Sorry. I'm understanding what you're saying. Really. They're good suggestions. Thanks. I better get going. I'll try to do better. It's just that we've never spent much time on learning essays, how to do them, I mean. You never tell us how much of our grade they'll count for."

"Well, you just have to work on them."

"But I don't think I understand the idea real good. And there isn't enough time in class usually. Forty minutes goes too quick."

"I'm aware it's not a lot of time, but just keep trying to do your best."

"It just isn't working for me. I can't do it. Maybe if there was more time sometimes . . ."

"*Okay, okay,*" his teacher interrupts. He stares for a long moment at his faded map of the world. "I know it goes quickly, just continue trying . . . ," he mumbles and shrugs then, a slow, forlorn shrug that tells Andy the guy's back is against the wall with everyone else's. "We'd all like less pressure. Maybe it will be better for you when the classes go back to fifty minutes. You come to me if you want any more help on any of these things, okay?" He picks up a stack of ungraded quizzes on his desk and rolls them into a tube.

"Okay."

"And good luck with the SAT."

"I'm kind of nervous about it. I don't know exactly if I get the math. If I don't score eleven fifty or twelve hundred, I'm probably screwed forever."

"Just do your best."

"I don't know what I'll do if I mess up. I took it once already. Did I tell you that? If I screw up, well, I don't know. My mom says . . ."

"*Andy.* Don't do that to yourself." He grimaces, squeezes his tube of quizzes a little tighter. "If you've done your best, that's all you or anyone else can ask. And something else: It's an important test, but it's still just a test. Try to remember that. Maybe it will help."

"I'll try."

"Get a good night's sleep before."

"Okay."

"Try to relax."

"I'm just so tired."

Saturday, October 12. The SATs. Andy arrives at UCLA with his four sharpened No. 2 pencils. He sits down in the back of the classroom, closes his eyes, and breathes deeply. He hears throats clearing, and some kid in the corner sharpening pencils. There is just enough time for a last breath before a proctor distributes the exams. He feels calmer than he expected. The test goes fine; only on one reading-comprehension section and a few math problems does he feel utterly stumped.

When he gets home, he finds some Godiva chocolates lying on top of his stereo, a bow around them, along with a note from his mother asking if he has found himself an English tutor. He picks up his phone and calls five tutors, recommended by friends, asking for their rates, finally settling on a guy who says that he understands "the system" and how to play it. "Believe me, I know what your teachers expect from you and what you need," the tutor says. "We'll show you how to get ready for these things and help you if you want to put the effort in. Now, you asked me about our fees. Let me tell you the structure we have . . ."

"*Forty-five bucks an hour?*" his father asks incredulously over the phone that night.

"Well, it's the going rate for the top guys, Dad."

"Hey, Andy, I'm not complaining; you need it, and so I'm more than happy to pay it. It's just that maybe we should have all become professional tutors. Well, if you need it, you have to pay the piper, right? How many hours a week can he help you?"

"He said two."

"Tell him to make it three."

"Dad, we're still having lunch Tuesday, right?"

"Sure."

"You're gonna be there, right? I want to know, because Mom is coming, too."

"I know. Take care of the tutor."

———

Months later, Andy will say he wished that he had gone to Andy Gombiner for tutoring. In mid-October, with the SATs finished, the most popular outside educational resource around Beverly becomes twenty-three-year-old Andy Gombiner, head of the Andy Gombiner Tutoring Service, located just two blocks from Beverly. Gombiner, a 1980 graduate of Beverly, has a staff of fifteen tutors and three office assistants who handle correspondence and the computer billing of students at rates beginning at twenty-five dollars an hour for the least-experienced tutors. Gombiner will not discuss the rate for his own personal services except to say that "I'm at the top end because I'm well known around here, and I can do a lot for them." He has a private room for parent and student conferences. "I'll go that extra mile," he says. "If you're a student, it is nice to have somebody like me on your side. It does not come cheaply, but this town can afford somebody like me. I can cut deals with teachers. If a kid has all F's, I'll propose to the teacher that if the kid gets all A's the rest of the way, then the teacher should give him a C, rather than a D. Or I'll ask a teacher what a kid will have to do to come up to a B. . . . I'll show kids how to negotiate with teachers and ask to do extra credit. Because even if the teacher says no, the teacher will remember the kid asked.

"It's harder to get teachers to make concessions for A's. It is really not very fair to ask a teacher to make concessions for A's. But the kids want A's. They think they have to have them. I get B students who want A's, and A students who want A-pluses. They're digging in for a long hard grind, I guess."

He says it matter-of-factly. "I like being with kids. Every day, if I do my job right, I feel like I'm making a little difference. I talk with them a lot, too, because they often have nonacademic reasons for failure. Maybe a kid feels he is a social misfit. If he does, it is hard to concentrate on a book. If I notice any of that, then we'll talk. Some parents call me to ask about their kids. I know their kids a lot better than they do usually. Even popular kids say to me sometimes that there's no one close to them, no one they can really open up to. They say they'd like to be able to talk to someone. I become that person for some students, I guess."

He sounds at once proud and worried about this. "I don't know, it's strange thinking that you're the one — a relative stranger — that some of these kids need to talk with. Isn't that a bit . . . *different?* . . . Shouldn't that be reason for worry?

"I can effect change with some parents' attitudes. Some, though, well, they don't even want to see me. . . . If a parent says, 'God, he only gets B's and C's,' well, then, I have to talk to the parents about that attitude, because that might be one of the problems for the kid, believing that he is a failure in the eyes of his parents. For some of those parents, college is like a status symbol. That attitude rubs off on their kids, I think. The pressure can make them miserable. . . . I'll tell you something about my own high school career: I worked harder at Beverly than I ever have at UCLA, except for one quarter."

Does he think he'll be tutoring after he receives his college degree? He laughs. "Oh, yeah. This is going great, and I love it. I go that extra mile. And, as I said, this city can afford someone like me."

———

Wednesday, October 16. Andy's English teacher gives him a B-minus on the *Canterbury Tales* essay that his new tutor rewrote for him. In his next class, his government teacher returns essays on the legitimacy of capital punishment, writing at the top of Andy's, "Sloppy reasoning." Andy decided to say he was for it, not knowing why. The tutor didn't help much, which pissed Andy off, especially since he had to give the guy his father's check for ninety bucks at the end of two hours. You'd think for ninety, a tutor would be able to deliver a B-plus. When he walks out of class, a girl he knows tells him that he looks gay with mousse in his hair.

As if his day hasn't been bad enough, he must meet his parents for lunch at Spago. His parents have come together over a pizza to get advice from a private counselor, about college admissions. Andy arrives fifteen minutes late. The counselor, devouring a salad, tells his parents that having Andy apply to an Ivy League school would be "like shooting for Jupiter when we should be satisfied with a nice trip to San Diego."

"I'm hoping for something fairly prestigious," says his mother.

"Wouldn't we all?" the counselor says blithely, shrugging. "But San Diego State and Arizona State will take him. Then there is graduate school to think of. There is no reason why, at a place like Arizona State, Andrew couldn't graduate with a three-point-nine or a four-o and go to medical school or law school wherever he would like."

"I think a three-point-nine at Harvard or Yale, though, would take Andy a lot farther," his father interjects.

"Am I correct in saying that we're all friends here?" The man has spread his hands and placed them on the center of their table, palms up, ready to sell. "I think that Andrew is as fine a young man as anyone could hope to meet, but what is working against us here are figures — norms, averages, high ends and low ends. I am advising you to consider seriously Arizona State, San Diego State, a couple of the U.C.'s on the bottom end, the state colleges, Claremont College — which, incidentally, I see as a top-end school for Andrew — along with the University of Colorado, the University of San Francisco, and the College of the Pacific. And this is my reasoning. . . ."

Andy doesn't hear any of the reasoning, his mind having been numbed by the crushing disappointment of what he's heard, head down, teeth absently working on the pizza in front of him, chew, chew, chew, a dumb animal reduced to grazing.

"Andy, do you have anything that you want to add?" he hears his father saying.

"Uh, no." His mother is frowning. What has he done wrong? "I mean, I understand," Andy says. "Maybe I'll get a miracle on the SAT. Maybe Harvard will suddenly want to take a lazy and shiftless white kid."

"That's not the positive kind of attitude that you want to have, going in," the counselor says, amiably. His business is finished here. "You're a wonderful candidate, Andrew, and we're going to find you a wonderful school."

His father stands to leave with the counselor, murmuring, "Nice to see you again," in the direction of his ex-wife, while looking over her shoulder for the exit.

"Never embarrass me again with that faraway stuff," his mother says to Andy after the two men have gone.

She pays the check, tips the parking guy, and tells him to be home by seven as she climbs into her car. He is finished with school for the day but goes back anyway now, unsure why, except that maybe he'll find someone with whom he can hang out for a while. Pulling up in front of the school, he sees two kids from his government class sitting on the Swim-Gym steps. They say that at three thirty they're going to see Hello Day. Andy had forgotten about it. Every year, on Hello Day, the upper classes put on skits to welcome the freshmen. The two kids say they know someone in the senior class skit. Andy tags along with them to watch.

Traditionally, the skits are funny, or at least try to be. The senior class skit, "It's a Wonderful Grade," with music from *Cats, Grease II, Can't Stop the Music,* and *Oklahoma,* is about a Beverly girl who attempts suicide after being deprived of an A in a science course. The girl overdoses on Ex-Lax. There is a smattering of laughter in the auditorium. Andy sits there smiling, as if in on the joke, too, though not quite understanding. ". . . Why on earth would you want to be dead?" an angel on stage asks the despondent girl.

"Because I got a lousy B in AP chem," answers the girl.

Murmurs in the auditorium. A Beverly student *had* killed herself two years earlier after receiving a B in AP chemistry. Is this a takeoff on that? he wonders. A student seated at a desk, behind a stack of books, has broken into a song called "Midterm."

". . . Help me — doesn't anyone hear me — Won't someone tell me — what a DNA does — If you help me to understand my chemistry lab then I might have half a chance."

Looking down the row, Andy hears his government classmates laughing and sharing a story about some geek who broke down and started crying in English because the teacher refused to give him an A. On stage, the girl who dreams of dying looks into the middle-distance. "What do you remember most about being a junior?" the angel asks her. The girl thinks about this. "The varsity football team," she says. "They were such hunks! But brains, brains the size of atomic nuclei. *Thank God* all their body parts weren't that small. . . ."

His government classmates roar, but Andy notices many people sitting in silence. After the skit ends, a boy whom he knows vaguely from a geometry class a couple of years ago says angrily, *"I can't believe they did a skit about a fucking suicide."* The boy never raised his hand or spoke in geometry, just turned in his problem sets each day and sat there waiting for the next ones, Andy recalls. "They think that is funny?" the boy shouts. "Somebody kills himself and they laugh? *Shit. What idiots, what idiots . . ."* He slaps a wall. A couple of people discreetly move away.

———

A Sunday afternoon, in early October. Paul, Tony, Randy, and Tony's cousin, Adam, watch a playoff game between the Dodgers and the Cardinals, on a television set by Tony's pool. Randy has made margaritas for everyone. Paul, having come from a workout at the Sports Connection, says that next summer he'll be able to work on his tan because he'll no longer care about people seeing his body. "I'm really gonna get down by April," he says.

"You mean you're going to lay off tacos and beans?" Randy snickers.

Paul smiles. "No problem, dude."

"Yeah, *right*," Randy says. "Have another margarita, Moose."

Adam laughs. Randy puts another margarita in front of him with
a chuckle.

Assholes. Backstabbing faggots. "I've been working out for a couple of weeks now," Paul says coolly. "Randy, you should come down
with me. You could work on those toothpicks you call arms."

"Actually," says Tony, wheeling around to face Randy, "I think
Paul is trying to say you're a woos and a faggot. And personally, I agree."

Tony smiles and looks around at the others. Adam laughs and
spits up some of his margarita. Randy's safely back where he belongs —
right there at the bottom of their little clique. Weasel. Girls might dig
him for his wavy black hair and blue eyes, but his close male friends know
him to be a wimp, someone to be tolerated because he will bring a little
fun and, sometimes, a lot of blow their way. Whenever Randy opens his
mouth for very long though, Paul wants to get rid of him.

But his best friend is different. Tony you can listen to for hours;
he knows about music and vineyards and exotic vacation spots like Bora
Bora. He reads *happening* books, and goes out sometimes with older
UCLA girls who call *him* for dates. But Tony never makes a move or
utters a sound that isn't carefully weighed for its impact on his social
standing. When the conversation runs down and Tony falls quiet, Paul
knows to be quiet, too, which is fine, he thinks, though sometimes he
feels this distance between them, wonders if they are together simply
because each feels the need, like a simpering third-grader, to say that he
has a best friend. Then, just when he has begun doubting everything
about their friendship, Tony will say something that he has never re-
vealed before, the closest thing to a confidence coming from the iceman.
"Do I ever look to you like I'm acting weird?" he asked once. "Sometimes
I think people see me as kind of weird, you know, acting weird, I don't
know."

Tony continues mocking Randy while passing tortilla chips
around. Paul eats them, guiltily. A flash of humiliation comes: He sees a
cute girl from a party last night throwing his arm off her shoulder,
revolted. He had been drunk. The girl said to one of her friends that he
had grossed her out with the way he porked out on guacamole and tortilla
chips. Paul went home afterwards and marked a big black X on his special
calendar, the one he keeps hidden in his bedroom chest. At the end of
each day, if he remembers, he makes an X over the box with the appropriate date, a red X if the day has been "exceptionally hot," a green X for
an average day, or a black X for an awful one. After writing down a color-
coded X, he might jot one or two words in the box, like "good swim" or

"excellent j" for excellent joint, or "biz grl at T," which means, bizarre girl at Tony's. All his highlights are on the calendar. Last April, he wrote, "four-bagger" over a red X, which means he got his wish with a Uni High sophomore after giving her a little coke. Last night, after marking a deep black X into the day's box, he printed in pencil over it, "Blub."

Blubber.

Around friends, he tries to hide the occasional pain, remaining self-assured and funny for them, cracking self-deprecating jokes about his sex life. "If you're Ivy League material and you're *cut*, like cut good so that your arm muscles look real buff, like you got the hot bod, then you're going to get action every week if you want," he tells his friends. "But if you don't, you're the Lone Ranger."

"Why the Lone Ranger?" Tony asks him.

"Because you might as well be alone with a fucking mask on."

Everyone has a couple more margaritas and watches the game. Paul falls asleep in the sixth inning.

"Dodgers lose," Tony tells him when he wakes up. Paul has one more margarita, goes home, and watches a couple of "Star Treks" with Bones.

Later, Tony calls and asks him if he wants to go along to *Rocky IV*, only everybody changes their mind on the way to the theater and they end up at Carney's eating hamburgers.

"Cheryl is late," says Randy.

Cheryl is a Beverly sophomore with whom Randy has been sleeping, off and on, since the summer before her freshman year.

"Is she preg or not?" Tony asks.

"I don't know," Randy says, flagging down a waitress and borrowing her pen. He is looking at a picture of Hulk Hogan in *People* and sketching Hulk's face onto his napkin. "Probably. It happened to her once before. She'll get an abortion if she is. No problem. She thought I was going to bail after she told me, but I said, 'We can handle this, no problem.' "

"Did her parents know, the last time?" Paul asks.

"Be real," says Randy. Paul feels bad for him. Most parents are only too glad to get their kids birth control to stop them from getting knocked up. But if a kid screws up and gets herself pregnant, she's suddenly scum.

"My sister told my mom when *she* got preggers," Adam says.

"Your sister still breathing these days?" Paul asks.

"The deal is that I'm not sure I was the only one making it with her," says Randy. "There's two sophomore guys who she is good friends with, because, you know, I'm not around with her as much as I used to be, because I got other things to do. . . ."

Paul can't help laughing. "And their names are Suzie, Kathy, and Alicia."

"I gotta put in something else here." Staring at his little sketch, Randy waves to a second waitress and borrows her red felt-tip pen. "I think one of those sophomore guys fucked her, but she couldn't ever say something to them, because what if they can't pay for it, right? Then she would have to pay for it all by herself. So, it's me. I don't give a shit. It doesn't cost that much. What do you think of this?" He shows off his sketch. Rowdy Roddy Piper is biting Hulk's leg, and the Hulkster, oblivious to the ravages being done to his body, holds a water bong that says AC/DC on it.

"Classic," says Adam.

"I think you should make her pay for about eighty bucks' worth," says Tony. "She didn't come protected."

"You want to go see a movie or what?" asks Paul.

Randy sketches Ronald Reagan in a biker's jacket, with greased-back hair. "I'd like to party a little," says Adam.

"Whatever," says Tony.

They take a drive over the canyon to Encino to pick up one of Adam's friends, who says he can score some good coke for them at a cheap price, if they let him have a little of it. "Okay," says Paul, "but this better not be a scam." They get the coke and everybody does a couple of lines at Adam's house while watching "Wild Kingdom."

"I heard about this lion that ripped off someone's arm at one of those places you drive through," says Randy. "The geek had her car window down and the lion got her."

"She got *busted*," laughs Adam's friend, who is doing a lot more free blow than Paul thinks he deserves.

Tony says he's bored shitless. He wants to go to an arcade. Everyone piles into Tony's car. They head toward a freeway. "Wait," says Adam. "*Look at that.*"

Two men, having just gotten out of a red Monte Carlo, put their arms around each other.

"Shit," says Adam.

"I'm gonna say something," says Randy.

"No, *don't, don't,*" Adam says. "We'll do something else."

The two men, arm in arm, walk down the street and disappear from sight. Adam jumps out, walks over to the Monte Carlo, and carves FFF onto its body with a key. It all happens very quickly. Paul's mind tries making sense of these letters: FFF. *Fucking Faggots . . .* But what would the last F mean? Randy appears out of nowhere with a tire iron and splinters the Monte Carlo's windshield.

Paul feels himself getting excited. "Fucking break the window over *there*," Adam yells at Randy.

Randy rushes over to the driver's side and hits the window five, ten times with the tire iron before it finally gives way. Adam takes his key and, inside the car, begins carving FFF onto the upholstery.

"Get the tape deck," Randy screeches.

"There isn't one," Adam shouts back, still carving FFF.

"Go for it," yells Paul. "*Hurry up, hurry up.*"

"Intense," chortles Tony.

An elderly couple is crossing the street toward them. "*Let's go,*" Randy screams. They jump into the car and Tony floors it. A couple of blocks down the road, Adam yells to stop again, climbs out, and scratches FFF all over a mailbox and the paint of two more cars. "Yeah, yeah," Paul murmurs under his breath, his adrenaline pumping so hard he can feel little pulses throbbing in his neck. The car once more rockets toward the freeway, Tony pounding his dashboard maniacally, Adam and Randy leaning out the window, cutting loose with Rebel screams. "*What's FFF?*" Paul shouts, trying to be heard above the din. They can't hear him. The car squeals and slides onto a freeway on-ramp. "*What's FFF? What is it?*"

"Fight for Freedom, dude," Adam shouts back.

"*What?*" Paul, unable to hear Adam in the tumult, is so excited that everything he says comes out an octave higher, a beat faster. "*What is it? What is it?*"

"Fight for Freedom," screams Adam. "*FFF. Fight for Freedom.*"

"*Fucking faggots,*" Randy shouts out the window, over and over again.

In his government class the next day, Paul's teacher asks for some opinions about the "morality" of racial discrimination. Only a couple of kids raise their hands. Paul writes U2 all over his notebook. The teacher gets indignant with the class. "Aren't any of you interested in this?" he demands.

Murmurs from the class.

One girl raises her hand and says meekly that she is against it.
"Against what?"

"Against what you're talking about. The discrimination stuff."

"Anybody else?" asks the teacher.

Nobody else.

The teacher sighs.

"I don't know what he wanted us to say about it," Paul says
afterward. "It's so boring talking about that shit. Nobody talks about
political stuff. What difference does it make? You can be on one side or
the other, but everybody lives the same way. Everybody does the same
thing even if they say it a different way. It's all bullshit. The teachers
know that. So why do they want everybody to be political guys? I
think you're smart if you just don't believe in anything and go for it
on your own."

He believes philosophies and idealism, liberal or conservative, to
be naïve and obsolete, that what counts most is for individuals to adopt
strategies to fit the moment. "Nobody stays with what they believe all the
time," Paul says. "They stay with it as long as it lasts and then they talk
about whatever is popular next. They talk about dirty air for a while, and
then they talk about making sure Russia is being kept down. Whatever
will work with voters, they'll say. It's kind of a popularity contest. Everybody knows that."

In his seventeen years, the prevailing causes have risen and fallen
so quickly around him as to be reduced to fads in his eyes, mocking their
very existence, suggesting all along that they were merely the props of
politicians — The Environment, Hunger, Nuclear Disarmament, Cen-
tral America, Tax Reform, South Africa, El Salvador, Nicaragua . . . He
thinks he has seen the truth: There are no issues, only ambitions. The
cynicism runs like a thread through most students at Beverly. Whether in
politics or business, a "cause" remains alive, believes Steven, the young
Republican activist, only so long as its sponsoring politicians believe it to
be "sexy." He saw the term in a *People* magazine article.

———

The next week, Andy goes to see a couple of small garage bands play at a
hole-in-the-wall club in Hollywood. "They have these guys playing 'sixties stuff, like the Stones," he says. "Everybody comes wearing all these
'sixties clothes. Some have long hair like the hippies did, and they wear
all this peace stuff. I'm very 'sixties in a way." He says this while combing

his hair with a brush, trying to get the streaked wave on one side just right. "They knew how to party and I like to party. They didn't get too bummed about things. They chanted and smoked grass — not *everybody* did acid, you know — and you didn't have to scam as much to have sex probably, because people were into free love. It was an excellent time. People did things then, you know? I got this when I was at the club."

He fingers a button on his jeans jacket. The button has a white dove on it, set against a sky-blue background. "Some guy told me that he got it at a Bob Dylan concert a long time ago. He sold it to me for ten dollars. He wanted twenty-five but I got him to go down to ten. I faked him out. I told him it was all I had." He polishes the button with his thumb and forefinger. "That must have been a cool time. One day a guy at school noticed the button and asked me if I was ' 'sixties.' He asked it real sarcastically, like a real dick, but I just told him, 'Yeah, I guess I kind of am.' I'm proud of it, they were cool. You know, they had a lot of belief in peace, and cool-looking clothes and hair however you want it and massive partying. I love to hear about the 'sixties, but it must have been a lot better just living in it. At least, there was something *happening* then. I am kind of 'sixties. It's my point of view."

———

Hillary has got an audition for a good-paying part-time gig — modeling swimsuits. She could use the bucks: Her mom has been a bit tighter with her money lately, acting like it was a big deal when she asked for fifty for a skirt last weekend, then giving her eighty anyway. A secretary hands Hillary and a dozen or so other girls slinky black, one-piece bathing suits, leads them to a series of dressing cubicles with partitions, and instructs them to change. Her boss and the photographer will see them in a few minutes, the woman says, explaining that preliminary photos will then be taken, with four girls to be chosen as models for the next day's summer catalog shoot.

Hillary changes into the suit, and sits on a bench waiting, listening to a few of the other girls complain about straps too tight or suits that are riding too high up on asses. A balding old guy enters the room carrying meters and cameras. She's disappointed, had hoped for a handsome photographer, someone with whom she could flirt during the poses. Now she'll have to forget about flirting and conjure up some sexy mood all by herself. The old man is walking around measuring the light with his meters. A second man enters the room then, considerably younger, nods at the boss, and, in one motion, picks up a camera, points it at a group of girls, and playfully rattles off a quick burst of Polaroid shots. "I feel good today," he says to no one in particular, smiling. "Ready to roll. Everybody with me? I'm Jeremy."

He is the photographer, not the old man, who is picking up equipment and arranging tripods, clearly the assistant here, the young man admonishing him, "Joe, don't be giving those love-hugs of yours to any of these nice girls." The girls laugh. The young man says, "I'm just going to play a little bit here," and he scrutinizes all the girls through the lenses of a couple of cameras, not taking any shots, just examining how photogenic they may be. "Oh, I like *you*," he says, studying a blonde. The girl blushes. Hillary feels envious. He is slim and very handsome, with the kind of steel-blue eyes Hillary feels could stare right through her if they wanted to. When the surveying eyes finally come to rest upon her, Hillary summons the most inviting smile she can find, then a sexy pout, laughing, all charged up. She feels as though she could play to those eyes all day and night.

At the end of the session, she gets the job and her wish. "Want to get a drink with me?" Jeremy asks her, on the way out.

He has an accent that she cannot place, something foreign sounding, mixed in with a little Southern. He tells her he's *Cajun*. She only knows they're from the South somewhere.

He's twenty-three. She would have guessed twenty-seven, twenty-eight, perhaps even thirty. He has a bearing, an easy confidence, that makes him look like a contemporary to the older suited men drinking at this bar.

"How old are *you*?"

A pause. She decides not to lie. "Seventeen."

"Maybe, sometime we could go take pictures or go to dinner, if you'd like," he says. "I don't know your situation."

"That'd be nice," she says, trying her best to sound casual.

She has a *crush*, she thinks, a half-hour later, saying goodbye to him and rushing for home so that she can get on the phone and share the good news with someone.

Once inside her house, she closes her bedroom door and calls her best friend, Karen. An answering machine says, "Hi, I'm fried. Leave a message." Hillary says hi, hangs up. She goes downstairs and sits at a table in the den, listening to an album and trying to write an essay for her government class on whether she favors or opposes the Equal Rights Amendment. She sees her mother striding into the living room, fumbling with some earrings. "Mom, how do you feel about ERA?"

She shrugs, looks distracted. "I guess I'm in favor. Look, sweetheart, I have to talk to you about something. This might sound peculiar, but I need to know. Do you like Harry?"

"He's all right."

"You've been very nice about him. I want you to know how much I love you for not complaining to me and for giving him a chance. In other words, I'm telling you that your tolerance did not go unnoticed. You couldn't have handled this more beautifully, sweetheart."

"Mom, everyone has a life to lead, I know that," she says philosophically.

"I'm glad you're so sensitive to that, dear. I have to ask you something else. Would Harry be the kind of man you'd eventually like to see me with for a long time?"

Uh-oh. Warning lights go off in her head. So this is what her mom has been leading up to all along. She gets pictures in her mind: She can already see the bastard sitting in his robe in the den, hogging the television, spreading his *L.A. Times* and *Wall Street Journal* over the small oak table at breakfast, yucking it up with a tray of double scotches with his cronies on a football weekend, sweetly asking her to lower the stereo, noisily padding up and down the stairwell in those slippers that flip-flop like wooden sandals; coughing, burping, smoking, stealing her privacy and usurping her rule over this kingdom of three bedrooms, three baths, den, and "fun pit." She has thought until now that her mom slept with him simply out of a need for companionship, a partner for sex and a date for the endless charity functions and gallery exhibitions she attended. So convinced has Hillary been of Harry's escort status that she rarely said more than hello on the weekends that he slept over, treating him much the way a motel maid would a brief guest. All the while, her mom would be massaging Harry's back, with all of its dark, curlicue hairs. Hair covered his thick body like a bear mat. With his low bulging forehead and immense jaw, he looked, in such moments, like no one so much as Java man. Oh, shit: Her mother is studying her expression. Hillary does her best to smile, feigning mock surprise and gushing, "Whoa, Mom."

Her mom puts her hands on her hips, the way she always does when she suspects her daughter is not being forthright. "I need to know what you really think, Hillary," she says. "I want your input here."

"He's nice."

"Why do I get the feeling that isn't all you're feeling?"

"Mom, don't ask me to make your decisions for you. Especially after somebody has slept here ten times. What do you want me to say?

That he's wonderful? Okay, I think he's wonderful. Is that what you wanted me to say?"

Her mother's hands come off her hips, and she slumps, unable to look at her daughter, dropping one of the earrings that had been a gift from some long since abandoned boyfriend. Hillary puts a hand on her mother's shoulder and says, "I'm sorry," though, in truth, she isn't. She simply doesn't want to hear another word about any of her mother's boyfriends, past or present.

When, immediately following the divorce, her mother began dating an architect named Marshall, who had a deep tan and rugged complexion, she began popping into Hillary's bedroom with questions: Did she think Marshall was "charismatic"? Did she like his mustache? Did she think that, at fifty-two, he was too old? In the beginning, Hillary had been flattered that her mom wanted her advice. Yet, as the months passed and Marshall gave way to Jerome who gave way to Larry who gave way to David, the bloom of sophistication derived from making girl-talk with her mother faded to drudgery. Meanwhile, the questions had become more intimate: Did Hillary think David had a nice tush? Did she think he had been "pawing that blonde" at the croquet party in Malibu? Hillary wanted neither to hear the questions nor to supply the acceptable answers any longer, weary of playing Big Sister, convinced moreover that her mother did not want honest opinions so much as enthusiastic confirmation that she was dating princes. By the time Harry appeared on the scene, Hillary had taken to concocting excuses for not being able to play gossip partner anymore.

Her mom still looks hurt. Patting her shoulder, Hillary sighs. "It was a mean thing for me to say, Mom. I know it. I *really* am sorry."

Her mother wipes at an eye. "All I'm asking, Hillary, is that you have some regard for my feelings. I'll listen to what you have to say. I promise. Harry has become very important in my life and you are my daughter. I need to know what you think."

"I don't really like him a lot."

"Then you *would* have objections?"

"To you two marrying? Yeah, for sure."

Mom nods, smiles, strokes Hillary's hair and giggles. "Well, you don't have to worry then. We're not marrying."

"I didn't think you were serious, to be honest, Mom."

"But, I think, he might be moving in with us."

"You're kidding!"

"No. We would like to see if we're compatible. It'd give you a chance to get to know him, too."

"I don't want to get to know him."

"Now try to help me on this thing."

"But why *him*? And why do you need him living in the house? You see him all the time. He doesn't need to be around here every second."

"Sweetheart, I have needs, too. I'm a human being like everyone else. I've always tried to be honest with you and I think I can, because you're getting to be grown up. I'd like to have a man I care about, a friend, a companion. I'd like affection. I'd like to be with a man in bed at night."

"That's so gross, Mom."

"It's just a human reaction . . ."

"*Pleeeeze.*"

After an hour of fruitless discussion, Hillary says she has to make a phone call about a modeling assignment. She goes upstairs to her bedroom, shuts the door, and calls Karen.

"Java man is moving in," she says. "I can't believe it."

The next day, she drives to Hermosa Beach for her modeling assignment. She's given a pink bikini to put on. A hot-pink bikini, with barely any material covering her ass. She can't think of anything except all of that skin showing. One of the other models tells her that she looks nice. Another girl says she has a great figure. No reason to freak, Hillary realizes. She begins smiling and frolicking with the other girls. The session, declares Jeremy five hours later, has been a gas. Almost in unison, the girls say, "Thanks."

On the way to the beach's parking lot, Jeremy turns to her and says softly, "Keep next Saturday night open, okay?"

Harry comes to the house for dinner, bearing roses. Hillary tries to avoid looking at him. "Oh, aren't you the sweetest," her mom squeals as he hands over the flowers, kissing him, open-mouthed, Hillary making no effort to hide her revulsion, turning her back on them and eating the macadamias that her mom has set aside in a bowl for Harry and ordered her not to touch.

"Hillary, I have something for you, too," Harry says, and, as she turns, places in her hand a bottle of perfume.

"I told him how much you'd like it," her mom interjects quickly.

"Thank you," she says, picking up on her mom's cue, though trying not to sound too enthusiastic. Her mom stares at her. Hillary does not want a scene here. "Thank you very much. You'll have to excuse me. I have a lot of homework to do."

"You haven't eaten yet," her mother says. "You have to eat sometime. Eat with us."

"I had something to eat earlier," she says.

"Well, just sit down and have a glass of wine with us," Harry says. "We never have a chance to talk."

They sit at the formal table in the dining room. Hillary cannot stop staring at the fur on Harry's forearms. Five minutes into their leg of lamb, Harry clears his throat and gently places his hand upon Hillary's. "I gotta tell you how happy I am, Hillary, getting a chance to sit down with you like this, around a table, with your mother here, a beautiful dinner, and an opportunity to talk as long as we want."

"That's nice," says Hillary.

"I know the news that your mom gave you was a shock. But I also know something else: I want to be your friend. I want to make you happy. I'll do anything to make this work. I love your mother, I care about you, and I think the first thing we should do is consider what the three of us can do together."

"How about a trip to the zoo or the art museum?" her mom asks.

The zoo? Hillary has to stop herself from laughing. Her mom's *totally gone.* "My class has been to the art museum already," she says.

"But that was last year," her mom reminds her.

"Last year was enough."

"Well the zoo sounds great," says Harry.

"I'm allergic to the animals, I think."

"Well, we'll do something," Harry insists.

"Fine," she says.

After dinner, her mom helps Harry hang his clothes and install his exercycle in the den, and makes room on her bedroom desk for his dictaphone. Hillary reaches Karen.

"The bear is in," she says.

"Why don't you think it will work?" Jeremy asks her Saturday night on their date.

"Because he's just too weird," she says. "He's only been there a few days, and he's already got his jazz on, walking around the house making these noises — 'bah–bah–boop–boop–la–boop' — you know, these jazz sounds, and he does 'em when he rides his exercycle in the den, too. It drives me crazy. I got up real early, you know, in the morning like five, because I couldn't sleep, and there he is, on the fucking exercycle, making his sounds. He's *so* weird." She sighs, tells herself not to let thoughts of Harry ruin this date. "Could I have a glass of wine?"

They have returned to Jeremy's apartment after an evening of dancing at a local club, her head floating free from the three vodka tonics that she got with her fake ID, but the certainty that they are about to make love is making her pulse pound; she needs some wine to relax her. Seemingly all night he has had his arm around her, going so far during one dance as to grind his pelvis into hers and deliver a kiss that tempted her to ask if he might want to go back to his apartment right then. They danced for a half-hour more, downed another drink, and then he said, "Want to listen to some records at my place?" They are now into a third Police album. Jeremy pours her another glass of Chablis. She congratulates herself for having put her diaphragm in at home.

For thirty minutes, he talks about photography, showing her his favorite pictures, Hillary at once fascinated and disappointed — for he does not seem to be warming here to what she wants, what she came prepared for. "Want to play some backgammon?" she asks, and, in a couple of minutes, they are stretched out upon his waterbed setting up the red and black markers. "Can I go with you sometime when you go to the desert?" she blurts. "Or to the beach or a mountain to take pictures? Wherever you go, I'd like to come, if that is all right."

"S-u-ure," he says, in his funny half-drawl.

They play backgammon for a couple of hours, drink a bottle of wine, and then he bends down and gives her a long kiss.

At the door.

Good night.

On a balmy Tuesday night, in mid-October, Steven calls Laura, who says she can't go with him to the local library to study. She has a date. The way she says it reminds him of times, in elementary school, when he would ask if she'd like to play and she would shake her head and run off, to jump rope with the girls. They have known each other since fifth grade, when they had crushes on each other and she'd slip him notes asking whether he would like to go swimming at her house. Then she met a seventh-grader and her crush ended, though his did not. One night at a party, during his freshman year at Beverly, he found her stretched out on a chaise longue by a pool with some senior football star whose picture had appeared in the school paper's sports section. The senior was nuzzling her neck, and she had her head buried in his chest. Steven got drunk on a six-pack of Heineken's and sat in a corner of the patio. He stripped down to his underwear and sat in a hot tub. He whistled Van Halen tunes. He did his Bogart imitation for passing girls, none of whom seemed to notice. A couple of kids in his English class pointed at him, laughed, and shouted, "Lightweight." They were right. He couldn't even hold a couple beers. He understood why a lot of party posters distributed around the school said, "No Freshmen." He felt anonymous and worthless. He also felt on the verge of passing out, the alcohol and the hot tub's heat having dangerously dehydrated him, and so he weakly climbed out and managed to put on his pants and shirt. He walked over and took a seat on a chair, and the next thing he remembered were arms gently shaking him. "Hey, Steven, wake up. *Wake up, Steven.*" Laura stood over him. He had fallen asleep.

"Where's that guy?" he managed to ask in a stupor.

She was looking into a mug of coffee. "He went off with some of his friends and a couple of girls on the swim team."

Steven thought he saw an opportunity. "Maybe we should go into the hot tub, just the two of us."

She laughed. "I don't think so, Steven." She patted his arm. "Don't you want to drink some coffee? If you sober up, then you could drive me home. Oh, fuck, I keep forgetting that freshman guys don't have licenses. Drink some coffee anyway."

He drank. "Most freshman girls are such bitches," he said. "They fuck seniors and juniors but they don't even look at freshmen."

"Meaning you."

"Right."

"You know, there are some seniors who won't even touch a freshman," she told him. "They think freshman girls might say something to somebody, or that they're too young to be on the pill or have a diaphragm."

They sat on a chaise longue for a long while swapping gossip: Who in the class had slept with whom? What girls did boys think had the hottest bodies? What boys did the girls think were studs? Which girls were considered easy lays? Who had done oral sex? It sounded gross, said Laura. Steven thought about it, then said he made it a rule in his life to remain open to all forms of experimentation.

"Don't be a geek, Steven, okay?"

"Okay."

He walked her home that night, and they talked about their worries on the way — worries over getting lost in the Beverly crowd, over being friendless, over getting bad grades, over doing too many drugs or the wrong kinds, worries over sex and performing adequately (hers) and worries over perhaps not getting a chance to perform at all (his). At her front door, she invited him inside, told him to be quiet, and gave him another cup of coffee. Within a month, they had become inseparable buddies. They went to all-night parties, all-night diners, all-night movies. They went on midnight grunion-hunting adventures at the beach, a drunk Steven scooping the spawning little silver fish into a burlap sack while a squealing Laura sat in the surf drinking canned margaritas. Whispers circulated that they slept together when Laura's parents went out of town, though, in truth, they had become nothing more than good friends, maybe best friends. Steven didn't even consider scamming on her anymore, the thought of having sex with her having become *too weird*. Most of the time she seemed to treat him like a brother. One afternoon, during their sophomore year, after they had finished watching some videos, she suddenly began taking off her blouse while reaching for a drawer.

"What are you doing? *What are you doing?*" Steven demanded.

She faced him in her bra. "Relax. I'm just putting on a sweater. Did you think I was doing something *else? God*, Steven."

He stared at the bra. It occurred to him that he had never seen her in even a partial state of undress before. Rather than think about it any longer, he walked over and kissed her. She kissed him even harder. He undid her bra and they had sex, and then they held each other through another half-hour of videos.

They did not go to the movies together that night or the next, did not talk to each other for the entire weekend, a curious tension having gripped them. By the following Monday, it lifted. An unspoken understanding had passed between them. Effortlessly they picked up where they had left off, neither uttering what both felt: that, as boyfriend and girlfriend, they could never make it; but as friends, they were inseparable.

At the root of their affection rested a realization that each could talk to the other about things that neither would dare utter to friends of the same sex. He couldn't tell his buddies at the beach he felt afraid of ski slopes or cocaine. She couldn't admit to her girlfriends she had no confidence in dressing herself. Being together was a source of liberation. They could pour out their doubts to each other at no risk. Then there came the bonus of being admitted to heretofore locked rooms. Laura regularly told him what girls liked during lovemaking (which meant largely what *she* liked), and Steven reciprocated by explaining what boys liked (which meant largely what the *Playboy* Advisor liked). He had never found a friend whose company he so appreciated. During the summer after junior year, they talked about the possibility of applying to the same colleges and being roommates at Berkeley or UCLA. "That would be so cool," Laura said one August night, before remembering she had to call her sister. "I have to go to Magic Mountain with my cousins and some of their friends. It's going to be so boring."

He phoned her a half-dozen times that night, until reaching her at 1:30 A.M., two hours after she was supposed to have gotten back. She sounded drunk. "I met this guy named Aaron," she slurred in a whisper. "He's *here*, Steven. He's twenty-five or something. He's gorgeous. I *have* to keep my voice low. He's talking with my sister. I have to go. Call you tomorrow."

In the weeks since the start of school, she has been spending more and more time with Aaron. Steven has stopped by to see her three times in the last week, only to find Aaron in her den, playing video games. He thought that going with her to the library tonight might be a way to cut the older guy loose. On the other end of the line, she's mumbling that she has to get off the phone.

"What time are you going to be home?" he asks her.

"I don't know, really," she says. "My parents aren't home tonight so I might stay over at his place."

"Aaron's?"

"Of course. *God*, who else would it be?"

"Whatever," he says.

"I don't know if he loves me," she says. "But I think I kind of care about him a lot. I'm on the pill now. I don't know if I told you that. I'm thinking that it might be smart for me to go to UCLA just so I can be close to him next year." He feels less jealous than simply out of place, an intruder, and so when she asks when they might be able to get together for lunch, his mind tells him to stay away. He concocts some excuses: He wants to do some volunteer work at a local Republican club, he says; he has some telephone solicitations to make for a hunger project. "Are you going to that Beer-Bong Madness party on Friday?" she asks.

"Maybe. Probably not."

"Oh, *come*. We're going."

We're. He doesn't need a threesome. He changes the subject.

"Your friend Vickie's been kind of flirting with me. She never used to. Now she's all over me."

"She's nice. She talks a lot, but she's not stuck-up, if that's what you've heard, Steven. Are you going to take her out?"

"I don't know."

"She went out with some guy from Santa Cruz for a while, but she's not now. She's pretty wild, Steven." She giggles.

He wishes he could talk to her more, but a gruff voice in the background says, "We've got to get going, babe."

"Aaron is here," she says. "I have to jet."

Still able to hear Laura's words — "You'll have a good time . . ." — he invites Vickie to a party on Saturday night and then a late dinner at Gladstone's, at the beach. She is as good as advertised. She rubs his forearm throughout dinner, as they stare at the ocean. "My brother tells me that you can get into whatever college you apply to," she says.

"That would be excellent," he says, modestly, "but I wouldn't promise it."

"He said *anywhere*."

Steven had been in a P.E. class with her brother Ben, a nervous, frail kid who tried ingratiating himself to everybody by telling them how great they were. "Ben told me that your SATs clinch it for you," she says, giggling and rubbing his arm again. "How did you get so smart? You *used* to be so quiet all the time." He shrugs, feigning embarrassment. "But you were always cute," she adds, and falls silent, staring up at him while resting her chin upon her palm, waiting for him to return the compliment. He doesn't know what to say. "I always wondered, when I was a freshman, what you were like," he admits uneasily. When he was a geek. When she and the other girls in her circle were untouchables for him. He tries to smile. "I was in your algebra class," he says, "but you probably don't remember." She doesn't. His face reddens. "I was also at your older sister's party, and I went in your hot tub once by myself. I was kinda drunk, but you probably didn't see me." She shrugs, smiles, thinks it's sweet that his brain would have filed her image permanently away, and leans over, right there, in the restaurant, and kisses his cheek. She wants him. He likes the thought of getting her alone in that same hot tub where he'd made an ass of himself freshman year. A chance to redeem himself. She strokes his cheek with her index finger. More girls than ever have been giving off these signals to him, though his sex life has changed little. His fault. Last spring he went to bed with a couple of girls, but he did little over the summer with his dates except to make out with them on the beach before driving them home. He thinks some of the girls know of his geek past, worries they may be too seasoned for him. He doesn't want to disappoint. "Why don't we take off our shoes and walk down there?" Vickie asks. She points at the beach.

They walk, barefoot, in the wet sand, Vickie giggling, Steven feeling cold, thinking that he'll need to start surfing soon in a wetsuit.

"I didn't know if you'd ever ask me out," she says. "But Ben told me you weren't as shy as you used to be."

She bounces ahead of him. Nice ass. Tan arms, good legs. What does she look like in a hot tub? They walk back to the parking lot. They make out in the car a little. He tells her he wishes he were a little more comfortable at parties. She tells him she has always been insecure about her abilities in school, suspects people think she's dumb.

"You give good talk," he says, smiling.

She laughs. "You're excellent, too."

———

A lonely and frightened girl has few intimate conversations. When Kelly makes plans to get together with people, she worries about slipping any farther down the social ladder. She wears the leather skirt tonight. And black pantyhose so that her legs will look as slim as possible. She joins Tina and two other girls, Shelly and Andrea, at the entrance to Club Lingerie. Shelly and Andrea are best friends. They usually like doing things alone, which is fine with Kelly and Tina, who generally prefer hanging out as just a twosome anyway. Tina and Andrea don't get along much of the time, just as Kelly and Shelly don't, but, what the hell, Tina told her the other day, once in a while it was more fun to go to clubs in a group of four or six. *Just be careful what you say around them*, Tina then warned. Kelly is always careful. She hangs back as the three other girls approach Club Lingerie's entrance and present their fake IDs to the doorman. "Did you get someone in a junior high printing shop to make these up for you?" the doorman asks them, and calls over a fellow employee to share in his amusement. "Hey, it says here that you three were born in nineteen fifty-seven," he announces to the spurned girls. "Tell me how it feels to be twenty-eight years old?"

In the midst of the doorman's guffaws and her friends' embarrassment, Kelly feels relieved that she wore the skirt and heavy makeup. The doorman nods at her ID and motions her through. She hesitates, wondering if she should strand the others, but Shelly and Andrea motion to her to go on and even Tina doesn't seem to mind, shouting, "Gimme a call later." Kelly waves goodbye and walks inside toward the bar, where, she has heard, young musicians like to hang out when they come to L.A. Which is not tonight. There are gaggles of USC and UCLA guys challenging each other to a drinking contest and checking out any woman who enters their domain. Kelly can feel eyes giving her a microscopic examination that starts with her face and ends somewhere around the black pantyhose. A guy comes up and introduces himself. He is the president of some fraternity, the name of which she forgets as soon as he says it. Something Greek. Theta-Beta-Chug-A-Lug Gator. He wants to dance. She would guess by his scent he's on his fifth or sixth beer and second tray of beer nuts. She obliges him, then dances with one of his friends, who buys her a margarita. Another boy gets her a rum and Coke. They are all a little dull. And they'd all like to lay her, she's convinced. After two or three drinks, she thinks disgustedly, college and high school boys, without girls for the night, get erections at anything with breasts and a little eyeliner. Even a pudgy girl. She knows.

The truth is she could have gone out quite a few times with two boys from Beverly last year, if only she had been willing to have sex with them. As it was, she had one date with each, both evenings ending in disaster when she refused to shed so much as her blouse for either boy. One of them, spurned on Halloween night in an empty, darkened beach parking lot after he had lost consecutive battles first to seduce her and then forcibly to strip her of the ballerina costume she'd rented, reacted by punching his car stereo and driving her home. She cried in humiliation, suddenly understanding that for this boy the whole evening had been an exercise in *getting it off her*, the very phrase that Tina's old boyfriend and his buddies regularly used on the school's Third-Floor Patio when talking about girls whom they wouldn't mind *porking, nailing, getting. Getting it off her*. The second boy with whom she had gone out had been even more obnoxious, predicting early in their date that they'd be going to bed before the night's end, and later, in the face of her adamant refusals, grinning and telling her that he liked a challenge, that he was going to turn her on and *get it out of her* before they said goodnight. He hadn't, and he never called her again. She didn't feel bad for long, knowing that some of her friends, including Tina, had been burned by Beverly studs who, after having sex with them, wouldn't give them as much as a smile at school, acting as if the girls had done the chasing all along. She won't allow herself to get hurt.

She'd like to have sex with a high school boy rather than one of those older dudes on the Strip, but it would have to be someone sweet, not necessarily a babe head over heels in love with her but one at least who says there will be a next time, someone with whom the possibility exists for a relationship of sorts, someone with whom she shares emotional power, whom *she* could dump, if it came to that. Romance always means someone is losing and being rejected in favor of someone else who's winning. She loved burning the asshole who predicted, *I'm going to get it out of you,* as if what she had down there was a tiny oil well that, after being drilled and pumped, would be just a dried up, worthless hole. She had liked that beaten expression on his face when he dropped her off at her house, not even bothering to walk her to the door.

She's getting a little bitchy, knows it, but she's not about to give in now to a bunch of college guys who look like something out of "Happy Days." She has a couple more drinks, then bids the frat boys goodnight and goes to Baskin-Robbins.

"Well, tell me what you've been up to," her father asks at dinner the next night.

"I've just been around, doing things. I don't know."

"Well, tell me a little bit about *those things.*"

"I don't know. I study, see my friends, go to a party on weekends. I don't do *so* much, Dad."

"Your mother says you're always gone."

"I guess I am a lot. So is she. So are you."

He purses his lips, nods, folds his hands, the professional establishing order and control here. "Let's talk about school. Let's be honest with each other. I didn't always do so great either."

"My grades aren't awful."

"Your mother says that you never study."

"I do. Sometimes. I'm not failing. Dad, I get a little tired of these talks. I see you once every few weeks or a month, and I get this check-up from you and then you're like gone until the next check-up."

"Well, your mother and I might not be married anymore but we're still very concerned about you and love you and we're trying to invest a little more time now and do whatever . . ."

"I know, Dad," she interrupts. "*I know.*"

"I'm writing this check. So if you need anything . . ."

"Thanks."

"And you and your mother are supposed to do something tomorrow, right?"

"We're supposed to go to the Ahmanson to see some play."

"Good. As I said, if you need anything . . ."

"Okay."

"Mom is such a goddamn bullshitter," Kelly says abruptly then, not quite knowing why. She tries to think of how to explain this to her stunned father. A week before, her mother suggested that, perhaps, they could go skiing in the Sierras over Thanksgiving, and stay in a little chalet co-owned by Kelly's uncle Chuck. "It'd be nice to do something together," said her mom, a not-so-subtle admission, thought Kelly, that the two of them hadn't been spending enough time together lately. Everything was arranged, her mom said.

That night, when she arrived home with a new ski cap on her head, her mother put an arm around her. "Sweetheart, we're going to have to postpone our trip," she said. "Unless you wouldn't mind settling for going skiing on Thanksgiving and that Friday. I've just been told that there is going to be some board meeting at which I'll have to be present on the Saturday of that week. Whatever you want to do, we'll do. You want to go, we'll go. But only for a couple of days, I'm afraid."

"No, that's all right, never mind."

"Why would you say *Mom is a bullshitter?*" her father keeps asking. "What would prompt you to think that?"

No point, she realizes. No point in telling him.

———

A perspiring Melinda rides the stationary bike in the corner of the family den, halfheartedly listening to her mother read aloud from another newspaper article about winning admission to the top private colleges, mostly Eastern. Melinda's heard this stuff forty, fifty times already, and tries to tune the omnipresent voice out, staring at the handlebars, concentrating on her own heavy breathing, feeling sweat streaking her face. A few of her mom's words seep through anyway. She faintly hears a name — "Haverford College" — but doesn't catch what must have been the rest of a list and the point of the story. She doesn't pay attention to people as often as she should, she knows. "I think you should take a good look at some of these colleges, maybe tour a couple of their campuses while you're back there again," her mother says, turning to solicit an opinion from Melinda's father. "What do you think, Jeffrey? If she didn't get into the Ivies, she'd have the others to fall back on, don't you imagine? *Jeffrey?*"

With a start, he glances up from the legal journals strewn over the couch and his lap, looking a little stunned, and smiles good-naturedly at his youngest daughter. He loves having her around, this last child in his nest; wonders sadly, in private moments, what it will be like in his big house when she leaves next year. They seldom sit for father and daughter heart-to-hearts, but this is only because his emotional makeup has left him with an instinctive reticence, an aversion to gushiness and open displays of affection that Melinda inherited. What words drop from his lips do so grudgingly, as if rationed, the remainder hoarded for necessities — family discussions with stakes involved, crises, business matters, important social occasions. Melinda has never minded his silences, enjoys the solitude of being with him for hours in this room, riding the bike and glancing at the TV while he scrutinizes his papers, their serenity punctuated every so often by a punchy remark or sarcastic aside from him. It does not hurt that he has a wry, deadpan wit and isn't above dropping in an occasional irreverent zinger about someone. It cracks her up. She likes it that he still has the capacity to shock her. Few people do. And, afterwards, she appreciates the quiet again. Wordlessly, they reach across one another to grab snacks, change channels, reach for law journals and high school work sheets, and exchange positions on the bike and couch, some invisible tether keeping them together here, until the moment inevitably comes when she has to leave for her bedroom and a couple hours of homework. Sometimes he speaks then, asks if she'd like to stay and watch "Santa Barbara" or one of her other soap opera tapes.

She's always sensed he likes her nearby. From atop the bicycle seat, she looks down at him now, hearing her mother repeat the question: "What do you *think*, Jeffrey?"

Her father pushes horn-rims onto the top of his head, squints in thought, finally nods at his wife. "Yes, I think that'd be smart. The only difference between the Ivies and the Haverfords might be size and status. What's there to lose?"

His wife nods, satisfied. "Oh, here's a very interesting article about cocaine, Melinda," she says, proceeding to read a grim passage of ominous facts and figures. Melinda hates these not-so-subtle antidrug lectures. "I'm going to stick it on the refrigerator for you, dear, so you can look at it whenever you have a chance. You —"

"Mom," Melinda interrupts, "*don't be a geek.*"

She shouldn't have said that, she realizes. She has too much of a temper. Sometimes, at big family dinners with her parents and older siblings, she gets so frustrated over something said, something misinformed or idiotic or simply different from her own view, that she starts

telling them all to shut up. When bored or irritated, she can get obnoxious, she knows, wants to change this about herself. For starters, she
could cut her mom a little slack. But God, it's hard sometimes, especially
when her mom keeps reading those damn articles about teenagers and
then asking something like, "Melinda, are you careful not to drink when
you're driving? Because it says right here that . . ." Melinda usually cuts
her off cold then. She doesn't like questions that presume she lacks a
mature young woman's judgment, that she's still the family's baby.

"*Don't be a geek, Mom*": How often has she shouted that? Just
thinking about it embarrasses her a little. Her mom, having been severely
chided, has turned away, head buried in the business section of a newspaper. The woman reads everything. The *Los Angeles Times*, the *New York
Times, The Wall Street Journal, Time, Newsweek*. She's an encyclopedia
— always looking for columns and items that her children might use to
their advantage. Knowing that Melinda aspires to be an entrepreneur, she
often clips out long articles about soaring companies and magnates that
have succeeded from scratch — a candy-making wizard one week, a
clothing designer the next, a consulting company built by college kids
upon an initial investment of a few thousand — instructive, inspiring
stories that she bugs Melinda to read until the teenager relents with a
groan and reluctantly looks away from television for the ten minutes or so
it will take to scan a story.

Melinda has to admit it: Most of the pieces have been fairly
interesting. Her mom regularly fills in the articles' gaps, having known all
about the candy magnate, able even to tell Melinda about the beginnings
of her operation, making it all sound fascinating, as she manages to do
with nearly any subject that doesn't pertain to teenage vices. Melinda will
ask her questions about businesswomen or talk about her dreams. She
wishes she had half of her mom's ability to listen to people.

Her mom also has the capacity to forgive quickly. She's turned
back to her daughter, Melinda's insult about being a geek having been
forgotten, and asks if she has started packing for their trip to the East.
Melinda nods, head down, and pedals furiously.

"You two will be back when?" her father asks from the couch.

"Monday night," says her mom.

A five-day trip, thinks Melinda, panting on the bicycle. What
could be sweeter? She doesn't mind, at this moment, that there will be
school work to make up upon her return, doesn't even care that she may
miss an exam in physiology. "I wish it could be a month," she hears
herself panting.

On Thursday, touching down in New York, still heady from the ride on the jetstream, they hail a cab, drop off luggage at their hotel, and walk the Upper East Side, checking out brownstones and museums and standing in front of Rockefeller Plaza for a few minutes gawking at Manhattan street life. The next morning, they're off to Pennsylvania, on the train, getting a rental car at the Philadelphia station and inspecting the campuses of Haverford, Swarthmore, and the University of Pennsylvania. Melinda doesn't like any of them; Haverford, she thinks, is too small, Swarthmore too cloistered, U. Penn too gross.

They take the train back to New York and, the following afternoon, visit Columbia. The campus is all grays to Melinda. Worst of all, the guys look as pale and wimpy as the ones she saw at Harvard.

"Okay, what places do you like so far?" her mom asks.

"I don't know, not a lot of them on this trip," she says.

Her mom smiles. "Well, tomorrow will be enjoyable. We'll go see Heather, in New London, and she'll show us Connecticut College. Who knows? Maybe that will be the place. And Heather knows everything about it." Heather is one of her mom's old friends from Ohio, where they once lived, though that was more than ten years ago.

The next afternoon, when they arrive in New London, there are a torrent of hugs and kisses, Heather then leading them on the promised tour of Connecticut College, the two old friends reminiscing all the while, Melinda largely left alone to scrutinize the old quiet campus, deciding halfway through the tour that she won't be applying here. The afternoon ends with Heather taking them to a performance of a local gospel choir. She has become a Quaker, she tells them on the way back to her house. Melinda and her mom smile politely. It is not until they are in her living room and Heather has gone off to the kitchen to make tea that Melinda works up the nerve to ask her mom, "What's a Quaker?"

Heather has overheard. "Will somebody educate this child?"

Melinda bristles. She doesn't like being called a child nor being treated like an ignoramus. So she didn't know what a goddamn Quaker was. So fucking what? She looks around and laughs, a tad derisively. Her mom flashes her a look of warning.

It seems the uncomfortable moment might pass, except that Heather won't allow Melinda's laughter to go unanswered. She lectures the teenager about the cornerstones of Quaker teachings, as well as the price that modern-day pagans will one day have to pay for their excesses. Melinda thinks that this means her. When Heather says Quakers are beholden to no one but God, that they don't salute the flag or stand for judges, Melinda decides to challenge her. "I believe we *all* have responsibilities to our country because our country is made for everyone," she says. Out of the corner of her eye she sees her mom watching calmly, appreciates that she is remaining loyal to her by staying out of this. She'd like to nail this pious hag alone, though she wishes she were more articulate. "Quakers just can't decide by themselves not to fulfill their responsibilities," she declares. "They should have to stand for judges just like everybody else. They're not *special*. They're no better than anybody else. They have —"

"But your chief responsibility is to God, *no one else*," Heather interrupts loudly, cheeks flushed with passion. "And, my dear, if your first allegiance isn't to God, your life is empty. *Nothing but empty.*"

Melinda stays quiet. She has never been very religious, and this woman's shrill preachiness makes her uneasy. She tries to shift the subject by inquiring what the work load is like at Connecticut College. "I mean, how much do you think you have to study there?" she asks. "Compared to, like, Haverford or U. Penn or somewhere?"

Heather folds her hands primly. "Melinda, you go to school *in order* to study."

Bitch.

Heather's husband enters the room, hugs her mom, and stares at the mink coat she's wearing. "Well, aren't we looking like a wealthy Californian, today, in our mink?" he says with a laugh, and winks at his wife. "You trying to look like a movie star, Helen?" Melinda notices her mom's smile fading slightly. The husband isn't finished, the teasing getting a bit rough. "Heather, just look at your good friend's coat here. Very glamorous. Must be worth thousands. Talk about *lavish*. Everybody in California dress this way, Helen?"

Her mom keeps her smile, or what's left of it, in place.

Heather pipes in. "Zach, she can take off from Beverly Hills anytime and not worry because she's got a housekeeper doing everything. Imagine that?"

Her mom says nothing. Melinda thinks this ribbing is tactless and unfair. Her mom's a good and generous person. She doesn't deserve this.

"And let me guess . . . ," Heather says. ". . . You drive a . . ."

"Yes, Heather, I drive a Jaguar," her mom says evenly.

"Oh, that's fine," Heather says cheerfully, as if sensitive to the sudden neutralness of her friend's tone. "I didn't mean anything by that. It's a nice car, I'm sure. It's probably only that, back here, we live, you know, in just a different way. It's tradition and things, that's all I'm saying. You know, it's that Yankee thing about being spartan. People here probably, you know, just don't feel as comfortable in flaunting their wealth."

Her mom stays cool, manages even to grin. "Heather, we've learned where I live to enjoy our wealth."

It's all that an excited Melinda can do not to stand and shout, *All right, all right, take that, bitch.* Heather becomes quiet, the discussion of contrasting life-styles over, though, later, she makes some lame remark about hating the hot sun and preferring a cool climate. Melinda thinks it's all a little sad, watching her mom try to get through this: You go through life imagining you have your roots in faraway places and people, only to return one day and discover that the people and places and maybe even you have changed, that the roots have turned to dust. For as long as Melinda can remember, her mother liked to say that her strongest bonds would always be in the East; that most people in California were only your friends for a while before moving on to someone new. "Back East," she'd declare, "you have your friends *for life.*"

Now it is as if one of her friends for life has been reduced to a curious acquaintance, an oddball. On the drive back to New York, Melinda studies her mom, who does not look disheartened at all, noting enthusiastically that it has been a fine trip. "We came and saw what we wanted to," she says. "You have a better idea now of where you want to go and where you don't. I'm pleased." By the time their plane takes off, Heather has been forgotten, lost in the jetsam.

When she returns, late Monday night, having missed several days of school, she cancels a scheduled weekend visit to colleges in San Diego. "I've been traveling so much that I'm behind now," she says. "I have to catch up."

She spends the rest of the week preparing for two tests and reading the remainder of *The Canterbury Tales*. By Friday night she feels on top of school matters again. Pam calls. What can they do? Melinda suggests that they drive to a party at Pepperdine, and so they go, Melinda bringing Pam up to date on the way about prospective colleges, the wimpy guys whom she met back East, and a woman at the supermarket who had been a total bitch to her in the parking lot. These random thoughts and remembrances gush from her without checks; she feels absolutely secure around Pam. Melinda does the same thing with Cecilia, her other close friend, a girl as outgoing as Pam is shy, as fun and frivolous as Pam is intense and purposeful. The three rarely do things together, for Pam and

Cecilia are not close, but Melinda never talks about one without mentioning the other; they are a threesome in her mind. *Melinda, Pam and Cecilia: best friends, confidantes, co-conspirators.* Melinda will talk about anything with them — her apprehensions about the future, her worries over college, drugs, sex, her weight, her personality. Two friends do not represent, in her mind, a "circle," but she does not need a retinue, sensing that the soshes with cliques have to "play bullshit games and then they have to be worried about being careful. I never have to do that with Pam or Cecilia." Melinda's siblings have moved off to colleges and their own lives, but, at seventeen, she still spends the majority of weekday nights with her parents in their den, watching television, exchanging gossip, relating tiny worries, voicing the kind of thoughts that pass as taboos in the homes of many Beverly students. If she has social or financial needs, they usually meet them. Such an atmosphere has encouraged her to believe she needn't fear candid exchanges with friendly faces on the outside. Despite her earlier insistence that she would not talk about "personal stuff" at the community center volunteer gatherings, she has opened up occasionally, guarding her darkest secrets but disclosing enough that the other students in the group come away with considerable understanding of what she is about. She possesses enough self-assurance to know that, in the real world, some people like you and some people don't; that to be relatively open is a good and healthy thing. She is, quite simply, at peace with herself. "Yeah, things are pretty good," she says. "Maybe I get bored a little sometimes, but that is just a kid's kind of problem. I'm still a kid in my mind. But, like I'm not someone completely serious with a lot of worries, like some people I know. I feel more like a kid, I guess."

She is among the few here who do. "There are a lot of teenagers running around with adultlike burdens," Steven says. "This city grows them up fast."

NOVEMBER

Kelly stands outside the gates to the athletic field, licking a giant rainbow popsicle, ready to go through the gates to watch the varsity football team play Inglewood High School. She doesn't like football much, but where else can you see so many muscular boys?

Not many people here today. Not many people at any of the games when she thinks about it. Sports just aren't popular at Beverly. At some schools, athletes and cheerleaders were gods, but not here, where dumb and dull football players didn't go any farther than ordinary geeks. Only one boy on the team has ever truly excited Kelly and her friends, the team's blond flanker and kick returner, Gregg Silver, who's just limped to the sidelines with a severe groin pull. Kelly stands along with her friends, gasping as a trainer helps Silver to the bench and takes his helmet off. She's boy crazy, she knows it, but Gregg Silver is different, Gregg Silver is her Dream Boy, Gregg Silver has been her crush since ninth grade when he was in her English class, long before he became a football star. Long before he became the fantasy of some of her friends, or had his picture in the local papers, or started dating the Golden Girl Leslie Paul. She envies Leslie, though she can't bring herself to dislike this girl, who, though blonde and pretty, is sweet and easygoing with people. Just like Gregg, she thinks. They've been nominated for Homecoming King and Queen. Everybody knows they have the election in the bag. The perfect couple. It makes her a little sick with jealousy sometimes. You can't let it get to you, she tells herself, but still it does sometimes. She wonders why some people become popular, while others pass through a place ignored. Gregg's life, Leslie's life: They're so perfect. What she would give to feel like they must.

The next morning, on the Third-Floor Patio, where her friends sometimes hang out to eat and gossip, she's introduced to the younger brother of an acquaintance, a fifteen-year-old sophomore whose biting tongue annoys her a little, but who has blue-green eyes and a sexy smile she cannot stop looking at. When he relaxes finally, he becomes quite funny, doing impressions for her of different teachers. He has a nice body, with shoulders that look hot in a cut-off T-shirt. Does he have a girlfriend? she asks someone. She stops herself. *No, no, no.* This kid is *fifteen.* Her friends would think she was totally desperate, a full-on *desperado.* She then remembers that, during the summer, one of her friends dated a junior, very short and a Michael J. Fox look-alike, and another of her friends spent all of August drooling over an incoming *freshman.* She shouldn't write off this sophomore just yet. But she better begin doing something about her body, for this cute boy has just pinched a little of her flesh around the stomach and said, in a W. C. Field voice, "Oh, I see we have a little padding here." Turning away from him, she sees a little roll of undulating flesh around her tummy, and furtively picks at it. She has to get some more of those pills.

Between classes she goes to nearby Roxbury Park. She comes here often. She lies on the grass and removes from her purse a little plastic baggie, containing a few dried hallucinogenic mushrooms a guy gave her at a party the week before school started. He probably meant for her to save the mushrooms for some special Saturday night, but she can use a dose of something fun and pleasant right now. She ingests the mushrooms, with her skirt tucked primly between her legs and her head propped against her three-ring binder. Thirty minutes later, she is seeing a kaleidoscope of colors in the Roxbury Park trees. A couple of electric brown squirrels are fighting over a piece of bark that appears elastic, stretching like a giant rubber band. One squirrel lets it go. The bark slaps the other squirrel in the face, sending the little animal toppling and then racing like a comet up the tree trunk, leaving a trail of light. Kelly giggles. It looks like a 3-D cartoon: a spacy Road Runner vs. Wile E. Coyote. The squirrels chase each other, leap, appear to jump into space. She does not move for two hours.

At one thirty, back on campus, feeling giddy, she doodles through the rest of her afternoon classes, then races home to listen to the Go-Go's in her bedroom and experiment with different eye shadows, trying to forget she has only until tomorrow morning to write a persuasive essay on the issue of whether Hamlet is insane. She hasn't read the play yet. Maybe she can fake it with the Cliff Notes. A yell from the living room: Her mother wants her to turn down her stereo. Guests are arriving soon for a party. "And *please* put on something nice tonight," her mother shouts. "Why not your new skirt that I got you? Try something understated tonight, okay? And turn *off* the damn stereo, for God's sake. Help Ismelda with the ice, will you?"

Kelly puts on her Sergio Valente's, noticing the jeans feel tighter in the hips than when she bought them, two weeks ago. She needs to shed at least twenty pounds, she figures now. She throws on her pink cashmere sweater, and walks down the stairs.

"Aren't those jeans too small for you?" her mother asks.

Kelly ignores this. "I'll do the ice," she says. She strolls into the pantry, opens a freezer, and fills two buckets with ice; then, seeing no one else around, reaches above a wine cabinet to pull down an old, forgotten bottle of gin and makes herself a tall drink in a wineglass. She drinks it and makes another. She loves how smoothly gin goes down. God, you get an excellent buzz on it. She can hear Ismelda coming from the kitchen, gulps what is left, and sticks the glass in the refrigerator.

In the kitchen, her mom studies the octopus sushi hors d'oeuvres. "I don't know why the caterer made these so early," she says. "I don't see how they can be fresh, even with this little ice thing that he puts on top of it. I mean, aren't caterers supposed to come to your house anymore? Kelly, what kind of music do we have in the house to play?"

"I could put on some Phil Collins," she says. "That's something your friends could probably handle."

"I have an idea," her mom says. "Put on one of my old Neil Diamond tapes. They're below the television."

The ring of the doorbell and the entrance of guests enables Kelly to flee upstairs. She stretches out on her bed, another gin and tonic nestled on her lap. Downstairs, guests have arrived and Kelly can hear her mother's voice booming above everyone else's, urging people to try the octopus hors d'oeuvres, bantering about the rise in the value of jade, chortling over some joke that Kelly cannot quite make out. A jocular, corporate chortle. Kelly thinks her mom acquired it from her dad, who was always pounding on associates' backs and laughing over inside jokes about T-bills and IRAs that Kelly never understood. "Kelly, you have to show people that you know the ways of their club," her mom confided one night, after she had been in real estate for a couple of years. "You aren't really welcome playing tennis, golf, or cards with them, and you sure can't follow them into the bathroom, but what you can do for yourself is talk their language when you're around them. Not to be fake, really; it's just showing that you can follow the ball." Kelly hears a machine-gun laugh. "You and your *debentures*, Gary," her mother is shouting. "You're a *scream*. I *absolutely live* for you."

The phone rings. It is Tina, asking whether she understands the climactic passage in *Hamlet*.

"Not quite, but I think I know it good enough for the essay."

"Is he insane, or what?"

"I'm going to say, *totally*."

"Have you finished?"

"Almost," she lies. "I have the flu, I think. I might have to miss school tomorrow."

"Are you *sure* Hamlet's insane?"

"Radically insane. I have to go. My mom is calling."

Kelly hangs up and shoves the gin and tonic under her bed. A knock at her door.

Her mom walks in, drinking crème de menthe from a Bugs Bunny glass. Bugs looks frog green.

"Cute glass, Mom."

"Does it look silly? Judy — one of the sales reps — gave me a set of them as, you know, one of those joke gifts."

"It's kind of bizarre."

"She's very sensitive, so act like you like them when you go downstairs. Try to come down, sweetheart, if only for a minute. I want everyone to say hello to you."

"Okay."

"In a few minutes then?"

"Okay, Mom."

Her mom closes the door. Kelly changes from her jeans into a baggy skirt. She trudges downstairs. A couple of people say hi. She goes in the kitchen and makes herself another gin and tonic. Her mother chats with a few women from her real estate company whom Kelly has never seen before. The women are debating whether they should go on a weekend visit to Honolulu. "Men and more men at the Royal Hawaiian," says one of the women. "I think we could have a good hunt there."

Peels of laughter from her mother. "Oh, I'd *die* to go away with you guys. Let's *try* to do it. You know, the most special thing is just having you guys as friends."

After everyone leaves, her mother stretches out on the couch with a vodka tonic and asks Kelly whether she had a good time. "I didn't talk to many people," Kelly confesses.

"I didn't either," her mom says. "I don't know if it's me, but I don't have many friends I'm comfortable with. I don't have a lot of fun with that crowd."

"What about those women you're going to Hawaii with?"

"Oh, you've got to watch them. They are all so manipulative. They're fun at a dinner or a party, but you've gotta watch what you say around them. I'm always watching myself."

"But you said you were going with them to Honolulu."

"That probably won't happen. It might, but that will be just for fun. They're okay. I just wouldn't tell them anything."

———

For a moment, Steven cannot believe it. He's made it. Into the hot tub. With Luscious Vickie. She has led him here, taking his hand and persuading him to strip down. Her parents are in Palm Springs and the house is unoccupied, except for a sleeping housekeeper and Vickie's ten-year-old brother, who, obeying her order not to leave his bedroom, is watching television in his pajamas and hoping his sister doesn't remember that he was supposed to be asleep an hour ago. Settling into the hot tub, Steven has this nagging fear Little Brother is watching. "How can you be totally sure he isn't?" he asks Vickie, suddenly afraid to touch her. "How can you be certain?"

"You get so hyper, Steven," Vickie says. "*God, relax.* He's watching some movie. He knows he'll have to go to bed if he does anything. He's not going anywhere. Come here."

He takes hold of her outstretched hands, looking over her shoulder toward the window of her little brother's room, where the drapes are closed, but . . . well, it's just a vibe but he thinks he saw a shadow. Why is he always imagining things? He gets so paranoid.

"What are you looking at?" Vickie moans in disgust. "Oh, stop being so stupid, Steven. Come *here*." She yanks him against her, kissing him gently on the mouth. He laughingly ducks under her arm and goes under water. When he comes to the surface, she looks befuddled and wounded. "Are you cold?" she asks politely. "Would you like to get out and get something to drink?" She has misunderstood, thinks he doesn't want to be in the hot tub in the first place.

"No, this is nice," he says. "I just wanted to enjoy the water a little bit. You know, *first*."

She nods. "I'll be right back," she says, and jumps out of the hot tub in her nakedness, flipping on a light switch and opening a little cooler on the patio. Vickie's old boyfriend, who enjoyed boasting of his sexploits with her, did not lie: She has a dark brown birthmark on her ass. The flaw somehow makes her sexier. He gets bored with perfection; quirks turn him on. She wiggles back into the hot tub with a bottle of white wine.

"Damn, this feels good," he says, the water from the tub's jets pulsating onto the small of his back. He takes a position on the wall opposite from her, drinking some of the wine straight out of the bottle and letting the jets pound on him. He puts her legs into a hammerlock with his own and pulls her over to him. She squeals, laughing now, mockingly fighting him, finally yielding at just the right time.

They make love right there, standing up, both of them fighting for balance a bit as feet slip on the tiled bottom, Steven spinning so that he is facing the house, the two giggling, then groaning slowly, louder and louder, the moment about to arrive. His eyes, squinting in pleasure and exertion, dance upon the house. A little figure is peering at them from between drapes. "*Oh, fuck*," he shouts. "*Oh, fuck!*"

Vickie turns, doesn't understand for a moment, then gasps, leaping out of the hot tub and, in one movement, grabbing a towel and screaming, "I'm going to kick the shit out of you, Jimbo!" She begins the long run toward the side door of the house. The boy has a little time to kill. He grins at Steven and then puts his tiny index finger through a circle he's formed with two fingers on his other hand. He takes his index finger out of the circle, and then puts it back in. In and out. In and out.

"You fucking pervert," Steven shouts. The kid is whooping it up, waving at Steven. Where the fuck is Vickie? Ten years old and a perv. What the fuck is the world coming to?

"You asshole, Jimmy," he can hear Vickie screaming inside the house now. "Unlock that door *now*." There is no getting to the little boy. His face pressed against the window, he waves at Steven a last time and turns off his bedroom's lights. Steven can hear high giggles. The boy is loudly telling the story to a friend on his private telephone line.

———

On the second Thursday in November it is time for Melinda to do her volunteer work for the community center, to go to a house in West Los Angeles and spend time with a child in need of an older friend. She doesn't feel quite up to it. Back in September, when she entered the "Adopt-a-Friend" program, she thought it would be fun to play the benevolent older pal to special children, but today she's tired and would just as soon be home doing her physiology and English homework, and maybe making some headway on her college applications. Plus, she had imagined they'd give her a really cute six-year-old but she's been assigned to a kind of dull and sometimes bratty nine-year-old girl. She'll be spending at least a couple of hours each week with the kid. She wasn't aware this job would be so time-consuming, though she tells herself in the next instant she has a responsibility and, besides, the volunteer program will look good on her applications. When she arrives at the address she's been given, the little girl is all over her, arms outstretched, asking if they can play with one of her electronic games. The kid talks so fast Melinda wonders whether she may be hyperactive. *"Can we play?"* she shouts. *"Can we play?"* Sure, sure, Melinda says.

Melinda plays with her for three hours, then says it is time for her to go; that she'll be back next week at the same time.

"I don't want you to go," the girl protests, so loudly that Melinda stays with her for another forty-five minutes.

"I really have to go now," she finally tells her.

"Can I have your picture?"

Melinda hesitates for a second.

"Please, please."

"Sure. I'll bring one next week."

The little girl gives her a piece of candy. "You'll come next week on Thursday again?"

"Each week on Thursday, right."

The girl reaches up, hugs Melinda around the waist, closes her eyes.

A half-hour later, Melinda is rushing through her physiology and English assignments. Her English teacher has asked students to perform satires of *Hamlet* on videotape, this passing for a literature assignment in the 1985–1986 school year at Beverly, and Melinda finishes the videotape in two hours, just a little longer than it takes her to study for three *Hamlet* multiple-choice and true-false tests.

Over the next week, the *Hamlet* exams are administered upon the school's SCAN-TRON computer strips. With a freshly sharpened No. 2 pencil, Melinda makes marks in spaces correctly identifying dates, places, characters, and passages from the play, information she gathered by reading the play once and then watching *Hamlet*, the movie. She gets an A on the three tests, and says a couple of days later, "I'm leading

a real comfortable life right now. I think I have school pretty well figured out."

───────

Early in the afternoon, on the first Sunday in November, Paul comes
home from his Nautilus workout to find a note from his mom stuck to the
refrigerator. He wouldn't have noticed it except on top of the note was a
twenty. He takes the twenty and crumples up the note, knowing what it
says: She'll be out for the day. The money is for dinner and "a treat." He
would have liked forty. He looks under the other magnets for anything
else he should know. His mom keeps his schedule here — reminders of
dentist visits, dates for his college interviews, and a proposed schedule of
the tennis lessons which she'd like him to take, to speed his weight loss.
He scans tiny pieces of paper, tries to make out her cramped scrawlings: a
reminder to herself to buy a calculator for her husband; something about
asking him whether they might be able to use two complimentary airline
tickets to the Bahamas; a barely decipherable date on a piece of San
Francisco Hilton Hotel stationery, alongside more scribblings: "12/14/85,
marriage encounter intro, Sausalito, $680/per couple — ask Martin."
Martin his father. Martin who never had time to look at the notes. He
puts the twenty in his pocket and phones Tony, who says that everybody
is going to Hollywood. To do what? Paul asks.
      "Whatever," says Tony.
      An hour later, having driven into and out of Hollywood, they are
standing in front of a bank of video games in Westwood. Adam plays
Space Invaders. Randy pleads with Tony to share his blow.
      "I've already told you three times *no*, I don't have enough."
      "I wish you had gotten a little bit more, too," says Paul. "I would
have paid you for it."
      Tony flicks a gum wrapper at him. "Well, I didn't, so stop bitch-
ing about it."
      Adam, who has been silent for ten minutes, clears his throat. "I
have some, but I'm not just giving it away." Adam has dealt a little coke
on the side for a while. Tony's told Paul that his Valley cousin has some
kind of connection. "Well, do you guys have some bread for me or not?"
asks the kid. Randy looks pissed off. Adam doesn't take his eyes off the
video screen.
      "You're a dick," says Randy.
      "And you're a hungry black child who doesn't have a quarter in

his pocket, right? Don't be a dildo. If you want it, let me see something. *Fuck*, I always lose this game." He slams the sides of the video machine.

Randy gives him a hundred-dollar bill.

Adam comes across with the goods.

"You're not shitting me, Adam, right? This is a gram?"

"Absolutely."

Randy gives him the finger. "I think you should sell it for less to a friend. A *ger* for a hundred is *harsh*. Fuck, I know somebody who will sell me an eight-ball for two seventy-five."

"Then go to him next time," Adam says.

Paul, who has only the twenty in his pocket, glances at the tiny packet in Randy's hand.

"Paul, don't be looking at me for anything," says Randy, "not unless you're going to fork over some bucks."

That he should have to pay bothers him. He has always shared his blow with Tony and Randy. "I'll just have to forget it," he says.

"Shit, you don't have to do that," Adam says. "I'll give you some if you promise to pay me back."

"Well, that's cool."

"How much do you want?"

"How much can I have?"

"As much as you want if you're good for it."

"How about a couple of grams?"

"That's cool." Adam reaches into his pocket and gives it to him. Paul is instantly in debt to the Valley kid for two hundred.

"The Homecoming Dance sucked," Randy is saying the next afternoon, "so Alicia and I left early and went up to her sister's place on Mulholland." They are sitting in Carney's eating cheeseburgers and Paul is already a little pissed that Randy brought along his eighth-grade brother. "Only Alicia's sister wasn't home," Randy says. "But, Alicia had a key, so we watched a little TV and fucked in the guest room. Then her sister comes home with her date or somebody, all bummed that Alicia locked the door to the guest room and didn't call to say that she was coming. What a fucking bitch — like I'm sure you're going to leave the door unlocked after you've fucked and you're drunk."

Tony and Adam laugh, though when they turn their heads to the side, Paul notices, they're wearing the thinnest of smirks. What a dildo Randy has become. He once had some style, was as cool as anyone in junior high, but he's never learned when or how to keep his mouth shut.

"What are you going to do about Cheryl?" Tony asks then. *Cheryl*, the girl Randy may have impregnated. *Cheryl*, whom Randy has been seen talking to lately at lunch alone, in whispers, head bowed. Paul studies a ketchup bottle, doesn't want to hear Randy's answer, thinks it is a little cruel of Tony to have asked this so casually. He wants to say to Randy, *Don't talk, don't talk*, but he knows Randy will, Randy always does. And Paul, being among Randy's closest friends — at least from Randy's perspective — has heard it all. Randy will say anything to him, confess to his wildest dreams about sex or drugs or how he truly wanted to stab his little brother in the ass once, just because the kid was being a dick. Once he told everyone how he'd like to butt-fuck some woman teacher. The kid has never understood: You just don't say some things. Paul doesn't confide in anyone, except Tony, who, with rare exception, confides in no one. Tony is poking Randy in the shoulders now. "C'mon, Papa, what are you going to do about it?"

Randy shrugs. "It's over. She got the abortion."

"That's why she was so bummed at lunch all week?"

Randy dips a couple of french fries into a pool of ketchup. "Partly." His teeth chomp down on the fries. "I like her, but I thought it might be hard if we started seeing each other again. I told her I just wanted to be her friend."

Paul glances at Randy's little brother, who is eating a hot dog and looking at pictures of Van Halen in a magazine.

"I kind of feel bad for her," mumbles Randy.

"Sure you do," says Tony, who rolls his eyes. Adam giggles. Paul hears himself rising to Randy's defense, not quite knowing why, nudging him, murmuring, "You felt pretty fucked that she was bummed, huh?"

Randy nods.

Tony groans disgustedly. "Give us a break."

Randy stares into his french fries.

"*Boring*," Adam says. "Why don't we get out of here."

Paul is relieved to be gone. They make a quick stop at a liquor store where Tony uses his fake California driver's license to buy two six-packs of beer and a pint of Johnny Walker Red. "Where's the party tonight?" Adam asks.

"Nothing's fucking happening here," says Randy's little brother from the back seat. The kid is already on his second Lowenbrau, keeping the bottle between his feet on the floor and out of sight from the cops who are stuck in Sunset Boulevard traffic with them. "I'd love to do a little blow tonight," he says.

Adam elbows Paul. "Did you bring some?"

"I'm not giving any to a goddamn thirteen-year-old," Paul says.

"Don't give it to him, *sell* it to him."

"Fuck you," says Randy's little brother. "Give me a line."

Paul wheels around and glares menacingly at the boy. "Shut the fuck up before I rip your gay tongue out, you little prick."

The kid bends his head down to suck on his Lowenbrau, does not look up.

They drive for a half-hour, through the Hollywood hills, down Sunset, up Beverly Glen, finally reaching Mulholland at dusk, the sharp turns and cliffs in shadows. A car from behind roars around them and goes past, cruising eighty, ninety, around Mulholland's turns, and Randy's little brother mumbles, "Intense." As if pulled along by a demon magnet, Tony drives faster, too, doing seventy, seventy-five, the car careening. Without warning, he whips the car down a side street, slowing and looking around in a quiet residential neighborhood for signs of life. Adam, holding the Johnny Walker Red in his hands, tells Tony to pull over. "Watch this, dude," Adam says, and before Paul knows what's happening, Adam has leaped from the car and cracked a Mercedes's window with a tire iron. Glass splinters, and gives way. Tony screams, "*Yeah, yeah.*" Adam works an arm through the window and unlocks the door. He yanks on something that Paul cannot make out.

"*Intense,*" shouts Randy's little brother.

Adam is running back to the car with a stereo in his hands. "*That's a burn,*" shouts Randy.

"*Let's go, let's go,*" Adam screams, jumping in.

The car roars off.

"*Full-on,*" yells Randy's little brother.

"*What are you going to do with it?*" Randy shouts at Adam, as they hurtle down Mulholland. "*What are you going to do with it?*"

"*I don't know, I don't know,*" screams Adam.

———

Hillary cannot escape the hairy new presence in her house. She ties her robe tightly around herself on this Saturday, as she does each morning now, and walks gingerly downstairs to see Harry doing sit-ups on their living room floor in just his pajama bottoms. The hairy chest is glistening with sweat. He grosses her out. Why can't he do this at a gym?

"Did you sleep well?" he asks, and then, as if reading her mind, says: "I'm doing the sit-ups here because I won't have time to go to my club this morning. I'm playing golf at Rancho. Do you play golf? Maybe sometime we could go out to a driving range and hit some. Nine holes maybe. It's a beautiful day, huh?"

Besides everything else, the man is too damn cheery. She nods instinctively, stumbles in the kitchen to find a danish, and tears into it. She could munch forever. A model with a fat girl's psyche, she has to be careful. "Would you like some orange juice?" she asks him at the end of his sit-ups, this being part of her morning ritual with him, though he always acts surprised. Worse than anything, he's too goddamn polite.

"Well, aren't you thoughtful!" Harry beams. The juice is not fresh-squeezed but he still drinks it heartily, wiping his lips at the end with that bear paw of a left hand, still sweating from the sit-ups. "You are just a dear, dear, dear," he exclaims and gives her a big wet kiss on the cheek.

This won't be easy.

———

SAT reports arrive the second week of November. Paul receives a score in the low 1100s, far higher than he expected, considering that he missed two of his six preparatory sessions. When Andy's score arrives, he is in Culver City, practicing with his new garage band. His mother calls him and asks if she can open the envelope and read him his score; she can't bear the suspense any longer.

"No, wait until I come home," Andy says.

"When are you coming home?"

"Soon."

"When?"

"Oh, God, Mom, I don't know. We're practicing here. In a couple hours, probably."

"I guess I'll just have to take a long walk then."

"Oh, shit."

"Do you just expect me to sit here and wait?"

"Shit, I don't know."

"I guess I could just keep walking around the block."

"*All right*, I'll come home."

"You'll *hurry*, right?"

So many people living and dying upon his performance. He hangs up and tells the other guys that he has to split.

"Let me guess: You gotta go home for the big drama of ripping open the envelope," says Jason.

Andy nods. Jason smirks, grabs his throat as if choking, and snickers, "Feeling the pressure, dude?" The kid has a lot of wise-ass in him. "Well, wait until your score comes," Andy fires back. "You'll be pissing in your pants."

"Hey, Mr. Valedictorian, it's already here."

"Yeah?"

Jason grabs some drumsticks and gleefully taps out a little roll on the garage floor. "Say hello to the future graduate of UCLA. Slap five with the test-buster. Check the kid out. An exceptionally hot twelve thirty."

Andy grins and tries to show excitement, but he cannot help wondering whether his own score is even close to 1230. How did Jason do it? In the SAT preparatory classes, the kid did nothing but chew sunflower seeds and whisper to girls. He says congratulations, and heads for his car.

It is forty-five minutes before he arrives home, having driven around in circles so he could get calm. Walking through the front door, he sees his mother sitting on the piano bench, not playing, just staring blankly at sheet music. She does not acknowledge him.

"Sorry I took so long," he says.

"I finally took a long walk," she says. "I would have thought that you would have appreciated the state I was in. I put it on your dresser."

"Okay." He begins walking up the stairs.

"*Well*, I don't suppose you'll let me look at it, too."

"God, Mom, I'll show it to you."

The envelope rests atop his folded T-shirts. "Educational Testing Service . . . Princeton, New Jersey," says the return address on the envelope. He sits on his bed and opens it. The number all but leaps out of the envelope at him, black and bold. It is disaster. He has not even scored 1100. Oh, God.

"Tell me how you did," his mother says excitedly over his shoulder.

He wants her gone. "Here, take it," he says, handing over the test score. "I'm tired. Could you close the door?"

She glances at the score and, for a long moment, says nothing, just stands over his bed, looking down at him. She finally clears her throat. "Andy, do you have any feelings about this?"

"None, besides that I feel fucked, if that's what you mean."

"I hope you will believe me in the future when I tell you that you didn't study hard enough."

He closes his eyes and chuckles. "Mom, I don't like to say this: But you don't know what you're talking about. Why don't *you* take the test? See how much your *Sidney Sheldon* books help you. I prepared as much as I could. I went to those preparatory sessions. I read all the fucking booklets. I took all the practice tests. That's all I could do."

"Yes, but you didn't read enough during the summers, except for those strange novels that didn't help you a bit. We were always telling you that your mathematics score wasn't going to get any better if you didn't do a lot of work in the booklets. You had the time, but you chose to use it your own way."

In one motion, he rises and heads for the door. "Mom, I have to get out of here."

Within three days, calm has been restored. His mother has apologized for losing her temper, and, on Saturday morning, his father calls from Hawaii to ask whether he would like to have lunch when he gets back at a restaurant near LAX. "You just need a little change of pace," his father says. "Have some nice food, nice atmosphere. You've been under a lot of pressure. We all know that."

Andy doesn't say that, in the last few days, the pressure has actually diminished. He knows his fate now. Maybe he'll be all right.

"Don't give up on things, pal," his father says. "*I'll see you tomorrow.*"

"All right, Dad."

"Hang in there. Don't get despondent."

"Okay."

"If you have anything to talk about, *anything*, I want you to pick up the phone."

"Sure."

"Say that you will."

"Okay, Dad, I will."

"Do you need anything?"

"Not really. Maybe you could buy me a pineapple or something over there."

"You got it. And I'll bring you a surprise, too."

"Thanks, Dad."

"I'll let you get going. Just remember: Stay composed."

"Right, Dad."

"We have to get you together again with that private college counselor we hired," his father says to him the next day over lunch, still wearing his Hawaiian shirt and a lei that he bought just before boarding the United flight to Los Angeles. "Let's just get him to tell us which colleges look like possibilities, which ones look like certainties, and which ones aren't realistic for you. We'll just have him go down the list again."

"He's taking your money, Dad. I'll be happy at San Diego State, or some place like that. I've been thinking about it. I don't need anyplace else."

"*Use* his expertise: That's all I'm asking. My friends have some pull at some colleges, your uncle has some pull, and I have some pull. Maybe we can work something out somewhere. Use all of us in this thing. Use the counselor and anyone else you can, that's all we're asking. I know you are depressed, and your mother knows you're depressed. She called me. Which is why I thought you needed a present, though your birthday is three months away. These are yours. . . ." He gives Andy some car keys. "It's being delivered today. Hope you like it in silver. If you don't, well, we'll fix it so you get something you like." The keys go to a BMW 325i. "And here's a pineapple and a lei for you." Andy feels sweaty petals go around his neck. Dead flowers, laden with Hawaiian humidity. Oh, but getting a car: *a Beamer*. He can always count upon getting hot gifts in bad times. His parents don't give him a regular allowance, but when he wants money or anything else, he gets it, within reason. His mother, who vowed after the divorce never to speak to his father except in the event of an emergency (a dip in the currency exchange rate or a credit shutdown at Saks constituted a crisis), must have called him to wail that their disturbed progeny looked to be suicidal, homicidal, or something-cidal. Mom never quite knew the right words but her passion always got the message across. His father cannot look at him squarely in the eyes, seems to be stealing glances at the side of his face.

"Is that earring you got on *new?*" he finally asks.

"Oh, yeah. I forgot about it. I'm just wearing it outside of school, not in school, Dad. You don't hate it, do you?"

"It just surprised me when I saw it," his dad says, grinning. "But don't feel like you have to excuse it. Nobody has to excuse that kind of thing. I used to wear a bandanna and a ponytail. My bandanna was my own personal emblem, I guess. I understand what you're trying to say with your earring."

"Oh, *God*."

"What comes around goes around, pal. Get a good start on those applications."

Andy arrives home at four P.M. to find his new BMW has arrived. He takes it on a drive around the neighborhood, half-hoping someone will notice him, finally pulling into his driveway to see, through a window, his mother stretched out on their living room floor doing the deep-breathing exercises that mark the beginning of her daily meditation. She neither talks nor moves once her deep-breathing has begun, so he uses the opportunity to sneak into the kitchen and make himself a tall roast beef sandwich with mayo and all the other things that she's always saying will one day kill him. He'd like her to try meditating for about a week. Eating in peace, he washes down his sandwich with a Michelob and a 7 Up. He can afford the calories, skinnier than ever. Can't understand why, since he never exercises, though the doctor told him at his last check-up that he seems to have an extraordinarily fast metabolism, probably burned off calories just sitting and thinking. "Studying a lot these days, aren't you?" the doctor asked. Andy nodded earnestly, though the truth was that, after concentrated study sessions at the start of the school year, he has regressed to the point where he can go no longer than an hour or so before stopping, just like last year. He can't think through the tension, which is what has really burned off those calories, he knows. Tension over the bullshit, his grades, SAT and Achievement Test scores, tension over his lack of college prospects. Tension over the big black void in front of him.

Up in his bedroom, listening to a tape on his headphones, he dons a loose gray sports jacket, sleeves rolled up to his elbows, just like the one worn by the lead singer of Simple Minds. His mother appears at his bedroom door. Her meditation has ended early. She wants to know where he is going. He doesn't know where he is going. Just out somewhere, maybe a club, he says, with Jason and a couple of girls from Jason's high school. He's combed his hair a new way, down and to the side, to show off the new bleached white streaks that his hairdresser gave him yesterday.

His mother leans back against the bedroom wall and smiles. She is always temporarily mellow after one of her meditating sessions. "Who did your hair?"

"Selina."

"Very nice."

"Like you really like it."

"I really do. You don't look like every other kid these days, running around like some boring aristocrat in his Lacoste shirt. Your hair is getting a little longer, too, I notice. I think it all looks good."

"Mom, you're so *happening*," he groans.

"I hope I always will be, Andy. I hope, too, that you'll become a little nicer."

"Why don't you go out with us tonight and we'll get some beers and do some doobies."

"Andy, there is nothing that you could say that would shock me. I've been there. Your father has been there. You can't shock us."

What he finds most infuriating about these exchanges is her smug belief that he can do nothing that she hasn't done already, that he remains, at best, a child following in the footsteps of elders who blazed Decadence's trail in their Nehru suits and granny glasses and then matured to shed it all and make some serious bucks. *You cannot shock us.* Whenever he hears it, he feels stifled; indeed, would like to terrify his parents occasionally, if for no other reason than to feel like he is carving an identity apart from theirs, growing up. He's found himself with a perverse need to unnerve his mom lately. A few weeks ago, riding with her to the supermarket, he noticed her sucking in her breath at the sight of a boy on a corner who had stuck a safety pin through his ear and drawn a swastika on his shaved skull. Inside the market, as she fondled cauliflower, he casually remarked how it might be fun to go to a club some night with a nail sticking through his ear. Her hands stopped fondling the cauliflower.

"What do you mean, a *nail?*" she asked.

"A nail, Mom. You know what a nail is." He pantomimed pounding it into a board, then his ear. "Bang, bang, bang."

She stared numbly at the cauliflower, not moving for a few seconds, before saying softly, "God, you're crazy. Please, don't ever do that. Please."

She has never been as *radical* as she would have liked, Andy thinks, letting her feel the streaks in his hair as he puts on his socks. Still, she's capable of surprising him. A short time after the supermarket encounter, he came home in a purple cut-off shirt cut so high that his belly button was exposed, along with a few of his chest hairs. The shirt reminded Andy of something Prince had worn in a video. He waited for his mother to freak. She surveyed him, up and down, then said, "This unisex look isn't bad. I like it on you, Andy. Your father used to wear a pink bandanna. I just *flashed* on that." Andy has not worn the shirt since. Actually, the shirt looks gay to him.

At six thirty, Jason arrives with two girls. Andy's mother insists on meeting everyone. Introductions are made, and one of the girls says to Jason, "Oh, I didn't know Andy was in your band."

Jason shrugs. "Well, we're taking a look, kind of, to see how it will work out. He wrote an excellent song, though."

"What is it called?"

"We still don't have a title for it," Andy says. "But it's finished."

"It's real good," his mother pipes in.

The girl smiles at Andy. "Does it have words?"

His mother answers again. "No, it's just an instrumental."

"Mom, what are you talking about? *It has words.* God, you never know what you are saying. A rock song has *got* to have words. You never listen. I've sung it twenty times around here. You just don't pay attention to me." He turns to Jason. *"Let's bail. Fuck."*

"Chill out, Andy," Jason says.

"Thank you, Jason," says his mother.

"Will everybody leave me the hell alone?"

The next morning, his father calls. "I hear you flipped out last night."

"No more or less than any other night, Dad."

"Try to stay cool. Good news from the college counselor, pal. He gave me a list of a bunch of private schools where he thinks you have a chance. They're pretty good ones. He says the schools can't afford to be as selective now, something about more competition or something. So somebody with just decent scores has a chance sometimes . . ."

"Like dumbshit me."

"Claremont College. Reed College. The University of the Pacific. The list goes on and on. I'll drop it by. I think we have a better chance at some of those than others, but we should think about giving them all a try. You're still in the running, buddy. Don't get down."

"Well, I needed a piece of good news, I guess . . ."

"Want another? How would you like to come to Maui over Thanksgiving with me and some friends? You could stand the rest, I suppose. In the meantime, I'll set up another meeting with that college counselor for Wednesday."

"What do you think Mom will say?"

"Wednesday will probably be good for her, too."

"No. I mean me going on a trip, with Thanksgiving and all . . ."

His father doesn't understand. "What does she ever say?"

DECEMBER

It is getting darker sooner, Kelly notices. You get out of school, eat a late lunch, watch a soap opera and a few videos, and before you know it, it is four thirty, the sun has begun to drop, the day is over. Time already to think about dinner, homework, school the next day, the assignments you won't finish, the trouble you're in. Ever since she was in junior high, darkness has had the effect of making her feel small and trapped. A chilly wind fills her nostrils with a familiar scent that she has always associated with burning wood, maybe the smoke from chimneys, maybe something else. She used to think that she smelled fires but now thinks she is simply paranoid. On the Strip, she sits at a sidewalk table at Chin Chin's, with Tina, Andrea, and Shelly, wrapping her arms around herself and drinking hot tea while the others argue over Tina's obsession with a boy in her government class.

"He's going to fuck you over, Tina," says Andrea. "Just like he's done to other people."

"Get a *head*, Andrea. I'm not in love with the guy, it's only physical, I'm not lost in space. He knows what I like, I know what he likes . . ."

"You're gross."

Shelly feigns a yawn, taps her teacup with chopsticks for attention. "I don't know if you know, but Nancy hasn't gotten her period yet."

"Like I *really* care," says Andrea. "Nancy is a slut."

Tina giggles. "That's so *hard-core* for you to say, Andrea. Like you're perfect. *Puhleeze*. You act *so* jealous."

"Jealous of *what?*"

On the other side of the table, Shelly whacks her cup and whistles softly. "Oh, look. What a babe. Look *quick*. On the other side of the street. *Ooooh, look*. Oh, he's gone."

The others turn and crane their heads to see a Porsche drive off. Shelly grins and throws up her arms, as if to say, You guys lose. She's always made a point of trumpeting her sightings of babes whom they don't see, her chance encounters with babes whom they don't meet.

When a guy stopped liking someone in their group, Shelly would invariably tell the wounded victim she had seen the guy with someone new, adding angrily, just to cover her tracks, "The bastard." It gets on everyone's nerves.

"What did he look like?" Tina asks.

"Blond Adonis type. Nice buns, too. Too bad you missed him."

"You're so competitive, Shelly, sometimes," Tina says. "I mean, *no offense*, but it's like you're being too cool."

Shelly responds by looking down at her teacup and slowly rubbing her chopsticks together. Kelly stares at the headlights of passing cars on Sunset, wraps her arms around herself a little tighter. "Yeah, no offense," Shelly murmurs, "just rag on me like that. Go ahead. No offense. *Right*."

Andrea sighs and rolls her eyes, playing the exasperated peacemaker here. "I don't want to hear this. Get to the point, Tina. What are you going to do if this guy comes up to you in government and asks you out?"

"I already told you, it's *happened*," Tina says. "Even if it wasn't a date, we've *done* it, okay?"

"I still think it's kind of gross not knowing the guy. He looks gayish to me, besides. What if he *has* something?"

"He doesn't *have* anything, Andrea. *Get a head for once, okay?*"

Shelly tries to find a way back into the conversation. "Did you use something, at least, I hope?"

"He did," says Tina.

Shelly chuckles. "I hope he did use something, Tina, for your sake. Last summer, in Austria, when I met that German guy, I made him wear one all the time because I didn't know who he'd been with. I'm glad I did because all we did in afternoons was take drugs and have sex every kind of way. It was wild and he was great, but I still wanted him to use something."

"We've heard all about your Austrian Experience, Shelly," Tina sighs.

Kelly hasn't. She can't imagine Shelly on some hotel bed buttnaked doing mushrooms with some German stud and readying herself for the high, hard one. Jesus. Until last year, Shelly was always the straight one among them, the girl whom all the mothers still point to as the ideal toward which the other girls should aspire — the bearer of a 3.8 g.p.a., a supporter of student body events, and a summer camp counselor.

Kelly's mother screamed at her daughter last summer, "Why can't you be more like Shelly? Do you think Shelly ever does drugs or sleeps around? Do you? *Do you?*"

Shelly is saying loudly that a couple of other Austrian guys had begged to do a threesome with her, that she had been tempted, but only slept with the cute one. Why is the girl so insecure? Kelly wonders. She's heard you have chemicals in your brain, and you're either sane or you aren't, and maybe Shelly isn't, after all. No one who has had anal sex and done 'shrooms in Austria could be the perfect girl. It would be sordid to ask her for details, but Kelly can't help herself, coaxing them out of this girl so desperate to be liked that she unravels the whole story as Tina and Andrea giggle. Kelly sits there, shaking: *The perfect Shelly likes it in all positions.* Another piece of naïveté stripped away. She would have liked to believe in somebody, anyone, even a girl who gets on her nerves as much as Shelly. She feels soiled, listening. That's life, soiling yourself, she thinks. She can't understand herself sometimes. All these swirling thoughts, all these changes and contradictions. Actually, she wouldn't have minded trading places with Shelly in Austria, she has to admit, would give almost anything for the thrill of meeting a decent-looking guy right now. But her hunt for a high school lover the last few weeks has been futile. She's still too fleshy in the thighs, she's convinced. Tonight she'll have only a dinner salad for the third straight evening. She's so tired. Maybe some of her mother's iron pills would make her feel better. Or some No-Doz. She especially prefers the thought of No-Doz after being told by Andrea that iron bloats you. Andrea heard it from her manicurist. Andrea has a twenty-three-inch waist and a thirty-five-inch bust and, during the summer, receives regular bikini waxes. Iron was a no-no, said Andrea.

Friday, December 6: Junior/Senior Night, the annual competition between the two classes in events ranging from a pie-eating contest to a tug-of-war. Paul comes to cheer the senior entrants but he spends most of the time talking to a buxom junior girl in a pink sweater who has come to the Swim-Gym alone. The buxom girl doesn't seem too excited by all these dumb-ass games either. "It's a little boring," he says cautiously, trying to feel her out on this point.

She shrugs. "I kind of like it," she confesses, "because it is the only time our class has spirit. I've kind of thought about trying out to be a cheerleader but then I thought that not many people come and really cheer at the football games, so why do it, only I might want to, I don't know. You meet better people if you do, maybe."

Another confused, aspiring soshe. Paul looks over her shoulder to scope some other girls.

"But *you're* bored?" she asks, so softly that she has to repeat the question while pulling at his arm to lasso in his drifting eyes. The other girls alone here, he can see, are alone for a good reason: They look like Bones. He can't afford to be seen with any of them. He turns back to the buxom soshe and shakes his head. "Well, I'm kind of bored, I guess, yeah."

"So what are you going to do?"

"Oh, I'm probably going to go over to a friend's, maybe party a little."

"Yeah?"

"I'm gonna do a little coke, actually."

"That sounds nice."

Early Saturday morning, still upset that the junior girl with the enormous tits did a half-gram of his coke and then wouldn't sleep with him, wouldn't even make out with him, he goes to the Sports Connection, does a furious twenty minutes of sit-ups, then sits in the sauna for a half-hour, hoping to sweat the last traces of chemicals out of his system.

Afterward, he calls Tony, hoping for an invitation to come over and have a couple of beers. Tony says something about having to study. Somebody is giggling and whispering in the background.

"Who's over there?" Paul asks. "Randy is partying, isn't he? I'm coming over."

"Not today," says Tony. "*Tomorrow*, okay? I'll see you to-morrow."

"Cool," says Paul.

It wasn't Randy whispering, he knows. Not Adam either. It was a thin blond boy whom Paul met at a party a few weeks ago. He recognized that high little giggle immediately. The suspicion he has harbored all along grows a little stronger: Tony is gay. He has no evidence; it's always been merely a strange vibe coming from his best friend, maybe the way he'd walk away from foxes at a party to mumble and giggle with some guy, alone, in the corner of a living room. Whatever, Paul's felt it and denied it, until those giggles filled his brain like sirens. Is there a possibility Tony has never truly liked those girls who fell all over him? No, the guy has fucked some of them too many times not to enjoy it. What could account for Tony getting it on (he can't picture this and doesn't want to try) with the blond boy? Mere curiosity? You don't experiment with what you find the least bit repulsive. He has read in magazines that one's sexual orientation is fixed early in life, before the age of three. *We are what we are.* The thought chills him; all these chemicals in our brain swirling around telling us what we must be. What is he?

That night, Adam calls him, excited. "How much you got right now?" he asks.

"I don't know, five grams about, I guess," Paul says.

"Some kid who said he was from Uni High called me wanting some, and I thought he might be a narc, but he put his friend on, a guy I sold to once, so I know he's cool. Anyway, I don't want to drive over the hill to bring some to him, so I said maybe you could do it."

"How much did you say I'd sell it for?"

"A hundred and twenty apiece."

"Cool. I'll give them all five. Tell me the address."

Adam gives him directions to a house in Brentwood, where four kids, fifteen, maybe sixteen, are sitting on large wicker chairs on a front porch, drinking margaritas. "You the dude — Adam's friend?" one asks.

Paul nods. "What's goin' on?"

The kid points at the margarita pitcher, pulls another chair over, and hands Paul a salt-rimmed glass.

"Uh, no thanks, I got to get to work," he lies, still standing. "Listen, I'm kind of in a hurry. I've got it right here." In one motion, he puts the margarita glass back on a tray and takes the contraband from his pocket.

"That was ninety a gram, right?" the kid asks in midsip. "Adam was talking ninety, I kind of remember." The kid glances at his friend, then cocks his head, grinning at Paul.

He decides to stay cool. "Well, I'm almost sure that he said a hundred and twenty, but we can call him just to make sure," he says.

The kid wipes the foam off his mouth with a forearm, stares into his margarita glass. "Well, if we had thought it was a hundred and twenty we wouldn't have wanted you to drive all the way from Beverly Hills."

He can see this falling apart, doesn't care. "It's no problem. I can drive right back."

"Would ninety-five be fair?" The kid pours a fresh margarita, and offers the glass to Paul.

He shakes his head. "Sorry, guys, a hundred and twenty is the price."

"But that's a ripoff."

"That's what you agreed to with Adam."

"Well, you gotta negotiate," the kid says.

"Get going is what I gotta do."

He walks toward his car. "Should have kicked his ass," he hears a new voice saying from over his shoulder. Then, the first voice: "*Hey, wait, dude.*"

Paul turns around. The dealmaker is walking hurriedly to him, pulling money out of his pocket. "Six bills, dude. I've got 'em right here."

"Right," Paul says.

The kid gives him the dough. Paul pauses before turning the coke over. He taps the kid on his chest with an index finger. Hard. "Don't ever try to fuck me over again," he says, his finger thumping. "*Ever.* I'll kick your ass."

"Okay."

"*Ever.*"

"Hey, chill out."

He gives the kid the contraband, vowing on the way back to Beverly Hills never to go to a stranger's home alone again.

He feels himself shaking.

At home, he microwaves a Lean Cuisine and puts on a tape of an old "Gidget" episode with Sally Fields. The phone rings. It's Tony, saying he has just seen a killer Black Sabbath video. Tony usually hates videos and knows absolutely nothing about Black Sabbath, so Paul guesses he needed an excuse to call, that he wants to talk about something.

"I got 'Gidget' on," he tells Tony.

Tony laughs. "*Really?* Bizarre. I was just watching 'The Partridge Family.' That show with the babe on it. What's her name?"

"Oh yeah, Susan Dey. She's a fox."

"Edible, I'd say."

Tony doesn't mention the blond kid from last night. They talk about the Raiders, the Rams, Prince, their physiology teacher, and a rumor that coke is half as cheap in Saugus, a town somewhere out in the sticks, beyond even the San Fernando Valley. Paul wants to open up Tony's closet and bring the blond kid out of the dark.

"You hear that story on the news about how AIDS is way up?" he asks. "Fucking unreal, huh? *AIDS*. I'd shit if some guy I knew had it."

Tony doesn't take the bait. "Me, too. You gonna watch the Raiders Sunday?"

The conversation runs out of gas. The boys promise to talk the next day.

Paul puts on a tape of "Family Ties": A shy, kind, troubled boy is having problems adjusting to his school and community, but Paul knows that he will get help from Michael J. Fox, because, on television, the meek always inherit the earth and the good life with friends and a lot of babes.

"It's kind of like real life, 'Family Ties' is," he says later. "But it isn't exactly like it, because, you know, it is better than real life. That is what makes it interesting to watch. It's better than books or talks from people most of the time, that's for fucking sure. There's so much that just bores the shit out of you. At least, on TV, life is *happening*."

———

Melinda's physiology teacher has formed discussion panels in which students explore topics ranging from birth control to their own futures. Along the way, the teacher dispenses his own opinions. He is opposed to abortion, believes hard rock and roll desensitizes kids to morality, thinks women are fools to live with men outside of marriage, and does not accept the theory of evolution.

Melinda says, "He really can be obnoxious. One day, he told the class, 'I just can't accept evolution. Man did not come from the muck of the sea. If a man is made from the muck of the sea, then we are all mistakes. And if we are all mistakes, then we have no biological reason for existence.' "

Melinda shakes her head. "I wanted to hit him."

But she stayed quiet. She tuned his voice out and thought of watching "Santa Barbara" that afternoon.

"I never get mad at a teacher, because it will backfire on me," she says. "I have to remember my grades."

———

Hillary's modeling assignments have grown to include department store catalogs offering two, even three times what the sporting goods company paid her for swimsuit work. Her mother wants her to get an agent. "It's getting too big for us to handle on our own," she says. "We need advice so we don't get taken advantage of. Harry thinks you need an agent, too, and he has quite a bit of experience about these sort of things."

"*Harry? He's a doctor, Mom.*"

"Still, sweetheart, he knows the market and the financial world. His advice is to get it done, get the agent before everyone exploits you. I think we should carefully follow that."

Hillary rolls her eyes. "That's advice from an expert?"

Will Harry be controlling her allowance next? He has so completely settled in that he has taken control over the den, rearranging the gray couch that had been Hillary's favorite so it no longer sits opposite the television but instead rests, nonfunctional and for all purposes forgotten, against a side wall from which the television screen cannot be seen. A deep wine-colored leather chair with a matching foot-rest sits in its place, along with two smaller beige chairs with straight stiff backs. Harry says the guys who will be coming over to watch the football play-off games will like the leather chairs more than a couch where they would be rubbing shoulders and touching knees. "Part of a machismo thing," Harry explains. Hillary still thinks he's weird, particularly resents how he's moved her father's rosewood bookcase out of the room and into storage so that he could put an old pinball machine and a 1950s 7 Up dispenser in its place. She never even looked at most of the books in her father's case, but the presence of the rosewood was always a reminder of better times when her parents sat alongside each other on the gray couch, television off, reading selections that they had just received in the mail from a book club. Did they read together? She wonders how many of these old images are inventions of her wishful mind. Sometimes she has problems imagining a moment when Harry wasn't riding herd over the house.

——————

The morning produces a shocker in Steven's English class. *The Canterbury Tales* tests are corrected and returned, and Steven has received a pathetic B-minus. Seven of the multiple-choice answers he copied off the doctored edge of a friend's pencil had been wrong. "Fuck, I thought you said you knew this shit," he whispers to the guy as the teacher goes over the answers.

"I thought I did. I studied all night."

"You're a dildo."

After class, he walks to the parking lot, removes a cooler from the trunk of his car, and, in the privacy of his front seat, drinks a beer. Maybe seeing Vickie will make him feel better. He drives to her house and finds her mother hitting tennis balls on a backyard court with a young blond guy. She introduces him as "Frankie, from Munich." "*Franz*," the guy says, yawning, waving his tennis racquet, not turning around.

"Frankie, I want to work on my overhead," she says. Franz hits one, two, three lobs for her to smash back at him, while checking his right forearm, which is peeling. Tennis, sun, a few drinks with divorcées and other men's wives — life could not be too bad for Franz, Steven thinks.

"Steven, you're making me nervous just standing there like that," Vickie's mom says. "Victoria's sick and asleep and not to be disturbed. Why don't you go inside to the library and watch television until she gets up."

"What's wrong with her?"

"The flu, a cold, maybe."

He nods, and murmurs, "Later on, Frankie," who, staring at his peeling forearm, doesn't hear him. Inside the house, he grabs a ginger ale, finds a television to turn on in the library, and lies on a couch, the television's remote control in his hands, Steven not quite able to concentrate on the screen, still thinking about that B-minus. Shit, you work your ass off for four years, but one lousy grade could screw you. He can't afford to take any more chances. On the next English multiple-choice test, he'll be prepared, will come in with the answers beneath his sock, something like that. He wouldn't mind doing without the tiny crib sheets if all the nerds competing against him did the same. But they won't, and, down deep, he can't blame them: Kids who study four or five hours for an exam feel they deserve the answers, just in case their minds go blank. People everywhere like the guarantee of an easy scam. On the television, there is news: Five-foot-ten Sylvester Stallone has married a six-foot, twenty-two-year-old Danish model. Former San Diego mayor Roger Hedgecock, free pending appeal of a year's sentence for his conviction on charges of conspiracy to violate campaign disclosure laws and twelve counts of perjury, will become a San Diego talk-show host. Steven laughs. He can sympathize with a scam gone wrong: Ethics count, but not as much as the press always tries to make you believe. He likes reading the police blotter items in a local newspaper, just to see what notables in his neighborhood have run afoul of the law, maybe been arrested for drunk driving. The list of familiar names is surprisingly long sometimes. Life goes on. People forget. The smart ones never worry.

He hears a shout. Vickie? He walks down the hallway to the other end of the house, past the bedroom of her monstrous little brother. "Hey, dude," the little pervert says. "Here for my sister?"

Steven says nothing. He keeps walking and surprises Vickie, who is changing her clothes. She squeals, putting fingers to lips, and closes the bedroom door. Her mother, smashing Franz's lobs, will never know.

———

Kelly has noticed that her irritation with life in general has grown since she went on her latest diet: grapefruit at breakfast; tomatoes, carrots, and yogurt for lunch; a small piece of fish and two vegetables at dinner. In fifteen days, she's lost nearly ten pounds, but she has ten to go, and flesh is coming off painfully slowly now. In the last few days the headaches have resumed. There have been bouts of light-headedness. The other day, while shopping at Benetton's, she screamed at a woman who, from under her nose, had snatched a rugby shirt Kelly wanted to buy. She screamed so persistently that, finally, a security guard ordered her to leave the store. The diet has made her a little crazy. She tells herself she has no choice but to stay on it. "Boys don't like girls with big asses, face it," Andrea said to her last week at Chin Chin's, speaking of another girl with an enormous backside, though Kelly sensed this was meant as a piece of advice for her, too. If this diet doesn't work, what then?

A finger down the throat?

God, it's so gross. . . .

But she could do it, if necessary.

At home, she lies on her bed, trying to resist the urge to rush downstairs and plunge into a bowl of chocolate chips. The phone rings. It's Janet, the sister of the cute sophomore boy whom she's developed a crush on, calling to see if she wants to get together for lunch. She says sure. They gossip about a freshman girl who, rumor has it, got it on with three different seniors in the span of three evenings. "So many freshman sluts this year, you know?" says Kelly. The most bizarre things are coming out of her mouth these days. One nice thing about the occasional light-headedness from the diet is that it frees her of inhibitions. "Hey, could you put your brother on the phone?" she asks. In a couple of seconds, fifteen-year-old Kurt comes on, talking deeper than usual, she thinks.

She does not waste any time for fear of losing her courage. "Do you want to go to Westwood, see a movie, maybe just hang somewhere?"

"Okay."

It was so easy, she thinks, hanging up, rifling through her closet for anything black and slimming.

———

Saturday, December 14. Paul, Tony, Randy, and Adam set out in Tony's father's Cadillac for a town in Mexico. "We get down there, find a cantina, and we'll be stoked," says Tony. "Nobody can bring any shit, though. I'm not getting busted for possession down there. And we're not doing any lines in the car either. We'll have some brews. Then we can get some tamales at this great place my dad took me to." A pause, a click of the tongue. "There're chicks all over."

Paul wonders whether this last remark is meant for him. "Mexican girls," Tony adds, "all have hard bodies." Whatever else, the guy is a great actor. When he called Tony's house last night, he thought that he heard the fey laugh of the slim blond boy in the background, but then Tony rapped so excitedly about some hot babe at U.C. San Diego that Paul decided the blond guy couldn't be there after all. Maybe he'd never been there. Tony had too many girls to want to do it with a skinny blond geek, Paul had begun convincing himself, when he suddenly heard a high voice squealing, "*Oh, shit,*" and then bursting into effeminate giggles so loud that even Tony stopped talking about the UCSD babe and blurted, "Hey, my mom's freaking, let me call you back. Bye." When Tony swung by in the big Cadillac this morning, Paul fully expected him to have an explanation ready for that fey laugh. But Tony was laughing, wanting to tell him about something his father had said before turning the Caddy's keys over. "Adam and Randy have these shit-eating grins on their faces, because they already have a full-on buzz from their margaritas," Tony explains. "And so my father says to them, 'Hey, guys, don't go looking for the applause down there.' These dudes just looked at him like he was spaced. And my father says, 'You know, fellas, don't be bringing home the clap. *Clap. Applause.* Get it?' My mother looked at him like she was going to blow her breakfast."

"Your father was kind of weird," says Adam. "I really think he wanted to go with us."

"I think the guy was a full-on partyer when he was young," Tony tells them, laughing. "He still puts away the Cutty pretty good. And he's always talking about movie stars' bodies. Like he's totally into Nastassja Kinski. Hey, so am I. Did you see *Cat People*? Is she *tight* or what?"

Paul wishes his friend would stop playing the stud here. The act only serves to remind him of the way Tony jumped off the phone, muttering "Bye," in a panic, their whole conversation playing like a recording in his head now, especially the blond boy's high titters. He can't get those squeals out of his head. "*Oh, shit . . . Hee-hee-hee-hee.*"

He closes his eyes for a while. Adam and Randy drink their canned margaritas. Three hours later, when they cross over the border into Mexico, Randy is slouched across the back seat.

"Fucking drunk and asleep," Adam announces. "Such a light-weight."

Tony looks for a place to park.

"No, don't stop," Adam says. "Let's cruise for a while, check it out."

They finally stop at a restaurant and awaken Randy, who complains of a bad headache and dizziness.

"You just need a cold one, bud," says Adam. "Come on, let's go party."

With his first step onto the pavement, Randy lurches and begins blowing his breakfast all over the curb.

Tony and Adam applaud right there on the sidewalk.

"A *mahvellllous showing.*"

"*We must see this again sometime.*"

"*Yes, let's remind each other.*"

Fifteen minutes later, the three boys walk with their wobbly friend into a restaurant and order four beers. Eight locals, leaning against a bar, stare at Randy, who puts his head on the table and makes a retching sound.

"Just a dry heave," says Paul to the Mexicans, who do not seem to understand. "Nothing to worry about."

Randy rolls off his chair onto the floor. Paul smiles at the guys lined up along the bar. "*No problem,*" he says. "Come on, Randy. *Get up.*" Tony stares at a cocktail napkin. Paul is already heading for the door, his arm around the dazed, retching body that he and Adam half-drag behind them.

For a couple of hours the four boys walk around, Randy trying to clear his head, the others buying ponchos and hand-tooled leather belts that would go for fifty or sixty dollars in Beverly Hills but cost only five dollars in a land where poor artisans lay their merchandise out in the sun and haggle over prices. Tony gets one merchant to come down from forty dollars to fifteen dollars apiece on two ponchos. Paul buys six belts as Christmas presents for cousins in Chicago. Randy manages to drink another beer. When they reach the Seville, two cops are sitting on the hood.

"Excuse me, señors," Tony says. "*Our* car . . ."

The cops do not move.

"*Our car,*" Tony says, grinning to make it clear that he is not offended. "Pardon us, we must go. . . ."

With his hand, he pantomimes a car going.

The cops look at him blankly.

"Maybe if we get in the car, they'll know what we want," Randy says.

"Somehow, I think they know what we want," says Paul. "What do *they* want?"

What they want is sixty American dollars. The Seville, explains a street merchant whom the boys have persuaded to translate for them, has been parked illegally in a spot reserved for police vehicles. One of the cops mumbles something else to the merchant. "He announces," the merchant tells them, "be grateful your car not towed many miles. It's no problem. Just give the money and you go."

"Tell them there was no sign on the street," says Tony.

"Let's just pay and go," says Adam.

"Explain about the sign," repeats Tony.

"No, it no help," the merchant says.

"*Why?* Just tell them."

The merchant mumbles something in Spanish, patting the arm of one of the cops and turning around with a wan shrug to point to Tony, as if to suggest that this question is not his idea. The cops laugh. "It no help," the merchant says, turning back to Tony. "I say it no help. You go with them."

Paul feels frightened. The cops stand now, gesturing for the four boys to follow. Paul looks for a police car but the cops point to a small building up the street.

They march down the road into a police station, Adam whispering to Tony, urgently now, "Just pay, *pay* dammit. Please. Show them some money."

A police official, sitting behind a desk in a white shirt and tie, takes control from the two street cops and rattles off Tony's offense in Spanish. The only words Paul understands are "Cadillac Seville." This older official, his desk flooded in hot sunlight, listens to them with eyes half-closed, sipping an iced tea from a straw and dabbing at a perspiring forehead with a damp paper towel. Perhaps he does not understand English at all. He looks at Tony and finally says, "Your identification, please." His lips curl around the iced tea's straw.

Tony gives him his driver's license.

The official looks at it, straightens a little. "I like very much," he says laboriously, "Beverly Hills."

"Uh-huh." Tony looks unsure of what to say. "It's all right. I like it, too."

"The fine is sixty dollars, please."

"I don't have sixty dollars, and like I told these guys, there were no signs, so I don't think it's fair."

"There are, of course, signs," the desk man says congenially. "It's not like Beverly Hills, not like our signs are all over, but you can see them if you look, and if you don't look, there are fines. But you can pay it, yes?"

"I am not paying," Tony says. "I want to call the United States embassy. My father works for the State Department. I want to contact him immediately."

The desk man avoids Tony's stare, shuffles some papers. "Well, let me think. There is no reason for a problem. I'm sure we can talk, we can find some solution. If you don't have sixty, you pay what you have for now. Perhaps forty dollars."

"I'm paying nothing. I want to talk to my father. I want to call the State Department."

The advantage has swung, Paul senses. The desk man asks something of the two cops in Spanish. The cops shake their heads.

"They say your father's car has no diplomatic plates," the desk man says. "How can he be a diplomat?"

Caught in a lie, Tony shrugs. "Oh, put us in jail. You're just trying to rip us off. You probably do it all the time. I am not paying. That is my father's car. He knows where we are. And he'll come down here."

The desk man slaps his hands together and barks a command at the two street cops. The four boys are led to a small conference room with grammar school-like desks and a large blackboard. The cops point at the desks. The boys are a little slow in reacting.

"*Siéntense.*"

"*Sí*, sit," Paul says, so that these cops understand he is doing his best to cooperate. He tries to squeeze his large body into one of the desks, so tiny as to be absurdly funny to him, like something out of scale that belongs in a toddler's doll house. He feels his stomach and thighs getting caught in the desk and strains to straighten his legs, panting with such exertion one of the cops begins laughing at him. The second cop pantomimes his movements, waddling his butt back and forth, pointing at him.

"*El gordo,*" says the cop.

His companion laughs, puffing out his stomach and patting it.

Adam raps Paul on his shoulder. "You should have told him to pay the money," he says, gesturing at Tony.

Tony sighs. "Lighten up, Adam."

"Hey, Tony, you are the one who should mellow," shouts Adam. "Why didn't you just pay so we could leave? No, you had to be a stubborn asshole, you had to be fucking obnoxious." Paul has never seen Adam so upset. "You had to be so fucking stupid that we're locked up here and no one knows where we are. Do you know what they do to people in these kind of places? Do you? *Do you?*" The kid who is so street cool when he deals now looks on the verge of tears. Adam pounds his little desk. "*Asshole.* God, I don't want to spend the night in jail here." He whimpers.

"We'll be all right," Paul assures him.

"*Yeah, right.*" Adam burrows his head in his arms.

"I promise. We will."

Aside from Adam, everyone in the room remains composed. Tony stretches his legs out upon the desk in front of him and tries to nap. Randy stands and sketches rock and roll stars and logos on the blackboard — Robert Plant, Prince, an AC/DC emblem, Tina Turner. Chuckling, he then draws a mustachioed figure in a tie.

"Who's that supposed to be?" Paul asks.

"That's El *Putz.*"

"Who's El Putz?"

"The dude at the desk."

Paul laughs so hard his legs get twisted up in the desk again. "Fuck this thing," he says, kicking his way out of the desk. He lies on a conference table in the middle of the room. "Actually if this place only had cable, we'd be all right," says Randy, giving El Putz a sombrero. The door suddenly opens. The two cops are glaring at them, gesturing for Randy to get away from the blackboard and for Paul to get back to his desk.

"*Siéntense, siéntense.*"

One of the cops takes an eraser and furiously wipes away Randy's blackboard sketches, pausing when he gets to the figure that says, "El Putz," beneath it. He wheels around. *"Qué es esto?"* he asks the boys.

Randy grins. "He's on television. *Television*. Television commercial. *Fritos?"*

The cop stares at him harder, then looks back at the picture. *"Sì,* Fritos." He wipes the sketch away.

"Levántense," commands the other cop.

None of them understands.

"Levántense," the cop repeats, agitated, and the boys look at each other for help.

The cop pulls Adam from his chair, and motions to the other boys to follow Adam's lead, to stand, too. Adam is yelping, being pulled by his shirt collar.

"Take it easy, Adam," Paul says softly. "He just wants us to stand."

"Take your fucking hands off me," Adam screams at the cop, and shakes free. Paul is thinking, A bad move, a *very* bad move; waits for this fireplug of a cop to take out his baton and thump Adam.

Instead, the cop opens the door and motions for the boys to walk. They end up back at the front desk with El Putz. "How did you like your room?" he asks Tony.

A small joke. The man is trying to patch things up. Tony laughs. Adam looks at his feet. Randy is softly humming the Frito Bandito theme song. El Putz sighs. "Because, and only because, our plumbing is under repair today and we don't have much room in our jail, I am going to reduce your fine to ten dollars."

"Okay," says Tony. "I still don't think that's fair, but if we can go, I'll pay it."

"You are driving a Cadillac Seville," says the official. "You must be more careful parking it."

"Okay," says Tony, pulling out his wallet. *"Gracias."*

In five minutes they are outside, breathing the deep-fat-fried smells of tacos again. As they drive away, Randy sees an empty police cruiser, parked on a corner. Tony slows down, and Randy drags a key along the cruiser, leaving a deep gash on it.

"Payment for El Putz," Randy says.

They are strangely silent as they head for the border. It is not until they pass the agricultural inspection station and cross back into California that

Tony smiles and says, "I didn't like being in that room, but it was still a good day, pretty intense, huh?"

They all explode then, congratulating Tony on getting El Putz to give in, ribbing Randy about the Frito Bandito, Paul thinking to himself that maybe this is the closest he will ever feel to these guys, especially Randy, who surprised him by staying so cool in a hot situation; he would have expected the kid to fold like an accordion. Adam doesn't say much about his own disintegration and no one raises the subject. Paul suspects Adam freaked because he had some coke on him but doesn't want to ask. He doesn't want to fuck up the feeling they have for each other right now. Tony slides an old Van Halen tape into the cassette player. "I'd like to get home and get a Jacuzzi," he says. Paul considers asking with whom, thinks better of it. It's hard to explain why the two of them are so loyal to each other, he thinks. Maybe it's just the idea of hanging on to your best friend; it'd be too much of a hassle, at this stage, to start all over with someone new. He hopes Tony stays in the closet, doesn't know how he would deal with it if the guy ever wanted to talk. "I say we party some when we get back," Tony suggests.

"I know where to get the things we need," says Adam, having recovered from Mexico.

"Where is that?" asks Randy.

"You better not have brought anything," Tony says, turning around to stare at Adam in the back seat. "If you brought anything, I'm going to kick the shit out of you."

———

Hillary is watching "Moonlighting," and Cybill Shepherd is barking at the secretary with the funny voice. Something about, "You're sleeping on the job, Ms Dipesto" — and the secretary lifts her head from a desk, surveys Cybill Shepherd, and then mumbles, "That's right," before closing her eyes again. "That's what you look like, Hillary, whenever you do a bong-load," says a voice behind her, cackling while munching on the same brand of soggy cornflakes that he has been flicking on her, with his spoon, as long as she can remember.

Her brother, Matt, is home from college.

"We're going to be alone for a while," her brother says. "Do you want to do a bowl?"

"I'm not smoking much grass anymore," she says.

"You want to have a drink?"

"Not really."

"Do you like Mom's boyfriend? I kind of think he's playing dictator over her."

Hillary doesn't reply quickly enough and feels a bombardment of cornflakes on the back of her neck.

Last night, because he said she owed him two dollars, he chased her around the house. She screamed so loudly that finally Harry intercepted them and said, "Hey, pal, why don't you go easy on her, cool it a little, okay?" Matt looked at him as if he were a meddlesome old nut whom they might have encountered in a public park, and said, "Dude, this is *my* sister. *You* take it easy, okay?" Hillary liked seeing how Matt's words backed Harry the Hirsute Boyfriend right up against his reclining chair in the den. Hillary didn't like it so much when Matt resumed chasing her then, stepping on the heels of her shoes while she emitted death screeches, finally catching her in their backyard, wrestling her to the ground, and taking everything out of her pockets, which came to about eight dollars. He pocketed two bucks and a package of breath mints before putting the rest of the money on her stomach.

"Asshole," she murmured, lying there.

"I know, I'm fucked. I kind of wish I was back at school already. I just get so weird being at home, and being told what to do."

"I'm sick of it, too," she admitted.

"Are Mom and Harry always like this? All lovey-dovey?"

"Not until the last week or so. I think they're trying to get us to act like a family or something. Mom is putting on the big front for him. Sometimes she talks about marrying him. It's too bizarre."

"Everything is too bizarre."

"Yeah."

"I might drop out of school. Don't tell Mom."

He was looking up at the sky, hands squeezing the pair of dollar bills into something the size of a spitball, when he said it. She half-expected him to say, in the next instant, that he was joking, that he had fooled her again. He took a special delight in that, always had, as long back as his grammar school days. He had been the model child in the family then, the kid who always received straight A's, played a variety of instruments in recital groups, and received praise from the local tennis pro, who said he had a gift for the two-handed backhand. By twelve, he had begun reading the masters — Shakespeare, Milton, Faulkner, Steinbeck, Hemingway. Hillary had been nine, and sometimes she would open his bedroom door upon which he had hung a sign he had stolen somewhere: "Guard Dog on Patrol 24 Hours Every Day." He would be either reading or listening to music, and, if he deigned to look up and acknowledge her, it was usually to tell her to bring him a soft drink. At ten, she began daring to say no. He would then chase her, out of boredom mostly, and she would scream and run about the house for several minutes, Matt laughing, stepping on her heels and swatting at her ponytail until their parents intervened and told her to stay out of her brother's bedroom because he was *reading*. Their tone, when they used the word, was reverential, and remained so throughout grammar school and junior high, until, during his sophomore year at Beverly, Matt no longer received straight A's. He had stopped reading his school books altogether, burned out, he said, on all the crap they made you cram into your head. He would still have a book on his lap though, usually something like Hunter Thompson or Kurt Vonnegut, and sometimes he'd read her a crazed passage. She'd laugh, and they'd talk about their parents, who didn't seem to be getting along, and what weird things were happening at their schools. She liked talking with him and listening to his funny stories, but, as time passed, he ate fewer dinners at home, hanging out with his friends in Westwood. A couple of times, their father complained, and Matt answered, "Hey, you're at your law firm until nine o'clock some nights. You only eat with us once in a blue moon. Why are you on *my* case?" It was a sad moment, and Hillary would forever remember her father's silence, a tacit admission that life had not gone according to plan; that they were four loosely connected people who had to try harder to come together, though he did not know enough to propose how to do it.

Hillary resented her father not a bit, knew that he stayed at the firm late into the night because her mother was always screaming at him. Matt had seen their split coming very early. After his junior year at Beverly, he had persuaded them to send him to a summer school program at an elite prep academy in the East, making the case that, in the East, he would become academically inspired as he had not been since junior high. There he stayed all summer, even though school ended during the last week of July. He went canoeing in Maine, and scuba diving off Cape Cod, and hung out with a new group of friends in Harvard Square, calling home twice in three months to tell his mother he felt himself getting things together. A half-truth, a ruse to spare himself the agony of going home, and when he finally had to — his senior year at

Beverly having begun in September — he made it a point to come home from school as late as possible in the evenings, sometimes at ten or eleven, claiming he had had to study, had to talk with a counselor about college admissions, had to take care of some group video project for a class. Any excuse would do by then, for his parents did not want to cope with any new conflicts, overloaded as they were by the weight of property settlement papers and their own imminent separation. Sometimes Hillary would then go looking for her brother in his bedroom, surprised to discover him gone again. Only on Sunday mornings could she expect to find him home. Eating breakfast, trying to get through a hangover, he would flick cornflakes and chase her, and though she would emit her primal death screeches, she did not much mind the harassment, knowing at some point the chase would end and they'd sit in his bedroom and bullshit.

She thinks about all this now while another soggy cornflake bounces off the back of her neck.

"How long are you going to do that?" she asks.

A large errant flake sticks to the TV screen. "Until you're married and gone."

She snorts. "Oh, you'll still be around then, won't you, lazy ass?"

"Maybe. Why not?"

"Did you mean what you said about college?"

"I don't know. Probably. It's not working for me. I don't see why I'm there. I think I want to try to write movies or get into real estate."

"Maybe you should talk with Mom or Dad."

"I did. With Dad."

This surprises her, since Matt has long been alienated from their father. "I went over to his office to borrow some money, and I just said, 'What I would do to have school over with!' He said some bizarre things. He told me that he dropped out for a couple of quarters at UCLA during his sophomore year. Did you know that?"

Hillary has heard many of her father's college tales but never this one. "Maybe that was the time he went to work at that shoe store. Maybe he just needed to make money for the rest of college."

"No, it was nothing like that. He wanted to be a painter, he told me. He drew up a list of all the things around L.A. that he wanted to paint and painted them and then he went to New York and he did the same thing there. He lived in Greenwich Village and he didn't fuck around. He just painted and painted, and loved it, and he took some of his better watercolors and got ready to apply to an art school. Then his landlord evicted him because the apartment had started to look like a goddamn museum. Dad was backed up against the wall. There were too many paintings to put 'em all in storage. He had no choice but to fight this landlord in court, only he didn't have enough money, so he went to a library and read all the law books and did everything himself. He couldn't believe how much people could get screwed by the law if they didn't know it. And he decided then he had to become a lawyer. He loved painting, but law was more important. He said he still wonders what kind of painter he would have ended up being. He misses it."

"I always looked at that art table in his apartment and just thought he messed around with some sketches on the weekend," Hillary says.

Matt shrugs.

"What kind of advice did he give you?" she asks, peeling the soggy cornflake from the television screen.

Matt looks surprised. "It was just a good story. I enjoyed it. There wasn't any point."

"What did he say about *you?*"

"He said, 'Life kind of takes care of those things.' "

"I don't know, Matt. I'm not sure that's advice."

"I know it's one of his bullshit sayings. I didn't care. I didn't really know why I was there. But his story was pretty good. I kinda enjoyed picturing Dad as something other than a lawyer."

"You keep avoiding the question: What are you going to do?"

He shrugs.

"You gonna tell Mom?"

"No chance."

"Did Dad say *anything?*"

"Well, he said one thing."

"Yeah?"

"He said that I should try to do something to relax." On the screen, Cybill Shepherd is moaning to the whiny secretary that just when she feels like giving a piece of her heart to Bruce Willis, he turns around and acts so insensitively that she no longer believes she knows him. The world is full of disconnected people, thinks Hillary. What else hadn't their father told them about his life? You work or live under the same roof with people for almost twenty years, only to discover they have these lives you knew nothing about. Who is she to bitch? What has she ever told her mother or father? Even with her brother, she tries not to say anything that might throw into question his image of her. They are all amiable boarders here, careful not to disturb the calm. *Boarders:* Once four, now three. You can't count Harry the Hirsute Boyfriend as a boarder, not yet. Her mother's boyfriends have a nasty habit of vacating the premises without notice.

On Saturday, they all go shopping on Rodeo, Harry first taking them to lunch at the Mandarin, where they share Mai Tais and everyone begins to feel giddy and a little drunk. Hillary and Matt have each been given an American Express card by their mother. "Don't go hog-wild," she says. "Remember: Someone is going to have to pay for this eventually."

Hillary realizes who *someone* is. She knows her father can't afford to pick up her mother's shopping bills. They go into Gucci's, and while Harry inspects a thousand-dollar golf bag, her mother whispers to Matt, "You could show Harry how much you think of him if you got him something small here, like a wallet or something."

"Mom, a wallet here is *a hundred and fifty bucks.*"

"Don't worry. It's the thought. You can buy it. I'm giving you permission."

"Mom, this sounds kind of silly, doesn't it? I mean, he's paying for it, isn't he?"

"Why are you asking these questions, Matt? Enjoy the day. The holidays come once a year."

"I was only thinking that, as a present, maybe I should just let him save his money, Mom."

"*Hey, gentlemen and dobermen, look what we have here.*" Harry has returned, with a gift-wrapped golf bag strapped to his shoulder. "Going to give it to my brother, Ned, the orthodontist in Detroit I was telling you about." Hillary forces a smile. Her mother and Matt are still glaring at each other. "Hillary, may I show you something over here?" Harry asks, smiling and gesturing toward some luggage. He puts a fatherly arm around her, gently steering her away from Matt and her mother, and says, laughing, "I think a little tête-à-tête is going on over there, cutie."

She doesn't want him getting too familiar. "I don't know. Maybe they are talking about college."

"Would you like to know how you could make your mother very happy?"

"Hmm?"

"The makeup cases here are marvelous. And you know how she

loves that sort of thing. How about the two of us getting together on a case for her?"

He must be made to understand he is not her father. "I already got her something," she lies. "Thanks anyway. I did most of my holiday shopping last weekend when I saw my dad." She smiles again. "My dad helped me pick out something for her."

"Well, good. Very good," he says, bringing his arm back to his side. "Maybe another time for the case then, a birthday or something."

"Uh-huh."

Her mother and Matt have reached a truce. "Matt needs to go and buy some records for some of his friends," her mother announces. "So, he'll meet us back at the house."

"We'll be here for a while, Matt," says Harry. "In case you change your mind." He shrugs. *I've tried*, the shrug seems to say.

"Let's get a piece of cheesecake before we head down to Giorgio's," her mother says.

Harry presses a twenty in Matt's hands. "In case you need a little extra," says the older man. Matt looks solemnly at the bill, finally stuffs it in his shirt pocket.

Watching him walk out, her mother says to Harry, "I think he's just so preoccupied with school that he can't concentrate on other people."

Within fifteen minutes, Hillary has concocted an excuse to leave them.

"I think sometimes you expect too much from your mother," Jeremy says to her that night. They leave his cramped apartment and stroll in and out of Venice's little oceanfront shops. A goateed man flies by on a skateboard, yelling for the world to save itself. "Your mom has her own problems," Jeremy says, his black hair flung back by the ocean wind. "You have to let her figure herself out first before she can be of any help to anybody else."

"I'm a little frustrated is all, I guess."

"But think of how much you have: You have money to go to college; you have a nice car; your father is still in town; you're modeling kinda successfully, even though you're just seventeen; and we're happy. Aren't we?"

She smiles, pulls his head down, kisses him, keeps walking. "Yeah," she laughs. Does he see her as some spoiled society girl? "You have everything for a great life in your hands," he says, and pulls her toward him. "Merry Christmas." He drapes a necklace around her. She feels her eyes welling. He is my family, she thinks, burying her head in his chest.

———

Andy has received an early Christmas present, too, a copy of a letter of recommendation that his uncle in New York sent to his good friend, the dean of admissions at a small but prominent Northeastern college. *"Andy's imagination, ingenuity and social concern do not manifest themselves in the standard measure of grades,"* the recommendation reads.

> *He has spent, fortunately or unfortunately, depending on your perspective, little time with books, preferring to be in hospital wards helping patients, or in garages perfecting his bass guitar. But this year, having been told of the unfortunate reality that is the 1986 college admissions experience, Andy has pledged to show his prowess in the classroom, too. (I think, Norman, that his fall term will yield nothing but A's and B's.) Andy is a Renaissance man — a thinker, artist, and a young man of good character. It is my conviction that he qualifies as an outstanding candidate for admission at your institution and I hope and expect that when you review his record you will share in my judgment.*
>
>

Regards,
Phil

Along with his uncle's recommendation letter, Andy receives a photostat of the dean's reply:

> *Dear Phil,*
> *Thank you for your most heartily appreciated letter regarding the admissions application of your nephew Andrew. How is your knee doing? Those cement courts do it every time. I think that I can say with some degree of certainty that if Andy performs as you expect this year, we will doubtless be able to grant him a spot in the class of 1990. What do you hear from Flannery? I expect to see the two of you at the reunion.*
>
>

Best,
Norman

And paper-clipped to the dean's reply is a brief note in his uncle's handwriting:

Andy,
Your old man told me you were thinking of applying to my
alma mater, so what the hell, I took the liberty of sending a
flier to an old friend whom I did enough with during the old
days so that either one of us could jail the other for moral
turpitude. Maybe someday I'll fill you in on the sordid de-
tails. Anyway, kiddo, I've sent something else along in a
Saks box, but I expect you'll find the enclosed letters better
than anything I could get you at a department store. As you
might have gathered from the dean's note, a strong perfor-
mance this semester should get you in. He told me in a
telephone conversation that it's harder there these days to get
the cream of the crop, with kids applying to so many places.
This helps your chances, no offense meant. Your father has
got some young chickadee who's young enough to be your
sister, I hear. We've always liked them young. Some genetic
flaw, I suppose. Or is it a blessing? Everyone sends their
love, if not their booze. The Jim Beam goes to your dad and
the chickadee, though I imagine they're doing fine without
it. I am, if nothing else, old and envious. Merry Christmas.

Uncle Phil

The final exams in January might mean his future, he tells himself. He calls the hospital to explain that he will not be able to come for his volunteer shift during the next few weeks: He has too much studying to do before finals. He gets to his bedroom desk by four P.M. every afternoon, fighting the urge to turn on his stereo. There is only so much that can be changed. His study habits, dormant for so long, cannot possibly be reawakened and tuned in time for him to compete with Beverly's top students. So, on a couple of meaningless quizzes in December, he cheats in order to test the system before the January finals. Nearly everyone cheats at Beverly, he tells a couple of friends. Why not us? They use crib sheets, notes on their palms, multiple-choice answers on pens and pencils. They spend, Andy notices, almost the same amount of time devising cheating systems as they do studying. The tension is worse. He finds himself studying his teachers' movements during the quizzes, looking over his shoulder in between stealing glances at the letters on his pencil.

He gets A's on his English and physiology quizzes.

He is still in the running.

He is still top drawer.

His uncle and father will be so proud.

His father calls him the next evening: Would he like to play tennis? Andy thinks he should study, but, having been reading his books for an hour and a half, he already feels exhausted. How do people study like this for three or four hours at a stretch? He detests himself sometimes for having so little discipline. "Okay, Dad," he says.

"I'll come by at seven," his father mumbles. "I'll just honk."

This is so he doesn't have to come to the door and see his mother, Andy realizes. The boy vows to be ready and standing at the door five minutes early. His parents did not enjoy an amicable divorce, still shout at each other over alimony and child support checks arriving one day late in the mail, still exchange accusations that the other is not giving Andy adequate attention. It has not helped either that they continue picking at each other like an old married couple, his father muttering about her weight, his mother mumbling at his father once that he looked like a tourist from Iowa in his Hawaiian shirt, polyester shorts, and brown sandals.

"Well, my apologies," his father responded dryly. "I was fresh out of those shirts with the little alligators on the nipple. I see, though, that you're opting for style in those beat-me whip-me jeans."

Andy doesn't need to hear any of that shit tonight. He hurries upstairs to his bedroom, showers, and gets into his shorts and a T-shirt when the phone rings. It's Jason, asking how the studying is going. Andy hears amplified instruments in the background.

"You're practicing tonight, huh?" he murmurs, slowly, uneasily, hoping that Jason has not called to tell him the band can no longer use an absent member.

"Yeah. Hey, we got an offer to buy this synthesizer from a guy. It's state of the art. And we can get a little discount. Only problem is that it costs too much for Bobby to buy on his own. So I was thinking maybe we could all chip in, like five hundred apiece."

Andy sits down on his bed. "I don't know."

"Man, you just got a Beamer. You can't come up with some bucks?"

"I don't know if I can for *that*."

"For what?"

"For somebody else's synthesizer."

"It's everybody's, once we get it. Bobby just uses it because he's the one on the keyboards."

"Let me think about it."

"Cool. But tell me soon if you can't. I have to know."

"*Andy*." "*Andy*." Two different shouts, one deep and authoritative, the other squeaky and pleading, fly up the stairs, almost tossing him off the bed. He didn't hear his father arrive. Andy hangs up, half-screaming at Jason, "Guy, I've gotta go. *Later*." In one motion, he grabs his tennis racquet and equipment bag and runs out of the bedroom toward the stairs. He can hear his mother lecturing his father: "And you have to do it right in front of the boy, don't you?"

Andy pauses at the landing. He sees his mother on the bottom step, standing indignantly, one hand on her hip, like some old schoolmarm, jabbing her forefinger inches from his father's chest. "Always flaunting it right in front of the boy."

"Mom, why are you always calling me 'the boy'? I hate it."

The two heads below turn as if on swivels. "Andy, your father and I were just discussing something. Come on down. He's waiting for you."

Andy bounds down the stairs. "And what is this big thing that Dad is flaunting, Mom?" he asks, chuckling. But his parents do not hear him, having moved away from the bottom step toward the living room. A wall that adjoins the top half of the staircase momentarily blocks his view of them. "*Bastard*," he hears his mother whispering. "Showing *it* all around."

In a half-second he has taken five more steps, is past the wall, can see his mom and dad and a third adult now, a tan, nubile young woman wearing a gray tank top a size too small and a pair of faded blue Dolphin shorts revealing the bottoms of the cheeks of her ass. She has layered short brown hair that has been bleached with very pale jagged blonde streaks. This is not Joyce, his father's twenty-six-year-old UCLA girlfriend. This is someone new — and younger. Maybe the "chickadee" his uncle mentioned? Andy assumed the chickadee meant Joyce. Joyce, after all, has been the chickadee for six months. He stares at this new girl and then looks at his father, who has turned his back on all of them to study a damaged table leg, studying it longer than necessary, before turning and softly murmuring to his ex-wife, "Oh, I'll have to have that leg repaired for you. This table is worth three thousand, easy. The investment alone is worth the repair." His mother does not meet his glance, says nothing, continues staring at the girl, who is alternately scratching her hair and pulling down on the back of her rising shorts, evading the looks of all of them by studying her tennis racquet as if checking for broken strings. "Hi," Andy says to her, in a voice stiffly polite so that his mom understands he isn't cozying up to this girl. She smiles wanly and says, "I'm Stacey. Your dad told me a lot about you." She scratches her shoulder and her tank top drops a half-inch.

"Stacey is a dancer, Andy," his father adds.

"I'm just *beginning* at dance," she says, blushing. And then, genuinely interested: "You play in a band, right?" Her teeth gleam. Another scratch of the shoulder. Andy gets a glimpse of the tops of round, tan tits before the girl pulls her strap back. "Your father," she says, grinning, "is always telling me you're such a good tennis player."

Andy weakens for a moment. He could see himself, given the time and the right opportunity, fucking this girl. Does she think he's cute? That look she gave him was . . . No, no, forget that. Who knows? Maybe she was just trying to be friendly. But she couldn't be more than twenty-one. How could an old guy like his dad, who's forty-five, hope to keep pleasing a fox like this? "Well, my serve is real weak, you'll see . . . ," he begins and then, in his peripheral vision, notices his mother, hands still on her hips, shifting her weight from one pale, meaty leg to the other, her varicose veins unusually pronounced this afternoon, her body leaning heavily against the wall, suddenly spent. Andy knows this look, realizes that she is but a couple of minutes away from dissolving, prays that the three of them — he, his father, and this new bimbo — can be out the door before it starts.

"Mom," he says hurriedly, "I'll be back by about . . . ," he looks at his dad. "Ten, Dad?"

His father nods.

"*Ten*, Mom." His mother says nothing. He picks up his tennis bag and kisses her. It occurs to him that he never kisses her except in moments of fear or pity. His mom waves feebly. She is wearing faded red shorts which once fit her loosely when that was the fashion, a decade ago. Now the shorts, fashionable once more, are too tight and pinch the loose, milky flesh that began accumulating on her thighs five years and twenty-five pounds ago, the ravages of cellulite having stripped her in the early 'eighties of her sexy shape and whatever interest her husband may have had in her. He was never a discreet philanderer, Andy knows. He remembers being regularly awakened, while a little boy, by his parents' screaming matches, hearing, as an eight-year-old, a strange and foreboding-sounding word for the first time: "I know you are *screwing* her." His mother looked wonderful in those days, swimming regularly and playing tennis to stay trim, but even so she could not hold his father; there was always someone in the world younger and blonder and prettier for him, of course, and so at some point she just stopped trying, just gave up, surrendering herself to television, and meekly driving Andy to his dentist appointments and Little League games. Within a year, there were an extra ten pounds around her middle, and his father would find excuses to be in Chicago on weekend business. Why had she hung on to him so long? What must she feel now staring at this blonde thing? wonders Andy, who thinks that the girl looks like Bo Derek, except for those bottom cheeks of her ass. A little too big and round. She will be fat, too, will be supplanted just as surely as Joyce and his mom have been, and the woman before his mom, the woman he has never met, his father's first wife. There are only two kinds of relationships, he thinks: those that have failed and those that soon will. Sometimes his mother stumbles about the house in a daze, like one of those Vietnam vets he's read about who had that thing — what did they call it? . . . stress-syndrome, something like that — except that his mom's stupor involved munching mindlessly on cashews and marmalade toast. Sometimes her eyes become droopy, and other times she screams and hits Andy for nothing more than leaving his underwear on his bedroom floor. She has been traumatized, just another beaten soldier among the walking dead, and there have been no signs that her pain will go away soon. Especially now, Andy thinks, walking to the door with his father and this bimbo, wanting to turn and say something else to his mom that will make her feel a little less alone when the door closes. "Mom," he murmurs, just before pulling the door shut, "I recorded a couple movies off the Z Channel and put them on top of the TV if you want to watch them."

Stacey has a nice serve and a hard top-spin forehand. Andy figures her tennis skill must be one of the attractions for his father, a gung-ho competitor who hates to lose at games, but, at the same time, hates to play anyone who accepts defeat good-naturedly. He likes games to be tests of wills, if he can arrange it. Because they don't have a fourth player, he suggests that they play two against one, he being the one.

"That sounds like fun," Stacey says agreeably.

"I'll play net, okay?" Andy says to her.

They practice for a few minutes. He feels guilty, cannot get out of his mind the pained look on his mom's face while he and his father had been ogling this luscious babe. His father didn't need to say anything about Stacey being a dancer and a model. He sees the ball coming toward him, leans forward, and hits a backhand volley into the old philanderer's chest. He smiles. "Hey, Dad," he says, "so what's going on with Joyce anyway?"

When he gets home, his mother is asleep. A message from Jason is on the answering machine: "I need to know *soon*, guy. Just a reminder."

Andy wants to stay in the band, but coming up with five hundred dollars from his father will be a problem. His father will want a receipt to prove that the money has gone to a preparatory course for SATs or to the scuba-diving lessons that he has been urging Andy to take. He'll never go for a synthesizer, just as he hadn't gone for a waterbed, a home gymnasium, or a moped. "Most things are frivolous, Andy," his father said once, launching then into one of his 'sixties' eternal-peace-and-love-through-inner-realization-and-rejection-of-materialism speeches before adding, "And a side benefit is that if you see most things as frivolous, you can hold on to your money. My bank account, fortunately, is very nice."

The frivolous synthesizer is, therefore, out.

Unless he can swing its purchase through his other contacts.

By the end of the next afternoon he has raised the entire five hundred, having sold one of his extra stereo speakers to a friend for a hundred and fifty, an extra pair of K2 skis for a hundred and twenty, an aquarium tank with a filter for ninety, and borrowed a hundred from a kid whom he's promised to repay in January. His mother kicks in the other forty, unknowingly, when she gives him the money and tells him that he can go out to dinner over the weekend, because she will be gone with friends.

"Five hundred is easy to get," he tells Jason. "Two, three thousand, that would have been hard."

"You're a born scammer," Jason says admiringly.

"Don't say scammer like it's a bad thing," he corrects gently. "I scam. You scam. Everybody scams."

———

Christmas and Hannukah descend so suddenly that a few of them, particularly Andy and Kelly, find themselves consciously laboring to get into
the season's spirit. Steven, Paul, and Hillary go away for the holidays,
Andy and Kelly stay home with their mothers, and Melinda travels to the
Mexican vacation resort of Cabo San Lucas with her friend Cecilia. At
some point, the six celebrate Christmas or Hannukah with their families.
Some are happier than others. Paul's sister had a graduate paper to finish
in England so she didn't come home. Paul's stoked. His parents won't be
talking about her academic achievements every five goddamn minutes.
On the down side, he'll probably be expected to hang out with the
parental units a little more to compensate for her absence. He'll probably
have to go to a couple more of those lame family parties.

Paul and Steven attend religious services with their parents as
does Andy, who suspects that his parents come together on holidays only
for his sake. It is just the two of them alone with their son, the silences at
the table so excruciating at times that Andy intentionally slurps his soup
to provoke a complaint, some small sound, from his mother. The chatter
of relatives has never been heard at their holiday dinners. The relatives all
live in New York, and Andy isn't sure if he'd want strangers popping in
on them anyway; it's tense enough here.

None of the six spends the holidays with anyone who could be
loosely described as part of an extended family. Aside from her widowed
grandmother in San Diego, who visits every Thanksgiving, Kelly has had
no contact for years with any of her relatives, all of whom are scattered
along the Eastern Seaboard, except for an uncle working construction in
Houston, and an older cousin at last report dealing blackjack on the
Vegas Strip, though her grandmother says he may be in Atlantic City. In
any event, said her grandmother at last year's Thanksgiving, he was living
with the pitboss's daughter or a tennis instructor, in a suite. In any event,
he was at the Sands, unless it was the Hilton or Caesars. Twelve years
ago, nearly all of them lived within a thirty-mile radius of each other in
Connecticut, but then her Uncle Frank, a thriving building developer,
moved his firm to Florida in search of an even bigger bonanza, and soon
everyone else made the exodus. Kelly's parents moved the same year, and
she hasn't seen most of her relatives since. It matters not at all to her,
never crosses her mind that she should feel at all deprived. Some kids
have it worse, she suspects. The other day, on the Third-Floor Patio,
some girl she and Tina knew only vaguely said that her mother, back in
Indiana, wanted her to come visit for Christmas, but she didn't want to

go. She wanted to go to her father and stepmother's big Christmas party in Aspen and, hopefully, meet some cute skiers. Besides, the girl added, her real mother hadn't extended an invitation for about a year, so why get totally excited about her now? What was the big deal anyway? She wanted to go somewhere fun and Indiana wasn't it and that was that. Kelly felt sympathetic, wished she could split to a ski resort, too.

Melinda's parents and sisters do not mind that she wants to get away. There are flocks of Beverly kids in Colorado and the California Sierras on ski trips over Christmas vacation. Kids do not stay home anymore, Melinda tells her family. She wants to be somewhere else. Having done so well at Beverly, she deserves a small vacation, she argues. Her parents agree.

She flies with Cecilia to Mexico, where a routine develops. They go out on the town at about eleven P.M. each night, meeting new people and drinking rum and Cokes until four in the morning. "The people at the nightclubs are not like Mexicans," Melinda observes to Cecilia, by which she means they are not Mayan-dark, like most of the Hispanics whom she sees in housekeeping and gardening jobs in Beverly Hills. They are lighter, more European looking. One night, a native tells her that the lighter-skinned Mexicans are generally of Spanish heritage and more affluent than the darker Mayans. This confirms for Melinda that the light-skinned Mexicans are not "like Mexicans at all" and, thus, are acceptable in their party circle. And yet they are somehow different from the American boys whom she dates, "more fun," she confides giddily to Cecilia. "They dote on the girl. If a girl wants a drink, there is somebody there to get one for her. If she takes out a cigarette, all the guys will be pulling out their lighters. They pay for everything for a girl even if they don't know her."

"Sometimes they're awfully macho," says Cecilia, who has spent many vacations in Cabo San Lucas. "And they drink too much sometimes."

"I don't care," Melinda says. "I wish I could spend a few months here. I think I might not want to go to college for a while. Just go through Europe and Mexico and have a good time. I'm burnt on school."

Cecilia smiles. A new boy has brought her a piña colada. She goes through boyfriends like underwear, but, down here, her casualness suddenly seems appropriate to Melinda, who is enjoying the attention of a bevy of young Mexican men.

On New Year's Eve, she sneaks down to the beach with Pablo, the most attentive of the vacation week's suitors, a twenty-two-year-old

light-skinned student at the University of Mexico and the son of a prominent government official, which for some reason entitles him to walk
around with a bodyguard. He is not much taller than Melinda but he has
deep brown eyes and a nice smile, and he has become her playmate, if
only for this night, on this dark beach. They make out for a while, the
sounds of distant mariachis moving her as much as the kisses; she loves
this place. She must get away from Beverly Hills more often, she resolves.
Deferring college for a year sounds like the thing to do.

JANUARY

Sometimes, picturing Pablo and that luminous moonlit beach, she can't believe that she's back in this room, at the community center, listening to these people moan about their boring problems. At today's training meeting, Melinda and the volunteers are asked what they would do if they could change their sex for a week.

"If I was a guy," says one girl, "I'd scam off every girl, because as a girl, you can't scam. You have to worry about your reputation."

A guy nods, sympathizes with this. "Girls have it bad," he agrees. "I feel sorry for girls because if I was one somebody would want to come in my mouth."

Melinda thinks of the three hours of studying ahead of her tonight. She can't wait for spring. A group of friends, including Pablo, are making tentative plans to go on a skiing vacation at Mammoth Mountain over spring break. She shuts out the voice of the boy talking about the humiliation of having someone come in your mouth; thinks of herself careening down a crystal white slope. She needs a year away from these geeks.

At home that night, she watches a tape of "Santa Barbara," sitting on her father's side of the couch, listening to him pad around the kitchen, hoping she'll be able to finish watching the soap before he comes back and commandeers the television. She can think of no soap that better captures life than "Santa Barbara," nor a man more attractive than Mason Capwell, the character name of the golden-hearted lawyer in "Santa Barbara." "There are some guys on the show who flirt with a woman only for a while until the woman they really want is free. It's like *real*. It happens all the time on the show. If I was there I'd watch out for that. But, maybe I'd do something with Mason Capwell if I had the chance. I'm not in love with him or anything, but I do *like* him."

Only five minutes to go in this episode. Something tells her that she may not get through it. Her father moves with speed and urgency on this night, suddenly looming above her with a sheath of legal papers, motioning for her to move down the couch.

"Out of the hotseat," he says. " 'The Equalizer' is on."

They watch "The Equalizer," father, daughter, and Melinda's mother, who glances up from her *New York Times* and watches as the episode climaxes with the silver-haired Equalizer doing what he does so well every week, putting his clamps on another piece of urban vermin, roughing the scum up a little just in case the police don't. The slimeball makes the mistake of taunting the Equalizer. "The Equalizer can't really do that, can he?" Melinda asks, watching as the hero administers another thorough beating before turning the thug over to the police.

Her father, eyes glued to the screen, shakes his head. "It's just a television show, Melinda," he says.

"What it is, is kind of ridiculous," adds her mother.

Melinda throws up her hands. "Then why do they have it? Why do you watch it?"

"It's entertaining," her father answers.

The three smile at the irony of this: A video family in a video culture, they do not fight their urges, sit back to let "The Equalizer" wash over them, accepting television for what it is — the Muzak of the 'eighties, background noise against which they read professional periodicals, scan the *New York Times*, do homework, ride the stationary bicycle in the corner. From her spot on the couch, Melinda can look around the den and see her parents' modest library — books by Updike, Vonnegut, Cheever, and Mailer among others nestled between law books — but she has never read any of these giants, associates reading with the drudgery of schoolwork. Thank God her history teacher has given them alternatives to doing research papers. She's chosen to do a videotaped report on drug abuse. No heavy research or writing for her if she can help it.

The next afternoon, Pam comes over and the two girls do their videotaped report. They take most of the text for it from an article in *Glamour* magazine, and decide to spice up their tape by having Pam act out the part of a drug addict, filming her just as television would, with Pam's face in shadows and her voice slightly distorted. Pam giggles while reading the true-life story. They finish the project within an hour. "We're not doing anything serious with this assignment," Melinda says later. "I mean, drug abuse is serious, but like *we* didn't do anything really serious. I wouldn't want to do an essay. Not many people would, because it takes too much time. This was better. It was easy and we got a good grade. I learned something about addicts, a little at least. . . . I don't care that we took it from *Glamour. Everybody* does things like that. Who cares?"

———

Steven hasn't decided whether to sneak in the multiple-choice answers for his physiology and English finals on the edge of his pencils, or to play it safe and just take in a small crib sheet with names, dates, and key vocabulary words — a cheat-sheet the size of a Band-Aid perhaps. Yeah, a Band-Aid might work. He can get sets of answers from a couple of smart friends who will be taking the finals in earlier classes. But he can't be certain how prepared they'll be. He might be safer just studying hard and occasionally cheating off the SCAN-TRON answer sheets of the two 4.0s who seem indifferent to the way he is always craning his neck over their papers. Wrestling with the pros and cons of each cheating method, fearful of the disaster that awaits any cheater caught — an automatic F on the final exam would mean a final course grade of somewhere between a C and an F, killing his chances at the Ivies — he gets nervous. He turns on his stereo for a few minutes, lies on his bed, and closes his eyes. He'll be fine, he tells himself. He sets the alarm to allow himself a twenty-minute snooze, then arises and studies for five and a half hours, until one thirty A.M.

He cuts classes the next day so he can study at home all morning and afternoon, without interruption. Vickie persuades him to study over at her house that evening. When he arrives, both mother and little brother are eating ratatouille in front of the television, the brat complaining that his mother won't let him play Space Invaders on the television screen.

"Hi, Steven," says the mother, who flips her hand in a greeting of sorts.

Steven murmurs hi, tries not to look at the little brother.

"I think they're going to fool around in her bedroom, Mom," the little boy says.

"Shut up, frog face," says Vickie.

Mother turns to the boy. "Yes, shut up, Jimmy."

Smiling in satisfaction, Vickie takes Steven's hand and leads him to the bedroom, where she locks the door behind them. "I want you to be comfortable so you can work hard," she says. "I know how important these exams are for you. I want you to go to Stanford or Berkeley. It's *important*, I mean, about what happens for the future."

Important for *whom?* Does she envision herself in his future? He summons the most casual tone he can, aims for a line with a strong cryptic message. "The exams aren't that big of a deal. Nothing can be too big of a deal in high school."

She seems to have only half-heard this. "No, these exams are important. I know it. I'm going to help. I'm going to put a cushion against this chair so that your back is comfortable."

She likes the submissive role. He has long known it, enjoyed it in the beginning when she brought him sandwiches and cold drinks while he did homework. Then she began dropping the dangerous words — "we" and "we'll" — with increasing frequency. "We should start thinking about how *we're* going to do weekends with you at Berkeley or Stanford and me *wherever*," she said one night. Although he did not think a college weekend in the sack would be a bad deal, he did not want her booking his weekends for the next four years. Delicately, seeking to convey the suggestion that their relationship might not be the same in a year, he has shot other subtle hints in her direction, all of which have more or less misfired. "We can wait, I think, on worrying about college weekends," he says, "because who knows where we'll be and what we'll be doing." She has taken this to mean he has doubts whether he will be accepted to Berkeley or Stanford. She is, among other things, not too swift, he's discovered. Last week he overheard her saying to her mom, "I don't think Steven really wants to think about us being separated, so we aren't even talking about the fall. He's like a lovesick puppy sometimes. It's cute. We'll be fine."

We'll be fine: another of those *we* phrases; it gave him a chill. He feels one of her hands adjusting the pillow against his back now while the other strokes the nape of his neck. Nice hands. They could do many things. This desk isn't right, though. Not enough light, for one thing. "Could you maybe bring me another lamp?" he asks, stroking her leg, feeling himself getting aroused.

"You tell me if you need *anything* else, okay?" She is kissing his forehead while plugging in an additional lamp.

"Okay," he says, already burrowing his head inside his English book.

"I know you need quiet," she says. "I'll let you read."

He has studied for a little over two and a half hours when she excuses herself, goes into an adjoining bathroom, and emerges in her bra and panties. "I'm just a little hot with all these lamps on," she says, sitting in a lotus position on her bed, her government notes spread along an assortment of pink pillows. "This cotton bedspread feels so good against my skin, you should feel it."

"You sure your mom won't knock on the door or anything?" he asks, climbing onto the bed.

"Listen," she says. He hears nothing. *"Listen,"* she commands. He hears the faint sounds of a tennis ball being hit back and forth, followed by a woman's muted shout: *"Jimmy, just shut up."*

"Relax," says Vickie, brushing the pink pillows and her notes off the bed. "Close your eyes. I'm going to give you a massage."

He obeys.

"Doesn't that feel better?" she asks.

"Yeah."

"Do I really make you feel good?"

"Of course."

"Sometimes I guess I get insecure," she says then. "I know I'm not as smart as some people and you're *so* smart. I don't know, I get weirded during finals."

"That's all right. I do, too, kinda."

"If I said that I love you, Steven, would that make you uncomfortable?"

"No," he lies.

"Because I think I do." She lets that sink in, and, hearing nothing from him, adds, "I don't know how you feel."

"I'm not sure."

She presses her face against his chest. He feels a dampness to her cheeks.

"But that doesn't mean I don't care a lot," he says.

"God, I love you so much, Steven," she says. "Please just don't ever dump me."

He hugs her tightly, closing his eyes, not wanting to see her cry. There is so much pain around him. "I won't, I won't," he promises. "I really do care, Vickie."

Home by eleven, Steven turns on the television. One good thing about nightly television news: It reminds you, just in case you forget and start suffering from guilt, that the whole world is screwing each other, selling each other out, bombing, killing, and cheating. Some tired-looking anchorman on CNN reports that gunmen have killed another of opposition leader Corazon Aquino's local campaign leaders.

They're going to shoot Cory Aquino dead right in the streets: Steven knows it. Marcos, Haitian police, the South Africans, they're all crooks, when you get down to it. Worse, they're unstable crooks, Steven thinks. If pushed into a corner, who knows what will happen? They'd do anything to hold power. Does Marcos have the Bomb? On another channel comes an entertainment report: Initial reports from the investigation into the plane crash and death of singer Rick Nelson suggest that freebasing in the cabin of his private plane may have led to the accident. A young reporter segues into a story on how new statistics show cocaine use among the young and upwardly mobile to be reaching, in the reporter's words, "crisis level proportions, an *epidemic.*"

"Thank you for that fascinating update," the anchorman says at the report's end, his eyes narrowing to convey appropriate alarm. "Very troubling problem, isn't it?"

"*Very,*" says the young reporter, smiling. "And we'll have an update tomorrow at five and eleven."

"Thank you very much," says the anchorman, grimacing, shaking his head, as if suggesting he doesn't know a single, pathetic soul who snorts; that he pities the poor bastards who do. "There's just a whole world out there that we don't know about, isn't there?" he concludes jocularly. Yeah. Right. What a dickface. Why this hypocrisy every night, all these people pretending drugs don't touch their world? Lies, people live them and climb over the backs of others upon them — which is why he'll never do coke in front of anyone who isn't a close friend. You can never be sure who might be a narc, or who might have a grudge against whom, or who, just to bait their parents, will defiantly drop the news that they've done drugs with you. Some of his friends call him paranoid, but screw them, you better be paranoid in a school where people get fucked over with regularity simply in the name of competition. Coke: Who *doesn't* use it? But reporters need stories and cops need busts. He opens a notebook, begins scanning his English notes a last time. Everybody lying, cheating, exploiting. Protect number one.

Studying until three A.M. and skipping his first class, he gets to Beverly at ten forty-five A.M., exhausted, though he took a couple of No-Doz about an hour before. He arranges his books as a pillow on the school's front lawn, lies down, and closes his eyes. He tells himself, *Relax, relax.* Although the rest of his body feels as though it might collapse, his pulse is racing; probably the effect of the No-Doz and the tiny hit of speed he took when he awakened. Only the second time he's ever done speed, the first being before his chem final a year ago. No sense in taking a chance on having your brain turn off with a half-hour remaining on an exam. You can never be absolutely certain how things will go on a final, but, right now, he feels good. *Relax, relax.* The grass feels slightly dewy on the back of his khakis. He'll be fucking pissed off if there's a grass or water stain on them. He had to look for three hours around the mall before he found the perfect pair of khakis with the right waist and ass. And the crotch is just right, well, a little tight, but if you had to err, well, he knows what side he'll come down upon. . . . So much concern with bods at this place. Shit, he's just forgotten Chaucer's birthplace. He groans loudly, worrying what other facts are burning out in his short-circuiting brain. "Oh, fuck."

"Oh, fuck *yourself*," a voice says.

It's Laura.

Sitting two feet away from him.

"I didn't hear you," he says. "How long have you been sitting there?"

"About ten seconds," she says. "Don't worry, I didn't see you checking your crotch or anything."

"I never do that."

"You do it whenever you have on a tight pair of pants."

"Well, only to make sure they fit."

"Yeah. Right." She laughs. Something about the laugh and her discussion of his intimate quirks makes him think of the time she changed her bra in front of him. Did it ever happen? It seems more like a pleasant fantasy these days.

"Where's . . . ?" He has forgotten her boyfriend's name.

"*Aaron*," she says slowly, "is at work."

"Does he like it?"

She waves her hand to indicate she doesn't want to discuss the subject. "I haven't seen you in so long."

He thinks about letting her off easy, then decides, fuck it. He's tired, nervous, and his pulse is racing. Just say what's on his mind. "That wasn't my decision — not to see you."

"I know. I've just been busy."

"So is everybody."

She pats him on the arm, flashes a conciliatory smile. "How's Vickie?"

"Good."

"Are you two really into each other?"

"What's *into* each other?" He wonders why he is feeling so antagonistic.

She pouts. "Be nice." She tickles his stomach. "Will she be bummed if you go to college away from L.A.?"

"I don't know. I'm not in love with her or anything, you know. We have a lot of fun. Can we talk about something else? How are you doing?"

Laura sighs and lifts her calculus book, filled with worksheets of unanswered problems. "We haven't done anything in a real long time, you know. Want to have lunch sometime?"

"I've been saying that for four months," he reminds her.

She pinches his arm softly, and stands. She has to go to a review session for calculus. "Actually, I saw you adjusting your crotch twice," she says, and in a peel of giggles, hops off.

He takes a last No-Doz, just before walking into English. The final is easier than expected: He needs to steal only four or five multiple-choice answers from the 4.0 with pockmarks and black Brillo pad hair, next to him.

"Did you need much help?" the girl asks on the way out of class.

"Well, on a couple of questions, I looked at what you had," he admits. "Thanks. Those things on Chaucer were hard. Good thing I sit next to you." A jocular, self-conscious laugh. He feels himself being a bit too effusive. He must sound like a sniveling hypocrite to this Brain, to whom he has never spoken unless in need of an answer. "You're cool to let me do it," he says. "Thanks. Very cool."

She laughs. "It's nothing major," she says. "Maybe in return, though, you could score for me sometime."

He tries not to look too surprised. "I didn't know you partied."

"Well, not much. But I did some mushrooms with a couple of people from UCLA last week, and that was excellent."

"You *did?*"

She smiles contemptuously. *"That's* cute. You look real shocked."

"Almost totally," he confesses.

"God, you really take me for some geek, don't you?"

Actually, he did, but she needn't know this. "I just thought you had more sense than me."

She nods, her brain riffling through more test questions. "Did you know number twelve? Something about the Globe Theatre, its look, design, something like that."

"I read about that last night," Steven says. "I think I got that one."

She stops at her locker. "Good," she says. "Because I got that one off you."

FEBRUARY

"Two A's and three B's," his mother reads aloud from Andy's report card. "This is the most impressive report card I've ever seen from you. This is extraordinary."

"I hope it's worth more than dick," he says glumly.

"I wish you wouldn't talk that way," she whimpers. "I've told you that I've heard it all before. Don't tell me you talk that way all the time around your father and his girlfriend." She pauses, waiting, Andy suspects, less for some confirmation or denial of this than for a story about her ex and his latest nymph. Andy doesn't bite. His mother straightens, changes tack. "Anyway, no matter who admits you to their school, the most important thing you've proved with this report card is that you can succeed, dear. I think it's just terrific. And now you have nothing to worry about the rest of the way, since the colleges don't look at the final semester grades, right?"

"Uh-huh," he says.

Liberation, a friend called it the other day. Short of failing a course or being busted on a morals rap, nothing they could do as seniors in their second semester would matter. Months before, Andy dreamed of such freedom, believing that it would come at the precise moment finals ended in early February, but finals have passed and, though he skips second semester classes whenever he feels the urge, a new pressure has seized him. He cannot get his mind off his upcoming college interviews. The season of being judged by self-satisfied Yuppies in pinstripes and blue pinpoint Oxford shirts has begun.

He sat for an interview last Saturday. He drank three large glasses of water at home to prevent his nervous voice from cracking, but, by the time he got to the interviewer's home, he had to pee and didn't want to ask permission to go to the bathroom. The interviewer, an earnest, balding investment banker in his weekend Polo shirt and Top-Siders, told him he had been in the class of '73, explaining he should have graduated in '72 except that he took 1968 off to work for Eugene McCarthy. Andy didn't know who Eugene McCarthy was. The interviewer glanced at a pile of books on top of his television and asked Andy if he had ever read *Moby Dick*. Andy thought he had heard of the book once and guessed that this man mentioned earlier, Eugene McCarthy, probably had written it. "Not all of it," Andy said. "I've been very busy with school and finals, so I haven't gotten around to reading everything I should. So you're a big fan of Eugene McCarthy's writing, too, huh? I liked *Moby Dick* a lot." The interviewer's quizzical frown told Andy he had somehow blundered into saying something either confusing or stupid or both, and, suddenly self-conscious, he became aware of the twitching of his legs, his body's involuntary reaction to his chief physical need at the moment. The interviewer shifted the discussion to the subject of nuclear holocaust, leaning back on his couch, awaiting Andy's pronouncements. Andy said something about how he thought everybody should turn in all their weapons to the United Nations.

"The U.N. has no clout," the interviewer said, absently arranging a couple of sailing books on a side table. "They can't even get people to pay their dues. Trust me on this one. Money is my sphere."

At the end, Andy was convinced he could strike the private school off his list; the interviewer's impression of him seemed clear in the way he had limply shook his hand on the way out. Andy doesn't care. One dead application doesn't finish him. He has an interview this Sunday at the Brentwood house of an alumnus of a small New Hampshire college, and then an interview Monday afternoon in Century City.

"I don't feel exactly free from anything, Mom," he says to her, in the living room. "I feel real nervous about this college stuff. I don't think that guy on Saturday was exactly blown away by my intellectualness or whatever."

"You should bring up a topic of your own next time," she softly suggests. "And just be yourself. Your uncle and father will get you in with some help. Don't underestimate your uncle."

"He's a dick sometimes."

"I thought you liked him."

"He always makes you feel that he's going to be responsible for the things that happen to you when he helps."

"When has he ever helped you before?"

"Like when he helped me get into that computer summer camp after sixth grade. And I would have gotten in on my own anyway, because my teacher ranked me number two in our class. But Uncle Phil always said, 'Andy, aren't you happy I got you into that camp? Wasn't it a great camp?' Blah-blah-blah. He's so conceited. He makes you feel like you are nothing. Dad tries to run my life a lot, too."

"He's just trying to help."

"Mom, goddamn, don't stick up for him, okay? He trashes you and you get angry, and then when I get angry, you are like his big defender and I'm not allowed to get angry. I hate it."

"Your case is different than any discussions your father and I might have had. He wants you to get into a good college. So do I."

"Fine, Mom. Don't you start, okay? I always feel like he's saying, 'I'll take care of it. Just don't be fucking up anymore and we'll all be fine.' He thinks I'm a bumbler. Sometimes you make me feel the same way, like I do nothing worth noticing."

"Well, what do you want me to notice?"

"See? *Jesus Christ*."

"Well, what?"

"I don't know, God, you want me to name things. Am I that dull and stupid? *Goddamn*."

"I'm just asking. I'm not trying to make you upset."

"Mom, I play in a band. I work at a hospital. . . ."

"Which you stopped, incidentally."

A screech. "*Yeah, because of finals!* You never pay attention to the things I *can* do."

"That's not fair. We all know about the things you can do. We're just responsible for making sure you can do the other things well, too."

"Bullshit. You treat me like some twelve-year-old. Remember that night when I played that song I wrote and you said that the song didn't have words even though I sang words to it about a million times? You didn't even hear them. You're so wrapped up in your own problems I don't count, unless you've had enough Valium for the day."

"Well, now you're just being obnoxious."

"I'm gone," he shouts. He opens the front door and takes a last look back at his mother, who hangs her head. "Did you really mean that about the Valium?" she asks.

Within two hours, he is back home with a new turquoise earring that he got from a friend along with a little buzz from three Lowenbraus. His mother can never tell when he's smoked pot but she always smells a beer buzz. He doesn't know what will piss her off more — the earring or the buzz. "You've been drinking a lot of beer, haven't you?" she says, not looking up, her head burrowed in a paper. "You think you're allowed to do anything, don't you?"

"You're no angel, Mom. When I'm drinking beer, what do you do?"

She surprises him by turning and walking into their den, shoulders slumped, closing the thin French doors. He hears her sadly drop into the den chair, able, after so many years, to distinguish someone happily easing into the big round chair from someone disconsolately flopping. Another sound comes, not so easily identifiable. He takes a step closer. The noise seeps through the doors. No mistaking it now. She is crying. He opens the doors and blurts, "I'm sorry, Mom, I didn't mean any of that, I'm sorry."

"I'm sorry, too," she says. "I know I've been preoccupied with things." She is smiling. The whimpering has come not from her but the television, where a woman on "Hill Street Blues" has learned that her cop-husband has been wounded. "We could use another cable channel, Andy. There really isn't enough on the ones we have, do you think?" How could he have mistaken that moan for his mother's? "Things will be fine," she says at a commercial. "I'll get past this."

"That's all right, Mom, don't worry."

"You know I don't ignore you, don't you?"

"Yeah, it's okay."

"But take whatever help your uncle or father or this counselor can give you with colleges. And play the game when you meet new people."

That, actually, makes sense to Andy. For his interview on Sunday with the representative from the small New Hampshire school, Andy, remembering the preppie attire of his last interviewer, arrives in a natty blue blazer, powder blue shirt, khaki pants, and penny loafers with Argyle socks. The interviewer, a rawboned man in his early forties, is wearing jeans with weed stains and suspenders, a faded college sweatshirt, and brown boots. He pours each of them a glass of Kool-Aid from a plastic pitcher, and signals Andy to follow him outside to his backyard picnic table, which has an electric chain saw atop it.

"So what do you think?" the man asks.

"Of the college?"

"Well, sure, if that's what you think I meant. Actually, I was talking about my little outdoor workshop here. I keep all my tools on the patio. We use the picnic table as a workbench, though my wife seems to take some exception to it. She says it somehow attracts flies."

"Oh."

The man raises an eyebrow. "You mean you believe that?"

"No. I just thought that that was kind of funny, but I don't believe it."

"Good," says the man, "because that's kind of stupid, thinking that flies come to a workbench."

"Uh-huh."

"This fly business is absurd . . ."

"Sounds like it."

"Because when you think about it very carefully," says the man, jutting a forefinger into the air, "you realize that it is the *ants* of the world who have something against the professional and recreational builder."

"Ants."

"Of course. Developers and builders are always destroying their hills, correct?"

"I guess," says Andy carefully.

"So there you are. Do you follow me?" The man raises his eyebrow again.

"Sure," Andy says.

"You like crafts?"

"Well, a couple of times, I've helped this guy make surfboards."

The man wipes his mouth and spits. "That's not building, that's a sport. So you want to go on to college?"

"Uh-huh. Yes, sir. Very much."

"Why?"

"Well, I'm not real good with explanations, but I'll try . . ."

"How's your Kool-Aid?"

"Fine, sir."

"Son, don't answer that question I just asked you. Talk to me about whatever gets your blood pumping."

"Pardon me, sir?"

"You heard me. Building things gets my heart going. What does it for you?"

"Really?"

"Yes, son."

"Playing rock 'n' roll."

"Tell me about it."

Andy tells him about the band for the next twenty minutes. The interviewer uses the time to whittle and slap flies that land on his neck. "Okay," the man finally says, "why, if you like this rock 'n' roll so much, do you want to go to college?"

Andy figures he has nothing to lose. "I've thought about that," he says deliberately, "and kind of decided that, you know, whether I make it in rock 'n' roll or not, a college education can only make me better."

The man studies his whittling knife. "Well, I think a school like my old one can use someone like you, son," he says. "So I'm going to recommend you, and you can save all that mumbo-jumbo about your extracurricular activities at school for someone else. What do you think of that?"

Andy smiles. "Good."

Melinda receives straight A's for the fall-winter semester. "It's over now. I already feel like I'm kind of gone, even though I'm not," she says. "I just want it to be over and to be out of there." She skips out on her new second-semester Spanish class one morning. "I just didn't feel like getting out of bed," she says. "I have never done that before. But now, if I don't feel like doing anything at school, I don't. I want the pressure to be over. My grades don't count as far as colleges are concerned, so why not? And, on sunny days, I'm going to the beach and work on my tan. When it gets sunny, you don't want to stay in the house and watch TV in the afternoons. I won't even do that for 'Santa Barbara.' I'll tape it. Bike and tan: That's going to be my last semester."

Still, she has the college game to play out. Knowing the colleges receive a list of the spring courses taken by their applicants (though the grades will never count, for purposes of admission), Melinda has enrolled in classes which include solid and impressive course titles — applied economics, English literature, and finite math, which combines the teaching of statistics and probability. "They'll look good, that was the only thing left to think about," she says. "Now I just have to be careful and smart in the interviews."

Her interview for one elite Eastern school takes place on a Saturday afternoon at a house in the Hollywood Hills. "What current events are you interested in?" the interviewer asks. "How about Reaganomics? What do you think of that? The trickle-down theory? Have any thoughts on that?"

She remembers a phrase she heard in her first-semester government class. "You mean, Gramm-Rudman?" she asks.

The interviewer looks surprised. "Well, let's talk about Gramm-Rudman."

"Well, some people would like very much to make it unconstitutional," says Melinda, and then launches into an explanation of why some people like neither Gramm-Rudman nor Ronald Reagan. In the process, she doesn't say a word about what Reaganomics means, hopeful her long answer will conceal the fact that she doesn't know anything about economics, that she has tuned out her teacher whenever he started talking about Gramm-Rudman. "They think it's anti-Democrat and not fair or constitutional," she concludes.

"Yeah, uh-huh," the interviewer nods.

He doesn't understand Gramm-Rudman either, she realizes. *This guy can be bullshitted.* "Whatever we talked about, it sounded good," she says later. "It doesn't matter if the points are wrong, if you sound good. I worked in the things I was really interested in, like entrepreneurial things. And I talked about sign-language classes; how I'd seen them on TV and was curious. It went good."

The following Thursday, her family leaves for the airport for a six-day trip to Tahiti. Missing school days in the lame-duck semester concerns her not at all, but failing to finish her Harvard application by the weekend deadline would be a disaster, and so Melinda is writing the application's essay en route to the airport. "I wish for your sake that you'd finished it earlier so that there wouldn't be all this rushing now," her mom says, and Melinda groans, not wanting to hear this, particularly because her mother is right: She should have finished the application weeks ago. It is simply impossible to get motivated any longer, even for a Harvard application, though with 1260 on her SATs, her chances aren't very good for admission anyway, she tells herself. She feels like a robot, answering the same damn questions, more or less, on the dozen applications she's filled out. Give them what they want. Don't forget to mention the importance of taking an interest in the arts. Her words look a bit sloppy in blue ballpoint, but she has become too cynical to care. She drops the completed application in a mailbox next to an airport terminal, then gets on the plane.

———

Steven takes no trips, does not stop running. During the first week of the new semester, he does three more college interviews, signs up for a Tae Kwon Do class, and attends two UCLA Republican volunteer meetings for senatorial candidate Bobbi Fiedler, making a flurry of phone calls to college and high school acquaintances whom he met during fund-raising for the Ethiopian famine victims, trying to entice them into working for

Fiedler. Nearly all beg off, saying they're too busy with homework and classes, even most of the high school seniors whose spring grades will mean nothing, unable to change habits after so many years of the grind. You need kids unaccustomed to backbreaking routines for political or social work. Last spring, when he tried to recruit students to help with telephone canvassing for a food bank, he drew from among artistic types — writers and journalists, drama people and musicians — groups that traditionally demonstrated a tendency toward iconoclasm, but that, at Beverly, were usually composed of systematic, professionally oriented super-achievers, super-achievers being the only ones who could devote two to three hours, say, to the school newspaper or a play without imperiling their grades. Some of his friends on the school newspaper continued writing and editing the paper right through the January finals, unfazed by the exam pressures, their schedules accustomed to expanding to meet harsh deadlines, but they were the exceptions. Most people have never had time for anything other than school, except when a trendy cause like the Live Aid rock concerts came along, something hip, designer relief. Then, within a few weeks after the charity concerts ended, they forgot about the cause. It disgusts him, thinking about it. He doesn't agree with most of what the 'sixties kids wanted, but at least a few of them demonstrated some social commitment.

His friends don't care who wins or loses elections. He respects the few Beverly kids interested in politics, even those working for liberal causes. "At least they believe in *something*," he says. "Like there's this kid who wears this old button for Jerry Brown on his jean jacket. He gets involved in a lot of things. The only time anybody paid attention in class to the political things he was talking about was when he wore a Reagan button and drew a line through '*Reagan.*' Some kids said, 'You're defaming the President.' I didn't agree with him, but I respect him because at least he's involved. He made those nerds think. The button had good shock value."

He tries futilely to get Fiedler volunteers all evening. He does not get to bed until twelve thirty A.M. When his phone rings at six the next morning, it takes him five minutes before he can groggily roll across his bed to answer it. It's Vickie. She sounds frantic. "My period still hasn't come," she says. "Six days late now. *Six* days. *I've never* been that late before."

He sits bolt upright in his bed, tells himself to be calm. "I'm sure this is nothing," he says soothingly. "Girls are late a lot, right? I know Laura has been late before and . . ."

"I don't really need to hear about Laura right now."

"But there can't be any problem with you on the pill," he reminds her.

"I think I missed taking it for a few days," she confesses.

He hears words coming from his mouth. "You'd want an abortion, right?"

Silence.

Steven waits, finally murmurs, "You would, right?"

"Relax, Steven, I don't want a baby either. God, I don't want you and me trapped together with something we don't want — and married." This stings him. He would have thought that, in a year or two, she would have jumped at the chance to hitch herself to his star. He liked the delusion, would have preferred that she not ruin it for him.

"Uh-huh, right," he says.

"But an abortion sounds so awful, doesn't it?" she asks in a philosophical tone, like the one his physiology teacher always uses when lobbying against abortion in class panel discussions. "It just scares me, thinking about the way they tear up your body to do it. Wouldn't it scare you?"

"It sounds like they have the procedure down pretty good these days," he replies. "I don't think your body would get messed up any."

"Well, *your* body won't." She begins to cry. "Please just don't dump me. I'm *so* late. Don't dump me."

It is the second time now that she has made the plea. "I'd never do that," he says fiercely.

"I'm going to the doctor if it looks bad."

"I'll go with you if you want me to," he says.

———

Kelly's fall semester grades include one D and three C's, and so she has given up hope of being admitted to U.C. Santa Barbara or a Cal State University. She does not mention the bad news to her friends at Chin Chin's, careful to talk only about boys and the issue of whether her new Reeboks would look good with a turquoise skirt and a thick rhinestone-studded black belt. "The studs are ultra-glitzy, but I think it's a nice outfit for the Hard Rock," she says.

"I was just thinking I'm gonna be so bummed if I have to choose between Berkeley, Stanford, and some Ivy League school," chirps Shelly. "Because I'll miss you guys so much. If Berkeley *and* Stanford say yes, where do you guys think I should go?"

"Alabama," says Kelly.

"But *really*," says Shelly, ignoring this. "*Where?* And what do you think if I get into Brown and Harvard?"

"The guys are so cute back East," says Tina. "They're smart, and they have real cool looks. They don't have California tans, but they're still real cute. I saw a rugby game back there. *Foxes.*"

"I'd like to get married to a guy from a good school," says Shelly, pausing and waving a chopstick to indicate the momentousness of her next thought. "It's important for your kids, too, genes and all. I'd like to have a couple kids early while I'm getting my career going, and then it will be perfect. Just when my career is taking off, they'll be getting old enough so I won't have to spend so much time with them."

"I'm not so sure about marriage," says Tina.

"I can't even *see* myself getting married," says Kelly. "I don't know. Why are we talking about this anyway?"

"We were talking about cute guys in rugby shirts," says Tina.

"Maybe I'd live with someone," Kelly says.

"You do that and you get screwed," says Shelly. "My mother says if they split from you then, you won't get a cent — even with that palimony thing. It's hard to prove. I'm going to make sure I'm married after Berkeley or Stanford."

"I still think you should go to Alabama," says Kelly, standing, telling the three that she has to get going.

At seven P.M., after an idle drive to the beach and back, she opens the door to her house to hear some unrecognizable wailing coming from her mother's bedroom. She warily approaches the bedroom, able to make out the sounds of a muffled lilting voice over a whirring hair-dryer. Her mother's bedroom door is closed. Kelly knocks once, twice, and, hearing no answer, opens the door, sees her mother dressed in only a slip and a bra, holding a hair-dryer in one hand and a brush in the other. She is singing and dancing in front of her full-length mirror. She waves Kelly inside. Music pulsates from stereo speakers. Mom croons in time with Rod Stewart. Kelly gives her a half-smile. "Come on, sweetheart," cajoles her mother, "move those hips." Kelly grudgingly does a little dance step, stops, puts her hands on her hips. "What's going on?" she asks.

"Sweetheart, I can't talk now. Go into my jewelry drawer and pull out some nice earrings, maybe those gold ones, to go with my black backless dress, will you?"

"I didn't know you had a date tonight."

"I didn't either until a couple of hours ago."

"Who is it?"

"Remember Jay Marsh, the man from Seattle with the department store up there? Slightly graying. We had him over for dinner with that councilman."

"Uh-huh. He was nice."

"I'm going out with his son."

"*Son?*"

"Yes."

"How old is he?"

"I don't know. Twenty-eight, maybe, I think. Somebody told me he was, at least. He's either twenty-eight or twenty-six, something like that. Where are those earrings?"

"Here." Kelly hands the earrings over, and her mom slips them on while swishing her hips in front of the mirror, inspecting her dress. "It doesn't look too tight, does it? I feel a little nervous. I don't go to rock 'n' roll nightclubs much. And he goes a lot, I bet." She reaches for a watered-down rum and Coke on her dressing bureau and takes a drink.

"Have you had anything to eat, Mom?"

"Do you think this dress is hip-enough looking?"

"Sure, Mom. It's okay. Where did you meet this guy?"

"Why so many questions? Be a dear and turn up the music a little louder will you?" She smooths her lipstick, and closes her eyes. "Let me relax a bit before he comes, okay, sweetheart? You'll like him." The doorbell rings. Kelly's mother takes a deep breath. "Get that," she commands.

Kelly bounces down the stairs and answers the door. Her mom's date has on a pink jacket and a tuxedo shirt, undone to the middle of his chest, which is tan and hairy. Kelly thinks he looks like a young Mafia hit man or the greasy New York disc jockey she watches on a cable dance show.

"Hi, I'm Dennis," he says, rubbing her shoulder. "You're Kelly. Your mom told me all about you. You *really* go to Beverly Hills High School?"

"I really do."

"It sounds like a movie, you know? *Beverly Hills High*. Does everybody say that?"

"Yes. I'll get my mom. She'll be ready in a sec."

"You look a lot like her. She told me you were real cute."

Slimeball. "Thank you. Excuse me. Would you like to make yourself a drink? There's all sorts of things in the bar. I'll see how my mom's doing."

"Okay, Kel."

His tone is already familiar. He expects to be back later. God, she'll be so grossed if her mom has this greaser spend the night. She walks down the hall and sees her mother smoothing her dress. "What are you doing, Mom?"

"Tell me it doesn't look wrinkled."

"It looks great, Mom. What's wrong?"

"Nothing, nothing. I'm fine, I'm fine." She takes two deep breaths. "Well, tell me."

"He's okay."

"What do you think he's expecting?"

"Oh, Mom, just be yourself."

Her mom practices a smile into the mirror, then saunters down the hall, exchanging a peck on the mouth with the young man.

"We won't be back until one or two," Mom says to her at the door, hugging her. "So I'll talk to you tomorrow morning, sweetheart. There are all sorts of goodies in the refrigerator. Fix whatever you want."

"You mean Ismelda's not making dinner?"

"Oh, I sent Ismelda home. She hasn't had a weeknight off in so long."

The dapper greaseball takes her mom's arm. Kelly senses the twosome's plans for the evening's end have already been made. That's why Mom got rid of Ismelda. Gross. Without warning then, the greaseball leans down and kisses Kelly's cheek.

"Kel, it's been *super* meeting you," he says. "I'll be seeing you later."

She has a pizza and two glasses of wine, and falls asleep on the couch in the den. A cold hand awakens her several hours later. "Come on, sweetheart," she hears her mother saying. "Wake up. You'll be more comfortable in your bed. *Come on.*"

Mother helps daughter off the couch. Kelly's mind comes out of the fog, focuses on her mom in the backless dress, remembers why she is in it. "How was your date?" she asks, rubbing her eyes.

"Fine."

"You're home early, aren't you?"

"Not really. It's late."

"Is he gone?"

"Yes."

"Was it fun?"

"Don't ask so many questions, okay?"

"I thought you'd want me to."

"Only about the guys I think I might see again."

"God, Mom, I'm glad you cut him loose. He was too gross for words."

"Actually, I didn't really cut him loose."

"What time do you have to go to Salt Lake City?"

"Not until tomorrow afternoon. Want to have a breakfast together?"

"Okay." Kelly hasn't had breakfast with her mother in some time. "He was a geek, *really*, Mom. It'll be fun to have breakfast."

She doesn't want to hear about the date, depressed enough by her own problems with the opposite sex. Kurt, the cute sophomore brother of her good friend, has not asked her out since they went into Westwood to see a movie and play Pac-Man at the Video Arcade. She didn't even get a chance to make out with him. They left the movie to get chocolate chip cookies, talked about how much they had hated *Rambo*, and then she drove him home. She could not bring herself to put the moves on a fifteen-year-old boy. What if he rejected her? It would have been too hard to take, especially coming from a younger kid who would certainly share the news with all his jock buddies, not to mention his sister. God, she has to get slimmer. So does her mom. Even with a pretty face, her mom has no chance against those young babes unless she gets rid of ten pounds in her butt, and firms up those freckled, sun-ravaged arms, which, while thin, still have bits of flesh as flaccid as Jell-O hanging off them. Bouncing, bouncing, bouncing, the skin has forty-two-year-old written all over it. When her mom works out at the Matrix fitness center, she keeps her arms covered in one of the baggy old college sweatshirts Kelly's father left behind, careful always to highlight her strongest asset — her face — in the midst of tough competition from the twenty-five-year-old Superchicks. Kelly senses these acts of cover-up and sexual strategy bother her mom, an otherwise proud and strong woman who, as recently as last July, upon winning a role model recognition plaque from a women's group, declared, "We have, fortunately, arrived at an age where women are no longer expected to sculpt either their minds or bodies for men's pleasure."

She sculpts anyway, Kelly knows. *Feminism*. What does that mean exactly? Her grandmothers didn't go to college and slaved for their husbands at home, excluded from decisions of family finances, little more than their men's chattel. Her mother went to college and has existed on roughly equal terms with men, but she seldom looks happy, goes absolutely misty-eyed in moments over the prospect of never having another man with whom to cohabitate. Kelly's father, a hearty liberal attorney, had championed feminism in principle, but then, seeing it meant, among other things, that he would be eating Stouffer's three times a week during his wife's real estate training, he chafed and finally re-belled. Something of an asshole, her father, trying to hold her mom down to some mediocre, part-time position, so she could have his house clean and goose liver pâté ready when he came home, his empathy for her professional burdens coming only from a comfortable distance away in his oceanfront condo, after their separation. "I'll know better what to do with the next man," her mother confessed to her following the divorce.

But you better get your bod in shape, no matter what else you do, Kelly thinks, looking at her. She heard about a college study on television that said women have little chance of marrying once they turn thirty-five. Some people claimed the study was nonsense, but to Kelly the news says that you better get a guy while you're young. It scares her a little, the thought of being alone, of living like an old maid with only cats and birds for companions. Even if she cannot conceive of marriage, she wants to live with a man by the time she is in her early twenties, someone who will be around long enough at least for the next man to take his place. Along the way, maybe she'll find someone who thinks as she does, a permanent partner who does not believe in marriage either. She sees what may loom as her future, the pathetic consequence of failure, staring at a donut. It just isn't fair. Men can be such pigs, all of them so tits and ass–conscious.

Her mother's voice interrupts her reverie. "We have something else we have to talk about," she says, reaching for the donut and putting it on a dish, settling in for a long discussion. "We have to start thinking about you and college."

"Santa Monica City looks like it's it."

"I refuse to accept that. Loyola and USC and a couple of others still might be in the picture. I want you to call for the applications tomorrow."

"I don't think it's much use."

"I don't want you to be a defeatist, okay? I hope I don't ever sound like a defeatist."

"No, Mom, you don't."

"Does your father ever mention anxieties like mine?"

"Not really."

"He's having the time of his life, that's why, isn't he?"

"I don't know, Mom."

Mom takes a bite of the donut.

———

On Friday night, Paul sits with Tony, Randy, and several senior class luminaries at a Beverly basketball game. Randy points at a freshman girl in the far bleachers with whom he claims to have slept the week before. Tony stands, cranes his neck to see.

"Why would she sleep with you?" Paul asks him contemptuously.

Randy is not insulted. "I gave her some blow before," he explains amiably. "So she probably thought we were going to party some more. She was a little bummed when I ran out."

"Serves the bitch right," says Tony. "Girls who sleep with guys just to do their blow are the worst."

"They don't sleep with me even if I've got a snowball," Paul says. "I could wheel in Mount Everest and it wouldn't help."

Randy laughs. Tony gives him a look of sympathy he doesn't want. Paul leans back in the bleachers and feels a tap on his shoulder. Turning around, he catches a glimpse of blond whiskers and a torn jean jacket. Joey, his old grammar school friend, former brain, and current burnout, waves a tentative hello with his index finger. "How are you liking that book I gave you?" the erstwhile buddy asks Paul.

Paul forgot all about the book. He can't even remember its subject now. He stuffed it deep into a bedroom drawer on the September day Joey gave it to him, and he has not opened the drawer since. He tries to cover. "My father thinks it's real cool," he says quickly. "He borrowed it from me and still hasn't given it back. He's totally into it."

"What's the book about?" Randy asks.

"It's totally complicated," says Paul, then turns back to Joey. "What are you doing here?"

"Just hanging," Joey says, absently pulling a toothpick out of his jacket. "What are you guys doing after the game?"

Tony and Randy give Paul quick looks to suggest this interloper is not welcome in their evening's plans. "I gotta go home, because I have to be up early," he lies.

"Let's go to a movie or party down some night," the boy suggests. "My parents would like to see you, too."

"All right, take it easy, Joey." Paul pats his arm, a signal that their conversation is over for now.

Joey walks back up the bleachers and out of the Swim-Gym, though the game is only two minutes into the third quarter. Watching him, Paul feels a little guilty, would have liked to have done something with him, if Tony hadn't made it so clear that he didn't want a burnout in their crowd. His best friend can be a terrible snob. Paul tells them he'll be back, then gets up to walk around and get a candy bar. He waits until late in the fourth quarter to come back.

A Beverly player stands at the free-throw line with only six seconds left in the game. Beverly leads Inglewood High 39–38. The player shoots and misses. Inglewood scrambles downcourt and hits a twelve-foot jumper at the buzzer. Beverly loses, 40–39.

"The Beverly dude choked," Randy says on the way out.

"Choked and died," adds Tony.

Paul bristles, not quite knowing why. "Like you assholes could have made it, huh? God, you just pass judgment on everybody, don't you? Just trash everybody, why don't you?"

He's in such a bad mood that he decides to go to the gym and take a quick workout. Thirty-five minutes into it, he feels his legs cramping. He walks off the mat, bends his head over a water fountain, and gulps until he begins choking.

"Is that how water buffalo do it?" says a voice behind him.

Gagging, his eyes watering, he turns blindly to make out a chunky form in pink tights and a black sweatshirt. "Excuse me," he says. "Go ahead."

"No, it's too much fun watching you," the voice says.

Focusing now, looking for the face of his tormentor, he lifts his head to see a hand covering a laughing mouth, looks higher, sees a long narrow nose rising to meet two eyes set so closely together they look somewhat crossed. He knows this girl vaguely, tries to place where he saw her; then realizes the same face teased him a couple months ago when he was draped over this same water fountain. Said something then about saving a couple drops for the fish. She looks like an escapee from a fat farm.

"*Please* have a drink," he gasps, "before you resume grazing." He is still bent over, wiping the tears from his eyes, coughing.

"*What* did you say?" the girl demands.

He mumbles just loud enough for her to hear: "Please pick up your Gravy Train at the loading dock."

"*Excuse me?*"

"I said, 'Weigh in by the *meat hooks.*' "

"*You,*" she shouts, "are an asshole. *You* should talk."

"So I hear."

The girl storms away. Paul sits down on an exercise mat in an empty adjoining room, too tired to walk the twenty-five feet to the sauna. He lies down on the mat, closes his eyes, and hears a body drop down on the mat's other side. The chunky girl is doing sit-ups. He opens one eye, inspects her, closes it, waits for her to go away.

"Excuse me, would you mind telling me if I'm doing these right?" the girl asks him.

He lifts his head. "You're doing them fine." He lies back on the mat.

"You're not really looking, are you? Would you mind holding my feet?"

"You sure you want a water buffalo on your feet?" he asks.

"It's okay. Just so you're not around when I'm *grazing.*"

"Sorry I said that."

"That was the worst. I'm not mad now, but that was so weird of you. Would you just hold my feet for a minute?"

"I was choking. I just say what people say to me, I guess. Actually, I don't give a shit what they say."

"I'm pretty sensitive about it," she says.

"Me, too."

He holds her feet.

"Mooo," she says, bending into her first sit-up. "Mooo."

He laughs. "I said I'm sorry, okay? *Oink, oink.*"

She jabs at one of his tennis shoes with an elbow. "Are those Adidas?"

"Yeah."

"They're nice." She talks while doing sit-ups. She must be in reasonably decent shape even if her body doesn't show it. "I saw Rod Stewart on the street in Hollywood once and he was wearing Adidas," she says. "Or maybe Reeboks. He plays soccer. There was this girl with him and he had his hand on her butt the whole time."

"Rod Stewart seems like he can do anything he wants," observes Paul.

She grunts. "The girl didn't even seem to mind. She liked it. All these people wanted his autograph, but he just kept walking to his limousine. I saw him in concert once. He doesn't have good skin, even." She is sweating onto his arm. "Hold my feet harder."

"Okay," he says. Her eyes aren't bad, actually, once you get used to how close together they are. Big and brown, they glisten when she smiles. When she looks directly at him, though, she squints. Is this one of those bizarre facial tics he's read about? Maybe her eyesight is bad, and she can't see him without glasses. Chunky with four eyes: This chick is headed for a lot of lonely nights. "How many have you done now?" he asks.

"That's . . . thirty," she gasps.

"Why don't you take a rest?" Paul suggests.

"No. Got . . . to do . . ."

At sixty, she falls back, hands on her stomach, finished. It is a couple minutes before she can talk. "I used to hate it, but I don't any-more. It feels good at the end. And I've noticed a lot of difference. I ride horses and I think it's making me stronger."

"Where do you ride?"

"All over. Mostly Malibu. Friends of my parents have a ranch there. I jump. Plus I think the son likes me a little . . ."

"You take advantage of that," Paul interrupts.

"Well, a little, maybe." She laughs. A nice laugh. Her ass could stand to lose five, maybe ten pounds, a minor flaw, given that smile. Maybe her nights aren't that lonely after all. "Once I didn't look like a blimpola anymore, I got a lot more confidence," she says. "That's why when you said, *grazing*, it hurt, because I don't see myself that way now."

"You're not. I was just being an asshole because I thought you were being an asshole. I was choking. Plus, I feel fat myself."

"I've seen you here before. You've lost some weight. You're doing a lot better. Oh, my mom's here. Well, thanks for holding my feet."

"No problem. I'm Paul."

"Hi. I'm Roxanne."

"Later on, Roxanne."

"Bye, Buffalo."

He waves, watches her leave, then grabs his athletic bag and walks out to his car. What would Tony and everybody else think if he showed up with a four-eyed Chunky Beef at a party? God, you have to stop being such a kiss-ass, he tells himself.

Arriving home, he finds his father sitting in their den, feet propped up on a leg rest, doing a crossword puzzle and watching television. "I thought you weren't coming back from Milan for another couple of days," he says.

His father turns off the television, puts the crossword puzzle down, stands up and beams. "Hi, pal," he says, extending a wrinkled hand with gray hairs. Paul shakes it, the old hand suddenly unclasping from his own to pat him on the back, once, twice, three times. "I was supposed to come back Wednesday, but I worked like a fiend because I thought, 'I want to get home and spend a little time with my favorite pal.' "

"Great, Dad. How was Italy?"

A flick of the wrist. His father's hand moves up and down. "Wasn't horrible but it wasn't great either. The plane was stuck two hours on the ground because some goddamn bolt in the door was defective. A three-cent part, probably. You don't want to know about it. Sit down here. Tell me about colleges and everything else you've been up to. Start from the top."

Paul reports on the status of his grades, college applications, and social life. "Well, how are you liking the Laker tickets I gave you?" his father asks when he's finished.

"They're excellent."

"Uh-huh. What do you think of the Celtics?"

"They're hot. Oh, after the game the other night, I saw this guy in the Forum parking lot with a monkey that did things on his shoulders. It was so bizarre. The weirdest thing was . . ."

"A dervish, that guy, Bird, huh?"

He doesn't know basketball as well as his father, feels like he is muttering clichés. "Huh? Yeah, Bird, he's a superstar."

"And Parish, what a force he is, huh?"

"Which one is he?"

"The black one."

"I don't know much about him."

"He's good," his father says.

"Oh."

Father leans back. A pause. Another conversation running on empty. "Turn on the television if you'd like."

Father and son watch "The Love Connection" in silence, the older man looking now and then at his crossword puzzle, the boy tossing a tennis ball in the air and thinking of Tony and the chunky Roxanne.

Chuck Woolery, the TV host, is asking a woman contestant why she was so disappointed with her date.

"He showed up an hour late and he wasn't especially dressed nicely," the woman says. "I'd gotten dressed up nicely because I thought we were going to a good place, but instead he took us to this place like a coffee shop."

Paul's father chuckles.

"Hey, it was a sushi bar," her date interrupts.

"But not a very nice one and, besides, you never asked me if I liked those raw squiggly things," the woman protests.

"You didn't even *ask* her?" Chuck Woolery asks, turning to the male contestant. "Let me make sure I got this right: You took her to a sushi bar and didn't ask her if she liked raw squiggly things?" He winks at the camera.

"No, I didn't," says the man, "I just thought she would. . . ."

"You *thought* she would?" asks Chuck Woolery to raucous laughter.

"Well, yeah," the man shrugs, beaten and sullen.

"Dummy," Paul's father says to the television. He returns to his crossword puzzle. Paul can't stand to miss "The Love Connection." He loves listening to people confessing to spending the night with their dates or being totally disgusted by them; can't believe how foolishly candid these people are. He feels a little sorry, though, for this failed couple who suddenly look like some divorced friends of his parents, weathered, desperate, ready to step over the edge to get a last chance at . . . *what?* Companionship? Some primal urge to pair? "The Love Connection" shows you how fucked up things are, how many lonely souls are floating around out there. Chuck Woolery is leering at the camera. A cult masterpiece, thinks Paul. Just too goddamn *intense.* When the show ends, he excuses himself to eat the lasagna that their housekeeper has heated in the microwave.

"Well, you just sound like you're doing great," his father says. "Was there anything else going on?"

"That was kind of everything."

"Is there anything else we needed to talk about?"

His son shakes his head.

Nothing else to talk about.

The next morning he is late for his second class because his car won't start. His mom drops him off at the corner of Durant and Moreno, right in the heart of Persian Alley, and Paul sees his old friend Joey talking to an Iranian kid. Ducking his head down, he walks quickly along the school's front lawn, but Joey sees him, shouts for him to stop. He turns to see Joey running toward him, slows to wait.

"What's been going on?" Joey asks him, out of breath.

"I'm late for a class. I gotta hurry."

"I was talking to Rahim," says Joey.

"Who?" Paul looks at his watch.

"*Rahim.* You introduced us at the beginning of school, remember? You were there, and I made a trade with him for . . ."

Paul cuts him off. His old friend has nothing better to do than hang out at Persian Alley? *Loser.* "That's cool, Joey. I gotta jet. I'll see you real soon."

"I was wondering if you wanted to come over for dinner, sometime?"

How can he be tactful about this? "Can I let you know?" he asks, feeling guilty once more.

"Sure."

Paul hurries to class, vowing never to walk by Persian Alley again. He's twelve minutes late to English and out of breath, sweating like a pig. He has to get in better shape. He'll get serious about it, he vows, after he gets back from his three-day weekend trip to San Francisco with Tony and Randy.

"So how was your weekend?" Roxanne asks him the next week at the Sports Connection.

"I went up to San Francisco with some friends to see a basketball game," he says.

"You went all the way up to San Francisco for a *basketball game?*"

"We're really into it," he says. Actually, they went up in hopes of partying and meeting some girls. They spent over a hundred bucks on four college girls who ditched them at Saturday night's end. "We got to see Michael Jordan."

"Oh." She is lifting light weights for her shoulders. "Do you think girls can look too muscley?"

"I don't think you look too muscley."

"I was just wondering." She sighs and puts the weights down. "I went to Disneyland on Saturday."

"I haven't been there since I was a kid."

"Neither had I. Fantasyland has all these new things. And I saw somebody blow lunch all over the Matterhorn. Imagine losin' it at Disneyland. It was gross but it was intensely funny, too."

He finds himself laughing. During a party after their sixth-grade graduation, Tony blew lunch all over some teacher on Disneyland's "It's a Mad, Mad World" ride. "You went with somebody?" he asks her.

"Yeah, this guy who lives in Malibu. His father has that ranch I ride at."

"Uh-huh. You already told me about him."

"He almost flew right out of one of those spinning teacups. He's such a dork sometimes. I told him not to stand when the teacups were moving but he did anyway." She smiles. Very cute. "To San Francisco just to see basketball, huh? You must be insane about it."

"I am." He decides to take a chance. "Listen, you want to get some lunch with me and a friend?"

"Sure."

"Where do you want to graze? Just kidding, just kidding."

"C'mon, c'mon: So you like this girl?" Tony keeps asking him that night. Paul's trying to watch Stupid Pet Tricks on David Letterman. It's the first time he hasn't felt vaguely nervous, on edge, all day, and he'd like to tell Tony to be quiet: He just wants to relax and watch this. A parrot is whistling a couple of pop tunes. Once he thought of trying to get Bones on Stupid Pet Tricks, but gave up on the idea when another dog suddenly appeared on the show doing Bones's trick — opening a refrigerator door with his nose and bringing his master a beer. Might not have made any difference anyway: Bones is probably getting a little too old to do any tricks. His dog is asleep in the corner now. Wiped out, on its last legs. What will he do when Bones goes? Who will he watch TV with? What would he have done at home all these years without Bones for a companion? It depresses him to think about it. Tony won't shut up. "C'mon, *dude,* so you like her or *what?* C'mon, you're hot for her, I know it. You really like her, huh?"

He knows he has no choice. He gives in. "Yeah, I guess. I mean, she doesn't have a great body, but I think she has, you know, a nice face and I like her personality a lot. She's not one of those Tens that you go out with, dude, but she's real cool." He looks at Tony, who is filing his fingernails. Does he wear a condom? Does his partner? Who does it to whom?

"Well, I'm glad you met her," Tony says. "You sound happy about it, man."

"Well, it's not like we've gone out, but we'll see. I just have to work up the balls to ask her. She may have a boyfriend. That's a problem. It's not like your problem where you get to choose between four or five babes."

"God, I don't know about that."

"Who do you like the best?"

"I like all of them," he mumbles, turning the television louder.

"Really?"

"Yeah. Let's watch the show."

Paul watches Tony settle back into his chair, fingernail file working away, his mouth small, in the same way it would get when he was six years old and intently digging a little hole in one of their gardens with a toy shovel.

"Is this girl just a little overweight?" Tony asks.

"Why?"

"Randy met her, right?"

"Yeah."

"Oh."

"Oh, *what?*"

"Take it easy," Tony says, going back to his nails. "I'm just raggin' you."

No way I can ask her to a Beverly dance, Paul thinks. He looks over at Tony, who is scraping dirt out from beneath a nail. *Faggot,* he wants to scream.

———

Hillary must deal with her own fury, that week. Jeremy has made a confession: During late January, he saw two old flames while he was in New York on a photography assignment.

Yes, he slept with the women, he told Hillary a couple of nights ago.

No, he did not love either of them.

She felt nauseated. Then, perhaps because the nausea called to mind how she had been dumped by Dan in her junior year, a new fear gripped her. "Do you want to sleep with them again?" she asked.

No, he did not want to sleep with them again.

"Why did you go to bed with them?" she asked.

He shrugged. "At the moment, it was exciting, I can't explain it."

He breathed deeply. These admissions seemed to liberate him. Yes, he had slept with "a few, but only a few" teenage models before Hillary. Yes, there had been a "share" of one-night stands. No, he had not preferred specific physical types, having liked all types, just so long as they were pretty. A couple of them had even been guys, he said then.

She fled after that, certain that she would vomit in her car, but she didn't, and when she got home she found four messages on her machine from Jeremy. She called back immediately.

No, he had not slept with dozens of guys, he said.

Yes, his bisexuality had just been a "phase."

No, he didn't think he had had more than five or six male partners.

Yes, he still loved her, loved her more now than ever.

"Why did you tell me any of this?" she shrieked. "Why? Do you want to ruin my life? Why?"

"I was just feeling too guilty," he said. "I didn't even think I could be with you. Didn't you think it was weird that we hadn't made love since I got back?"

In fact, she hadn't. It had been only a week since he returned from New York. "I didn't really notice," she said.

"I couldn't sleep, let alone make love. I had to say something."

"Your idea of honesty sucks, Jeremy. What you've done and the way you've told me is just what I'd expect from some redneck hick. Fuck you."

"I'm sorry. *Please* don't give up." He sounded panicked.

She hung up, saying that they would talk in a couple of days when she felt calmer.

The thought of his infidelity continues to anger her, but it has nothing to do with her worries. How often has he been sleeping around? How many partners has he had? Could he have slept with someone who contracted AIDS?

It worries nearly all of them to some degree, this thought of being exposed to *something* by an infected sexual partner, and so their own thoughts about going to bed at a date's end have changed markedly. They feel reasonably certain that their peers at Beverly are "clean," uninfected, believe that a casual encounter there carries little or no possibility of danger. But the prospect of sex at private and public universities with new classmates concerns them. They worry who among the universities' most attractive will be closet gays or bisexuals, who will have slept around indiscriminately and become unwittingly exposed to the unthinkable. Kelly wonders occasionally whether any of her liaisons from her Sunset Strip days have left her marred. Melinda, with characteristic good sense, says she'll get to know college guys as good friends, becoming privy to all their secrets and desires, before going to bed with any of them. Hillary moves about in numb trepidation. "I just can't talk to you right now," she says to Jeremy's phone machine a couple of days after his confession, and takes her phone off the hook.

To make matters worse, her mother and Harry have had a fight. Harry stormed out of the house to play golf. When he comes home late that afternoon, her mother is the model of contrition, and Harry takes her in his arms, giving her a long kiss and a pat on the fanny. Her mom looks beatific, back in the graces of her rich doctor, head pressed against his chest, closing her eyes, the storm over. She kisses him again and again. "I was just being silly," she says.

"Ah, we all get silly," he says, patting her on the back of the head.

Hillary angrily goes out to the backyard to lie on the hammock her father hung there when she was a second-grader. From the house, she can still hear the sounds of wet kisses, her mom lapping at her new master's face. *Disgusting.* How does her mom get in these positions — just throwing away her self-respect like that? As if she were praying for a man, any benevolent man lenient enough to overlook her shortcomings and admit her to his kingdom. "I was just being silly," she hears the older woman repeating.

How long have women been murmuring such things to men in kitchens? Hillary wonders. It's so fucked, the deal females get — having to kiss men's asses all their lives, in kitchens, offices, and bedrooms. She's vowed to make it, *big*; doesn't know exactly how yet — whether in modeling, Hollywood, or business — but somehow she'll get the bucks to protect herself against becoming some guy's plaything. She'll do it alone. The idea of becoming involved one day in a women's rights organization sounds like too much work, not to mention that it'd probably be boring, and she's always looking for a little fun. Neither she nor any of her friends has ever paid any real attention to the women's movement. Asked what she thinks women must change most about their lives, she stares vacantly, as if being quizzed on current events, and finally guesses, "Equal

Rights Amendment?" She has never heard of Gloria Steinem. She has heard of Geraldine Ferraro, though she has a considerably easier time recalling that the woman did a Pepsi Light commercial than that she ran for vice-president. "The smart thing is to make money and make your own life whatever way you want it to be," she says. "Politics won't do it. After I have a lot of money, I'll be able to tell anybody who's an asshole that he's gone. That will be my solution."

Kelly and Melinda share such a philosophy. Melinda frankly professes a willingness to do nearly anything on the way up the corporate ladder, believing that when she hits the top, she'll be able to reshape anything undesirable. Kelly says, "I'll make sure that I have enough money when I live with a man so that I'm free to walk away."

Hillary has "an even better idea," she insists. "If I get married, I think I'd maybe want to do it with a man a little less successful than me, so that he'd have to be afraid of me walking out on him. I don't mean for it to sound cruel, but you need something to protect yourself."

For the moment, protecting herself means altering her relationship with Jeremy. She sees him that Friday at his apartment, tells him that, though she loves him, she feels too scared to sleep with him, that sex between them is over. He nods, apparently understanding, and then suddenly begins to cry. She rocks him.

"Oh, it's going to be all right," she says.

After fifteen minutes, he finally speaks: "What does all this mean exactly?"

"It means we can't be like boyfriend-girlfriend. I can't deal with that now."

He breaks down again. At some point, he finds his composure. They spend the next two hours talking, Jeremy telling her about his two former flames, Hillary revealing stories about the boy from junior year. Jeremy moves to touch her. She brushes his hand away. At the door, she tells him their adjustment will not come easily, but that, over the next few weeks, they'll become good friends. He shakes his head. "Trust me," she says.

———

Kelly has gone a second time to Westwood with Kurt, her sophomore crush, this time getting what she missed, a chance to fool around with him, making out with him so long in her car at a red light in Westwood that an amused motorist honks at them. "I was wearing these tight black jeans that I've had for a long time, *real* tight," Kelly says. "Black makes you look thinner and stuff, and I've been so weirded by my weight lately. The jeans were pretty uncomfortable, because they were scrunching all over whenever I turned, and he had kind of seen that and asked me if I was uncomfortable. I lied and said that they were new jeans. He asked me when we were in this coffee shop why I was wearing them if they were uncomfortable. Maybe he knew, maybe he didn't know, but I just told him I didn't feel real confident about the way my butt looked. He was real sweet. He just smiled and said, 'I like the way you look.' Then I said something like, 'I know I don't have as good a body as some girls do,' and he said, 'I think you're real pretty.' Then he told me he was really insecure about these zits he gets sometimes on his chin. We talked about a lot of things — like how we both like the beach but we're real bad at getting tan. We both like to water-ski and we talked about these places we went. I had fun. We talked for about three hours and then we went home."

They had sex that night and, though it was exciting, it matters not nearly so much to her as their talk in the coffee shop. They may or may not become boyfriend and girlfriend, may or may not date steadily, but they have seen each other twice since that night and will become nothing less than good friends, she thinks.

Being true friends matters to all of them, it seems. Despite the fact that she will no longer sleep with Jeremy, Hillary continues seeing him, going to movies and dinners, working with him on developing photographs, remaining close. Paul, who admits to feeling sex-starved and having serious doubts over whether he'll make it into bed with his new friend, Roxanne, nonetheless goes to workouts and lunches with her, happy to listen to her gibes, satisfied with having a funny pal who likes his jokes and can sympathize with what he is doing to lose weight.

Steven and Laura, since talking the morning of Steven's English final, have been hanging out together more, sharing secrets revolving largely around the pleasures and concerns of their respective romances. They confess to reservations in these relationships, but admit, only slightly sheepishly, to enjoying the sex. Steven and Laura's friendship is unique, even among their peers, in that they've been buddies for years — "*Tight buds*," Steven says — and can talk about anything. Steven first heard of a clitoris during freshman year from Laura. He had asked about what made a girl excited and, at some point, she told him about the clitoris. He laughed. She laughed. These days, he's been telling her that he wishes he and Vickie had a little bit more in common. Laura tells him that she wishes Aaron would relax. Sometimes, at Vickie's, while she is lounging in her pool, Steven will call Laura just to say hi. He finds himself thinking about her a lot lately.

February 28. The school's spring concert, featuring a new wave group called the Untouchables, kicks off in the Swim-Gym. Paul has come alone. He starts to sneak out of the dance early. Tony sees him, asks where he is going. "I have to pick up my old man at the airport," he lies. "He just got in from Milan."

"Well, we're all going to be supremely bummed," says Tony. "Adam is coming over later with some party shit. There's a party on Mulholland somewhere. Sure you can't come later?"

Paul can see them whipping around Mulholland, breaking car windows and carving FFF over an assortment of Mercedes and Porsches. He throws up his hands. "You know my old man: He'll want to know everything that's been happening, and have me sit around with him. It takes fucking forever."

"Okay."

"*Later.*" He watches Tony, whose date is waiting for him across the Swim-Gym. Tony is wandering, heading for the gym's corner to talk to the skinny blond boy whose fey laugh Paul can make out from here. The kid has grown himself the faintest of wispy mustaches. In the distant corner Tony shuffles his feet and stares at the gym floor. *He is not your brother,* Paul tells himself. *This is not your business.* He turns and walks out of the gym, headed for the Sports Connection to meet Roxanne.

Neither Andy nor Hillary goes to the dance. Andy has band practice. Hillary has finally agreed to go to dinner with her mom and Harry. Over dinner, her mom turns to her and says, "Harry and I have been giving some thought to some things, Hillary. We just want you to know that, if we decide on anything, you'll be the first to know."

"We both love you," says Harry, smiling and putting artichokes on her plate.

"Eat your dinner, dear," her mom says. "Model or no model, you need to eat."

"Don't lecture the girl, Marilyn," says Harry.

Her mom clears her throat, looks down.

Hillary excuses herself before dessert, making up a story that she has a date with Jeremy.

Outside the restaurant, she calls him. "I just need to get away so bad. My mom has gone fucking crazy."

———

Steven sits at home. Vickie cannot go to the dance, having come down with what she's told her mom is the intestinal flu, throwing up every hour, calling Steven every fifteen minutes, it seems, to tell him she'd like to die. Might be morning sickness, she cries. The phone rings again. Why won't she leave him alone? He doesn't answer it. A couple of times he's felt like getting in the car and driving someplace where they'd never be able to find him. The ringing stops. It's been *ten days* now. She's pregnant, she must be pregnant. What the hell will he tell his father? Can he tell his father? Probably a bad move. He'll be alone on this one. Jesus, how do you go about getting a doctor? The phone rings again. Five rings, ten rings, fifteen rings. She is going to let it ring all night. There's no escape. He finally picks up the phone and babbles that he just stepped out of the shower. She isn't listening. "God, I feel so drained," she says. "I feel like I'm going to die. But it's happened at least. We know now."

He'll have to get some money together, he tells himself.

"Well, I thought you'd at least *say* something," she moans.

"I'm sorry. I'm thinking so many things, I guess. If you're pregnant, we'll just have to deal with it."

"Didn't you listen to what I said? It's *happened,* I said. I've got my cramps. God, I really feel like I'm gonna die."

He's off the hook.

MARCH

One of the reasons that Andy dislikes band practice is that Jason's garage always reeks of Black Flag bug spray. Jason's father gets paranoid about mosquitoes and roaches, and so a box of spray cans always stands in the corner, on ready-alert. He sprays every weekend. You can't go into the garage without seeing a bunch of bugs, flat on their backs, legs up, like they were taking a nap or something. And the stench is awful. If not for that, Andy thinks, it would be a fairly decent place to practice, since neither of Jason's parents complains too often about the volume of the music or the harsh sounds that come out of the band's new synthesizer. In the beginning, everybody thought getting the synthesizer would improve their music tenfold and land them plenty of gigs on the party circuit, but they're all discovering that, unless a band has someone who can master the machine's array of bizarre sounds, it merely sounds amateurish, like something in a cheap wedding quartet. They all take turns fiddling with the synthesizer during breaks, but leave it alone when it actually comes to rehearsing a number. They'll practice a song for forty-five minutes or so, until someone says he needs a break. Whether they've mastered a song or not then, they move on to a new number so that no one gets too bored. They're not very good, Andy realizes. They're not going to get many party dates and, perhaps, not any. He doesn't care. It's worth it, knowing he has something to do two or three times a week.

His weekday schedule has returned to what it was before he had to study for finals and write his college applications. He studies for a half-hour, then, if not scheduled for a volunteer shift at the hospital, he'll see some Beverly friends or go to Jason's for practice. Once in a while, they don't get around to practicing. Sometimes, Jason wants to drive over to Baskin-Robbins or smoke a joint. Today, he wants to set off a couple of M-80s that he has in a toolbox, but Andy says he doesn't want to waste his time and that he'll leave if Jason takes out the fireworks. "Check this out," Jason says anyway, showing everybody a firecracker, lighting it, and firing it at a cat across the street. The cat streaks away. The firecracker goes off, and his mother opens a blind to look at them. Jason laughs, waves to her, and hides a second firecracker behind an amplifier. He's wearing a California Angels baseball cap, a cut-off T-shirt, and navy blue shorts with oil stains. "We're starting off with 'I Like That Old Time Rock 'n' Roll,' " he announces to the group. Gary, his nine-year-old brother, nods from behind the keyboard, chewing on a piece of root beer licorice and spitting juice in the direction of the Black Flag cases. The regular keyboardist had to work overtime at his grill job at a burger stand, so little Gary, who has taken piano lessons for two years, tries to fill in. "Gary, you just do your best," Jason says.

"I'm right there," says Gary, spitting again.

Jason sings lead vocals, doing his best to sound like Bob Seger, and he doesn't sound half-bad, except that "Old Time Rock 'n' Roll" is meant to be played on a piano and Gary can't play the keyboard worth a damn anyway. After twenty minutes, Andy can feel them all winding down, ready to quit.

"Did Jason show you the rat we captured?" little Gary asks him. Andy shakes his head, trying to ignore the kid and practice the rhythm to a David Bowie tune.

"Show them," Gary says to Jason.

In a second, their instruments are leaning forgotten against amplifiers and Gary has pulled out an old rug stored against a garage wall. A cage is behind the rug, with a rat inside. The rat has a tiny cardboard sign around its neck, tied there with a leather string. The sign looks like a miniature sandwich board. "Rat for Hire," it says. Discolored and mildewy, the sign has been on the rat for a while. Little Gary is taking a can out of one of the Black Flag cases.

"We cornered it in here last week," says Jason. "I stuck out this broom handle and he bit it, and I tossed him in the cage."

"Tell 'em what else," says Gary.

"I gave him a 'shroom and he got real dizzy. He was just stumbling around and bumping into the cage and shit. That's when we put the sign on him."

"*Ready?*" squeals Gary.

"Okay, but not too much," orders Jason.

Gary walks over and sprays the Black Flag into the cage.

"A little more," says Jason.

Andy doesn't feel like watching. You never could be sure about people: They might seem perfectly together, then one day they acted totally bizarre, demented, until you doubted whether you'd ever really known them in the first place. Shit, it's not like he himself isn't a total screw-up, like he doesn't have some radical problems of his own, but at least he hasn't sunk to torturing poor dumb rats behind bars. Jesus, you had to be bored shitless to get into this. Jason pokes the rat with the neck of a guitar to get it into position. Andy looks away. At least, at home, he has his video games and his grass for amusement. Gary gives the rat a second, third, fourth blast. Little clouds of spray form inside the cage. The dazed rat scrambles backward a couple of inches and leans against the cage's rear bars, burrowing his head in some crackers.

"We call it Rat for Hire because he puts on an act," Gary tells everyone. "An *act*, right, Jason?"

The rat's head has come out from under the crackers. It looks around, sniffs the rear bars of the cage, walks into them, bounces off, wheels around, and falls on its face.

Everyone laughs except little Gary.

"It wasn't supposed to fall then," says Gary, rapping the rat cage. "It's supposed to walk all around and bounce off the walls and *then* fall flat. This rat is *dumb*."

"Well, you sprayed too much on him again, pea-brain," says Jason. "You gotta do it slower." The rat tries to rise, takes another step, then falls like a tree.

"Timber," says the bass guitarist.

"Give him one more *short* spray," Jason tells his brother.

Gary gives him two.

The rat, semiconscious, begins biting at the air in a slow-motion stupor. Its mouth won't close. Gary is laughing so hard that spit comes out of his mouth.

"Well, that's Rat for Hire," says Jason. "Show's over. Don't tell my mom." Band practice is finished. Everyone leaves, except Andy, who goes inside the house with Jason and little Gary to have a Coke. Gary rushes into the kitchen to get the drinks. Jason stays by the back door.

"I don't want to go in there," he says. "My mom has her bridge group over, and they always stop you and ask you what you're doing, where you're going to college and all that shit."

"Where *are* you going?"

"Maybe UCLA," he says. "But if I get accepted and go there, my parents say I have to live at home. They say they couldn't afford to pay for the dorms or an apartment. My dad always gets worried about layoffs at his plant. Aerospace is real weird."

Jason's dad has a job making something on the wings of jets. What Andy best remembers about the job description is that the guy has to punch a time clock every day. Andy doesn't know anyone else whose father punches a time clock, but then he doesn't have many friends outside Beverly Hills either. Everyone in the group, except him, goes to Uni High and comes from, at most, a middle-class home where they'll be living throughout college unless scholarships miraculously arrive. He feels a little guilty, thinking about it, but not much. Shit, he's earned his life, he figures. He's put up with the Beverly bullshit for four years. Jason and his friends have been able to fuck around, set off M-80s, play with rats.

The boys trudge up the stairs to Jason's bedroom, dimly lit by some green neon lights. Jason has a poster of Christie Brinkley over his bed, except that he's cut off her head and pasted it on a poster of King Kong, right over where Kong's head should be. All of Jason's posters have been mutilated. Ozzie Osbourne's face has been glued on Ronald Reagan's body, Bruce Springsteen's on Gary Coleman's, and Barry Manilow's on Stevie Nicks's. He has put a photo of his girlfriend's head over Christie Brinkley's body but it looks totally fake, Andy thinks, because Jason's girlfriend has a thin, almost emaciated face and you can just tell it doesn't go on that killer body. How much time does Jason spend putting this shit together? He can't blame Jason, feels sympathetic actually. Boredom reeks here. What else is there for the guy to do? A framed cover from *Soldier of Fortune* magazine rests next to a Bruce Lee poster. From the ceiling hangs part of a ripped parachute that Jason says he found in the Saugus hills somewhere. Over the chute, he has painted in blue, "This parachute did not open," and, at its bottom, "Gone to Zeppelin Madness." There are cigarette holes in the chute, and, beneath one of them, someone has scrawled, "Do not toke." Andy sees pieces of driftwood and a broken surfboard attached to the underside of the parachute, making it look like an art piece. It's the first thing he really likes about the place. "That's very cool," he says, gesturing at the chute collage. Little Gary trips and spills his Coke all over the floor.

"Go get a paper towel from the kitchen and clean it up, peabrain," Jason commands. "And bring us more drinks while you're down there."

Gary opens the door and runs out of the room. Jason is taking a padlock off a little refrigerator sitting in a darkened corner of the room. "Want some ravioli?" he asks. Andy shakes his head. Jason takes a can of ravioli from the refrigerator and puts it on a hot plate, then reaches back into the refrigerator, pulls out a slice of ham, and pops it into his mouth. He bought the refrigerator for thirty-five dollars and stocks it with bread, luncheon meat, Spaghetti-O's, cans of ravioli, and cinnamon Pop-Ups. His ravioli heated, he takes it off the hot plate and, standing up, eats it right out of the can with a plastic spoon.

It is all kind of bizarre, thinks Andy, but he loves the idea of a guy his own age having a room that he can do absolutely anything in, that no one can make over, not a housekeeper or parent or interior designer. His own bedroom, even with all of its state-of-the-art stereo equipment and track lighting, is boring by comparison. It doesn't look like anyone even lives in it. "Where's my brother and those drinks?" Jason asks. "Hey, shout down to him and tell him to get his ass up here, will you?"

"*Gary, get yourself up here so that we can party,*" Andy screams down the stairs.

They cannot party for long. The bridge group breaks up in an hour, and Jason's mother shouts upstairs that she wants the garage swept and sprayed. Jason and little Gary trudge outside with brooms and Black Flag. Andy goes to McDonald's alone for dinner. His mother is out, having signed up for a Szechwan cooking class somewhere. She has never been crazy about Szechwan but the French course was filled when she got there. Two weeks into it, the Szechwan class has gone better than she expected. She thinks she might be able to make the sprout dish, and though she doesn't like those tiny vegetables any more now than when she began the course, she has met a set of funny, eclectic explorers like her former self, that is to say in the days before she lost a husband, gained twenty-five pounds, and got heavily into Valium and "Days of Our Lives." Next to her in the class, on one side, sits a friendly widower, roughly fifty-five, who wants to take her on an ocean swim; and, on the other side, a blonde Austrian woman, fiftyish with four grandchildren already, who is the tour director of a travel agency. After class at the end of the first week, Andy's mother went with her two new classmates for cappucino. When she arrived home that afternoon, she did not turn on "Days of Our Lives" but went straight to her ex-husband's old office and made lists of everything that she would need if she were ever to do Szechwan for a party. The next day, Andy heard her laughing on the phone. You could hear the laughter, a long trail of giggles, from as far away as his bedroom. Now she has left a message for him on their machine to come down to her class if he wants to try one of the dishes. "I love you," she says at the end. "And help yourself to the fortune cookies in the glass jar."

Fortunes change. His father calls him the next day to say that his uncle has made inroads on getting an admission's staff officer at a private Eastern college to give him serious consideration.

"Terrific," says Andy.

"Have you heard anything yet?"

"No. It's still too early yet, Dad. But all these guys at these private school interviews say my chances are better because a lot of people who they accept decide not to go there. Just like Uncle Phil says."

"That's good." His father's voice sounds flat.

"Do you have a cold, Dad?"

"No."

"I think I got one. I'm taking six vitamin C's a day."

"Good for you."

"How's Stacey?"

"I don't know."

"You're not seeing her anymore?"

"She's not seeing me anymore, okay? Don't you worry about it, though. Hey, did you get the tickets in the mail for that concert yet?"

A friend of his father, a record company executive, has gotten him two seats to a John Cougar Mellencamp concert along with passes to go backstage after the show.

Which reminds him: He needs a date for the concert. After he gets off the phone with his father, he calls a girl named Sandra whom he met at a teen club and had dessert with at a coffee shop. That was two or three months ago. He hasn't seen or talked to her since, has only a phone number, written on a pack of Nutra-Sweet. When the girl answers, she doesn't remember him.

"I met you at that club a few months ago," he reminds her, "and we were both alone and you came with me for pie and um . . ."

"Yeah, I remember. You said you were really into Annie Lennox, right?"

Did he? Annie Lennox of the Eurythmics? Maybe. He could have been trying to sound like a rock sophisticate. Then again maybe this girl goes to coffee shops with a lot of guys. "Right," he answers. "But I'm not into her anymore, I'm into something else."

"I kinda thought you might call. But it was so long ago, and then I forgot about it."

"I was calling to see whether or not you might want to see a John Cougar concert with me?"

She says, "Sure," then asks him what his last name is.

On the night of the concert, he picks her up in his new BMW. The evening goes well. Sandra likes the show and the chance to stare at members of the band backstage. "You must know a lot of important people to get tickets like that," she says on the way home.

"My father does actually, not me really," he admits.

"Did he give you this car?"

"Yes."

"You sound like it bothers you."

"No. I'm glad he could. I like it. I just don't like it when they hold it over me, like, 'Look at all we give you and you screw up and then we have to make things right.' "

"They do that?"

"Sometimes. Not a lot anymore. But enough that it bothers me still."

"Me, too. But not as much probably as you, because we're not rich. We have a pretty good family. I like my parents."

"You're lucky."

"You don't like yours?"

"No, I think they're okay. Usually I like my mom better than my dad, but that's just because he's been such a shit to her. And sometimes he acts like I'm kind of a dumbshit. I like them both when I don't have to think about it too much. I know that I could have had it harder. I know a lot of kids who do."

"Me, too."

"Want to go dancing for a while?"

"Okay."

They dance for an hour at a club, then go to a coffee shop for cheesecake. They talk for an hour about their families and college plans. She wants to be an archaeologist if she can afford the tuition through graduate school. "I'm really into ancient civilizations and dinosaurs," she says. He says he'll need some luck to make anything of himself. He thinks of something. Maybe, he says, they can go to the La Brea Tar Pits sometime and she can explain all the different dinosaurs and stuff under the tar. She says that sounds like fun. They talk about sex, and how neither of them likes the idea of sleeping with people immediately just because they look hot. She confides that she heard about a ninth-grader who hated oral sex but did it anyway to keep her tenth-grade boyfriend. He says oral sex sounds weird to him, but not half as weird as sleeping with someone on a waterbed. She laughs. "What do you have against water?" she asks. It is a first date, in March 1986.

———

At home, Hillary's mother cooks a roast in the microwave for Harry.

"Mom, are you thinking of making permanent plans with Harry?" Hillary asks her.

"Sweetheart, you know that we're both giving it some thought. Nothing has been decided."

"But do you *hope?*" Hillary whines.

Her mother shrugs and says, "We just want the best for all of us."

"But you can tell me what you're *thinking*, Mom. You don't have to bullshit me."

"I don't know and don't talk like that. We love each other: Does that help you understand? No, he hasn't asked me exactly."

Hillary feels her heartbeat slowing. She won't have to get accustomed to Java man as a stepfather just yet. "We'll just have to see what happens," her mom says, turning off the microwave for a moment. She dips a couple of her fingers into the roast's juices, tastes them with concern, then turns the microwave back on. "Very good, this roast. He's going to like it. You know, sweetheart, I think you should consider the fact that you're going off to college somewhere next year, and chances are that you won't be living at home much again. It's only going to be me here then. Having a man as wonderful as Harry here whom I could care about and love would be a very comforting and nice thing."

"You mean you'd be afraid of being lonely?"

"Not afraid. It's just not a good feeling."

"I guess not."

"Then start being less antagonistic about Harry."

"I'm not. I don't mean to be. It's just because he's in this house, a new person, it's weird."

"Try to be nicer. He may be in your life for a long time to come. I hope he likes this roast. God, I hope I didn't bungle the spices. It's funny how he gets so annoyed about his meat. I can only hope, huh?"

"Just don't be a *desperado*, Mom."

———

Paul's mother has told him that you feel good when you're doing things for others, that being the reason why she has plunged into heart funds and auxiliary balls and charity food baskets for the poor, but whenever he helps her with the baskets, he merely feels tired. The hardest thing about life, he thinks, is that not even in its best moments does it live up to your expectations. You buy front-row tickets for Springsteen, thinking that it will be one of the magical moments of your life, Bruce thirty feet away, you and your friends riding high on three hours of music so loud that you feel the vibrations of amplification in your seat, only, when it comes, there is an annoying feedback that makes some of the music sound distorted, and a concert in front of ninety thousand people isn't exactly an intimate club date anyway, even with front-row seats. A couple of your friends lose enough interest that they sneak out before intermission to get hot dogs. Even in the hottest moments something is usually missing and that old restlessness creeps up in you again to step over the line, get a little crazy. Dealing a little coke could be exciting. That might get rid of some of the restlessness.

"Just give me a little, I can sell it, don't be a tight-ass," he pleads to a distracted Adam, who sits in the bedroom of his Valley home, hunched over a computer, trying to figure his cost and price projections for April and May. Paul taps his shoulder. "You think I can't sell it, Adam?"

Adam slaps the side of the computer. "Hey, you *mind?* I'm concentrating here. Don't be a dickface. I'm going to screw up if you keep talking. Go into the refrigerator and bring us a couple of brews. See if Tony and Randy want anything."

He walks out of the bedroom, turns down a hallway, and finds himself in a tiny kitchen with faded beige wallpaper yellowed by years of cigarette smoke baked in by hot sunlight. Get too close to the walls and you get a whiff of a twenty-year stench. The kitchen has no microwave, computer-programmed stove, dishwasher, or automatic ice-maker. Paul wonders how Adam's mother can stand it. He sees Tony and Randy playing a video game on the television that sits in the corner of the cramped dining area just off the kitchen. He can't get over how depressing the room looks. Old *Times* and *Newsweeks* lie in crooked piles underneath the television, which stands on plastic wheels gouging permanent holes in the cheap green carpet. The carpet smells like wet dog hair, like Bones. Tony's father and Adam's father may be brothers, but that's about as far as the link goes. Adam's father, a pest controller, has to nickel and dime housewives for an extra ten or twenty bucks on a job, couldn't be making more than thirty or thirty-five grand a year. Still, Adam and Tony usually get along fine, the two cousins quietly aware that their places in life won't necessarily be the same as their fathers'; Adam, in particular, scamming every second in order to make certain this won't be the case. Paul opens the refrigerator and sees Budweisers and Bud Lights, but no Michelobs or Heinekens. The Valley. It figures. "Hey," he shouts at Tony and Randy, "you guys want something to drink?"

"Yeah," says Randy. "Why don't you put on a tape for us? Maybe you could make us a sandwich."

"I'm not your Mexican," Paul says, grabbing beers and taking three small steps from the kitchen to the television. He drops the Buds on their laps.

"Hey, Pablo, you forgot our glasses and the cheese spread," says Randy.

"Play the fucking game," Tony says.

"And clip the azaleas while you're at it."

"Play the fucking game."

"Where's that beer?" Adam shouts from his bedroom. Paul can't take his eyes off the carpet holes under the TV wheels. On top of the tube rests a big red plastic bowl and a popcorn maker with grease stains on the handles. He walks into the bedroom and tosses Adam a Bud. The computer's printer buzzes and spews out paper. "You'll let me have a little to sell, right?"

"It isn't that easy, dude," Adam says.

Paul wonders whether Adam isn't just a little worried about a rich Beverly Hills kid being cut into the operation and possibly taking it over. "*Lookit,*" he says, fumbling for words that will reassure Adam, "I'll be working for you and I'll sell whatever amount you want to give me."

"Forget it. I don't want to talk about it. I'll think about it. But drop it for now. Let's get out of here. Maybe we can go to Tony's and swim or something. Shit, I hate hanging here."

Swimming sounds like a good idea to everyone. They cruise over the hill to Tony's, where Tony's friend, the blond boy, is waiting by the door, talking to his mother. Paul thinks that Tony looks stunned for a second, though his friend quickly strolls up his driveway casually mumbling, "What's happening, David?" in the direction of the blond boy.

"David says that the two of you were supposed to see some exhibition at the observatory," his mother tells him.

Tony slaps his hand against his forehead theatrically. "Shit, I forgot. Goddammit, David, I'm sorry, man. I just completely forgot all about it."

"That's all right. No problem."

"Want to go swimming with us?"

The blond boy shakes his head, mumbles something about having to get to his job at a movie theater soon. Tony says he'll walk with him to his car. Adam and Randy pay no attention, already walking into the house and asking Tony's dad where they can change to go swimming. Paul lingers on the porch, small-talking with Tony's mom, keeping an eye fixed on the pair standing at the curb now, hands deep in pockets and heads down, hunched spies talking in soft voices that are meant not to carry. Tony straightens then, nods, says in a suddenly louder and jocular tone, "All right, later on, David." The blond boy nods slowly, gets in his Datsun, and roars off.

"That kid is pretty bizarre, I think," says Randy, who has come back onto the porch in his bathing suit.

Tony says, "He's okay."

"Tony, how could you forget about going to the observatory with someone, dear?" his mother asks.

Tony frowns. "I don't know. It's nothing. Let's not make a big deal about it, okay? I want to swim. I don't know, Mom. I just forgot. Okay?"

"Yeah, let's swim," says Paul.

"I'd kind of like a cold drink, if that's okay," says Randy.

"Sounds good," says Tony.

His mother stares at him. "Well, that doesn't make sense to me, Tony."

"Forget it, Mom."

"Something very strange has been going on for some time with that boy and you," says his dad. "We want you to tell us . . ."

"Leave me alone."

"Why was David so upset?" his mother persists. "He looked very upset to me."

"Mom, I'm going swimming."

"Tony, *what is going on?*"

Paul sees his friend's lip trembling. Do his parents know? "Just drop it, Mom," Tony mumbles.

Paul feels a chill, turns around so that he can look through the open front door of the house, through the big bay windows of the living room, out onto the pool's blue water, sighing then to feign boredom, closing his eyes, concentrating on a tinge of chlorine in the air. *Not here*, he is thinking. *Not here. Let Tony walk away* . . . Maybe his concern is as much for himself and the rest of this foursome as Tony; he doesn't think their friendships could survive the truth. Already, the other two boys sense something is very wrong, watching the fear that has gripped their leader, who has turned around to look out onto the pool, frozen, red-

faced. Tony's panicking: Paul can hear it in the tremors seeping through his pursed lips.

"If you want to talk alone, Tony, I'm sure everyone will excuse us," says his father.

Tony chokes on his first word, barely able to get it out: "*Asshole.*" He swallows, eyes misting. "He's an asshole. He's pissed off that I haven't paid him for some grass that I got from him in *junior* year. Real *early* in junior year."

A lie.

It works. Parents always buy a story with a confession. "*You bought pot?*" his father demands.

"A little, yes. A *long* time ago."

"I'll want to talk to you as soon as your friends leave, of course."

"Yes."

"*You realize this is a crime?*" his mother shouts.

"Was the guy going to narc to your parents if you didn't pay?" Randy whispers to him by the pool after his parents have gone. Tony shakes his head. Says he doesn't want to talk about it, except that David is an all right dude and that they both fucked up. Paul, sitting in the shallow end of the pool, can't help but smirk over this choice of words, knowing that this certainly means the end of David. Tony must have known as much when talking to the kid by his car. The lie fit neatly into his plans: He made sure David would never be allowed to set foot on his property again. At the curb, he must have told the kid that their late-night forays had come to an end. What did they call their get-togethers? *Meetings, affairs, flings, fucks?* How do gays talk to each other? In public, around the straights, the language must be a sort of coded shorthand. "Catch you later": Hadn't that been what Tony said to the kid at a party when Paul had come too close? How did Tony give him the news at the curb? The blond kid looked stunned and angry, which would explain in part why he made the Datsun burn rubber as he took off. Why did Tony dump the kid? Do gays "dump" other gays, like guys and girls do? Did Tony only rid himself of the kid because he sensed his parents' suspicions? Has he taken up with someone else? Does he have many partners? He must. Nobody can go without sex for too long, Paul thinks, and so if the blond boy was out, someone else must be in. Bad choice of words, but there's a joke there that he must remember. How does Tony *do it* exactly? Who's in what position? Has he ever gone to gay bars in West Hollywood to be picked up? He remembers Tony's complaining once about how filthy

West Hollywood had become. He seemed to know too much about the place for a kid who said he only went by there once in a while to buy clothes. And then there had been the night when Tony called him, asking for a ride home because his car had supposedly broken down and he couldn't find his Auto Club card. When Paul arrived, Tony had been standing with some guy whom he introduced as a motorist who had been nice enough to help push his car to the side of the road. The helpful motorist did not seem to know, at that moment, where his own car was.

He finds himself staring at Tony's pallor more intently than ever, looking for signs of sickness and weight loss. The other day, a girl in his government class, talking about AIDS, said she thought the solution might be found in quarantining AIDS carriers. She added it would also be better for the rest of us just to cut off their "things." The Beverly Hills board of education, reacting to the growing concern, has called for the creation of a panel of medical experts to review the cases of any students who contract AIDS, and to recommend whether they should be barred from school. "We like to be prepared," said a school board member. "We see AIDS as a possibility. It could happen in Beverly Hills." Could there possibly be a worse time at Beverly for a gay to come out of the closet?

At the other end of the pool, Randy and Adam assure Tony that they can score him good sinsemilla whenever he wants it. "Can we just forget about it?" Tony asks. "Shit, all these hassles. I want to swim."

"Do you want to go over to my house later on and watch *The Deep?*" Randy asks. "My father has it on cassette. It's that movie with Jacqueline Bissett in the wet T-shirt. She is *so fine.*"

"Yeah, she's hot," says Tony. "I could get into that."

"I'm going to take off soon," Paul shouts from the shallow end.

"Bullshit," says Tony. "Hang around, have something to drink."

"Okay, but I can't stay long."

Tony swims over to him. Paul waits until he gets close before saying, "David seemed pretty mad driving away, huh?"

"Yeah. Let's forget about it."

"Okay, but some time, you know, you might not want to forget about it."

Randy and Adam, absorbed in a water fight, do not hear what Tony says next.

"What does that mean?"

"I don't know."

"No, *tell me.* You said it. What do you *mean?*"

"I just think you're secretive about all kinds of shit."

"Secretive about what kind of shit?"

"Like everything."

"What does that mean?"

Paul backs off. He feels the chill again. He doesn't want a confrontation here. "I don't know. Lighten up, Tony."

Tony stares at him a long time. "I'm gonna get myself a couple of beers. Just forget about all this shit, okay?"

"I've got to bail," he says. "Roxanne's waiting for me at the gym. Shit, I'm twenty minutes late. I gotta go right now."

Another lie, his own. He has absolutely nothing to do for the next three hours, except maybe to return the call of some soshe who asked if he wanted to come by her house tonight, with a bunch of other people, to watch the Academy Awards and do some partying. Her father and mother, she said, would be at the Awards with some of her dad's studio colleagues, and going off to some gala at a hotel afterwards. They wouldn't be coming home at all tonight. Her house would be free. Paul was interested, before she added that they could do nothing more than drink some of her father's liquor. No coke, grass, or mushrooms. She's afraid her father will notice drug residue on their rug. "He freaks when the house isn't immaculate," she said. "He might not bust us harshly for the toot if he caught us. But if there is even a *speck* on that rug, I'm dead. He loves that rug. It's like totally everything to him. But we'll do up some tasty shooters. C'mon, Paul, you like tequila."

He told her that he'd think about it and call her back, just to get her off the phone. What a lightweight. Maybe it's just as well the party's bogus and he isn't doing any blow tonight. He feels a little burnt. Besides, his parents want him around this evening. What's Roxanne doing?

Roxanne. Even her name sounds good these days. He calls her. Two hours later, they are doing their one hundred sit-ups, after having finished an hour's worth of aerobics. He feels himself tiring on the slant-board halfway through, but Roxanne drags him along by telling him how great he is doing, how much slimmer he looks. He has lost another ten pounds in a span of six weeks, though he wishes it would come off faster because he would like to look decent enough to ask some hot Beverly girl to the prom. Roxanne would not be decent prom material in the eyes of his soshe friends, especially Tony, and he doesn't want to be talked about as the guy who brought some Fairfax girl only because he couldn't get a decent-looking babe from his own school. Her body is looking a little better all the time, but he doesn't want to take any chances. He forces himself through the last of the sit-ups, and tells Roxanne that he has to go; that he'll call her later.

His father has asked a Texas attorney from Shell Oil over to their house for dinner. Paul has been ordered to be ready by six and dressed nicely. He smokes a joint in the garage before the guy arrives, feels so stoned that he goes into the bathroom to check for bloodshot eyes. This Colombian shit may be *too* good. Over dinner the Shell Oil guy talks about the elasticity of the stock market, which must mean something bad, given the way the guy tilts his head and grunts whenever he says it. "Oil prices are down, too, ma'am," he says to Paul's mom. "We're really feeling it in Dallas. Office buildings closing down, people worrying 'bout whether they'll be able to afford their suites at the Cowboy games. You know, my own boss down there has an expression: The Republic is only as strong as our big, bad Lone Star State. Texas and America go hand in hand, economically, that is. So you'll pardon my French, when I say that I'm worried that we won't have a pot to piss in if this oil problem keeps on much longer."

Paul laughs. "C'mon, you've never *really* pissed in a pot, have you?"

"*Paul*," his mother snaps, "my goodness where did you learn to talk that way? *Apologize.*"

"He was the one talking about pissing in a pot," Paul says.

"Ray was speaking *figuratively*," his father clarifies. His father won't be dishing out any of his 'sixties marmalade skies tonight, not with this pinstriped Gary Cooper doing his Up With America bit.

"It's just a saying," says his mother.

"You better hope, son, five years from now," says the Shell Oil guy, "that there are pots left for *anything*. You're part of the generation that will suffer most if oil prices cave in. Damn right I'm concerned about having a good pot."

"Glad to have a man who feels the same way about pot that I do," Paul says.

Father stares at son's poker face, fixes him with a baleful stare in an attempt to bring him back into line. "It's just a vexing problem," says the Shell Oil man. "Just the most vexing thing in the world, as *vexing* as that Iran-Iraq thing, which is plumb awful, since those clowns are sitting on all that oil. But, our prices at home, that's a real sorry state."

"You couldn't have said it better, Ray," says Paul's father. "The slumping oil prices have had an effect all across the nation, even at Paul's high school. Paul knows something about this, don't you, Paul?"

"We have some oil wells at school," Paul says to Shell Oil. "Big, big, big ones. *Plenty* of room to piss there. I mean, they're *verrrry* big, Ray. V*errrry big.*"

"They're not making any money, Paul, that's the point of the story that Ray wanted us to see," his father says.

"Yes, it's one of our *vexing* problems, Ray," Paul says, wrinkling his forehead for effect. "Ray, did you know that graduating high school students regard the oil crisis in the Middle East and nuclear war as the world's second and third most serious problems?"

"What is the first?"

"Jock itch."

"Paul, why don't you help me serve?" his mother asks, guiding him from the room. In the kitchen, she tells him to shut his mouth. "I have no clue what has gotten into you," she says. *"Jock itch*, my God."

"It's one of the few times that we're having dinner together," Paul points out, "and Dad and this guy are monopolizing the conversation with a lot of talk about oils and politics. It's so boring. I can't stand it."

"You don't have to stand it, just eat politely and when you're finished, you can ask to be excused."

During dessert, the topic turns to whether the CIA should be used to undermine unfriendly foreign governments. Paul thinks about Tony's lip quivering and how his parents bought the pot buy story hook, line, and sinker. Parents seldom have a clue what's going on. Gayness, now that is a *real* problem for a kid, he thinks, listening to the two adults yap about some pissant African regime they want to bring down. If you're Tony and you're gay in 1986, you're screwed. There are just too many straights out there who won't allow you to fit in, who will do everything in their power to *stop* you from fitting in. On this night, teenage gayness is on the top of his personal list of societal problems, followed by pressure to be happy and get thin. The CIA means diddly squat to him, and George Bush and the value of the dollar even less. Politics is crap. The world is out of control, and politics couldn't stop that. Somebody could do something for a gay kid though. Or maybe somebody could do something for some guy scared to death about getting into the right college, or a kid whacked out of his mind by too much pressure and coke. Where were his dad and the Shell Oil guy and Tony's parents when all that shit came along? Just before he excuses himself from the dinner table, his father and the Shell Oil guy look over at him in earnest and ask what concerns him the most. Half-surprised, Paul wonders. He smiles.

"Bad sushi."

"Why do you have so many problems with your dad?" Roxanne asks him late that night.

They're sitting on her living room couch, listening to his Plasmatics tape on her tiny stereo and watching a tape of "Dallas," with the sound off. "I'm not sure," he admits. "It's probably a lot of things. My attitude hasn't been too good about stuff. And I just don't get the feeling he listens. He's not around much. We're real different, too. I just don't know the stuff he knows, the stock market, all the stuff in the news, sports. It bores the shit out of me. He thinks I don't care about anything. So we can't talk about stuff, which doesn't leave much else."

"You two never just sit around together?"

The question sounds funny, makes him think of old black-and-white cable reruns of "Father Knows Best," where Robert Young, wearing a suit and a tie, sits in a living room with his son, Bud, talking about their days. Watching the show stoned, Paul always feels like he's getting something of a history lesson since his only other knowledge of the 'fifties comes from textbooks and old *Life* magazines that his mom keeps around. He likes to look at old pictures in *Life* before he goes to bed. Nearly every adult in the pictures has a suit on, and those who don't, wear white shirts and ties. Even gathered in front of those old-looking televisions with their friends, they keep their ties on. Very weird, especially the way everybody looks so lovey-dovey with each other, so enraptured with the idea of Closeness — Mom, Dad, and kids sprawled on floors, nuzzling each other, with not enough elbow room to click the remote control, even if they had had one back then, just lying around admiring the tube and their own good fortune, little Sis and Bro so close together that it looks perverted. Didn't they ever want their space? *Bizarre.* The last time he and his parents gathered in front of the television together was for his father's 1985 Super Bowl party. His mother had been entrusted with the chore of keeping everyone's drinks fresh. Paul parked cars through the middle of the second quarter.

"No, my father and I don't exactly sit around," he tells Roxanne. "Don't be offended, but that's kind of a dumb question for you to ask."

"A *dumb question?*" She looks hurt.

"Yeah. The only thing we can really talk about is basketball maybe, and he knows a lot more about it than me. So it doesn't last too long. I think whenever he asks me what I think of Magic Johnson or somebody, he's thinking to himself, 'I'm going to try to relate to this kid, open him up.' It kind of pisses me off when he hasn't bothered to ask what the hell I've been doing for a week and then he slaps me on the back and says, '*Hey, pal, what did you think of Kareem the other night?*' I just want to tell him to fuck off."

"You shouldn't feel that way," Roxanne tells him. "He's your father. And he's been nice to you. He's given you all of those Laker seats, right?"

"Yeah, but he does that so he doesn't have to do anything else. You don't know. *You* don't have to live with him."

"Maybe you don't make enough of an effort either. You probably don't tell him what you do at nights."

"*Oh, yeah. Right.* Uh-huh. Like I'm going to race over there right now and tell him that I love nothing more than doing a jumbo line. Oh, that's a very *live* idea, Roxanne."

"Well, I don't see how you can complain so much if you don't want him to know what's going on in *your* life."

The Plasmatics tape ends. With the musical buffer gone, he's suddenly aware how loud their voices have become. They have never before shouted at each other. "I don't need a lecture from you, Roxanne. I don't care anymore. Okay?" He pauses, takes a deep breath, sees J.R. on the soundless television jabbing a finger in some poor sucker's chest. You have to rely on yourself. Anybody worth a shit knows it. J.R. His father. The Shell Oil guy.

Roxanne rubs his arm. He takes a deep breath. "Do you have beer or wine?" he asks.

"We're out of beer. My father has a little brandy, I think. Maybe it's peach brandy. That's all we keep."

"Shit. That sounds awful. Well, if that's all you have."

"Why don't we just sit here for a minute and relax?"

He is too tired to protest. "Okay. I was talking pretty loud. I hope we didn't wake up your parents."

"We haven't. Don't worry. You seem so tense."

"Would you mind if I smoked a joint outside and then came back in?"

Her voice becomes softly adamant. "Just stay here. I'll relax you. Don't move."

"Okay."

"You do too many drugs."

"I know."

"You need to talk more."

"I know."

She bends down and gives him a kiss.

"I was hoping you would do that sometime," he says.

"Well, you don't have to worry now," she laughs. "I've done it for you. You can too, if you want."

He marvels over how much slimmer she looks these days. Is it his imagination? "I'm not myself enough," he says. "I'm kind of an asshole once in a while. I got to be more my own person. All that stuff."

"Me, too," she admits.

This shocks him. "You?"

"Yeah, we all have to deal with things."

They make out for a few minutes, grappling with each other, and then turn over the Plasmatics tape.

With a short vacation from school, he spends every evening over at her house for the next week. Tony calls Roxanne's house to tell him that he, Randy, Adam, and a couple of Beverly juniors are going down to Palm Springs, where college students traditionally congregate during Spring Break.

"I can't go," Paul says.

"Why?"

"I'm stuck here with my delivery job," he says.

"You're not pissed at me for anything are you?"

"No, why?"

"Because I shouted at you the other day."

"No. I forgot all about that."

"You sure?" Tony sounds doubtful.

"I'm not bullshitting you."

"You must be bummed you can't go somewhere."

"Fuck, yes." Actually, he's glad to be staying home, though if he admits this now, the shit will hit the fan, Tony assuming that he has unlocked his dark secret about the blond boy. In fact, Tony has nothing to do with it. He just feels himself having gone adrift, needs a little time anchored to Roxanne's place, any place, actually, where he can rest for a few days and think. He has felt so tired and nervous lately. He can use the week to get his strength back.

"Well, shit, I'm bummed you can't go, man," Tony says.

Paul can hear a whirring sound in the background. "What are you guys doing?"

"Strawberry margaritas for the ride down tomorrow."

"Watch your asses," Paul warns. "There'll be highway patrol all over the place."

"We'll save you a thermos," Tony promises.

He hangs up, and gets on the scale in Roxanne's bedroom. He has gained back two pounds. "I'm glad you didn't go," she says.

"Don't be my mommy, okay?" he moans.

"I'm not. I just don't want you to get hurt."

"Just don't hassle me."

"Let's go work out," she suggests.

The phone rings. It's Paul's mom. *"Come home,"* she says. *"I* think your first college acceptance has arrived. *Hurry."*

"Something's come from a college," he tells Roxanne, heading for the door. He drives home, takes a thin envelope from his mother, and opens it in the foyer. "We are sorry to inform you . . . ," it begins.

"Oh, I feel so bad for you, dear," his mom gasps, putting an arm around him. "I *so* sorry." She calls her husband, who is in New York, to give him the news.

Paul drinks three Miller Lites, alone, in his bedroom.

———

Although most of the college acceptances and rejections will not be sent out for another month yet, a trickle of the decision letters begins making its way into Beverly Hills. Andy receives rejections from Claremont College and the private school that he coveted in New Hampshire. Hillary, rejected from U.C. San Diego, learns that she has been wait-listed at a private school in Colorado. Steven has been accepted by U.C. Berkeley, and Kelly, who dreads confessing she will be attending Santa Monica City College, tells her friends she will probably be admitted by San Diego State. Melinda, despite her 3.9 g.p.a., receives rejections from Berkeley and Pomona College. Late in the week, however, she learns from her counselor, who has been tipped off by admissions officers, that she remains under serious consideration by at least one Ivy League school. That leaves nine schools to hear from. Her parents are in England, her father delivering some legal lectures, and, because she hates to be alone in her home with only the housekeeper, she has asked her good friend

Pam to stay with her. It is difficult to think of anything other than college acceptances any longer. High school seems ridiculous now. She can't get motivated to do any work, has fallen behind in English, where she has yet to read *Catch-22*, one of the term's big assignments. "I don't think I *have* to read it," she says. "I watched the movie, and the teacher said that we don't even have to do a book report if we don't want to. The teacher said we could turn in a poster with phrases from the book on it, you know, a poster with pictures of World War II and quotes from the book around the pictures, done very neatly. I'm going to get the quotes right from the movie. I saw some war pictures that I can cut out from the *World Book*. It'll be easy. . . .

"I kind of have to do it that way, because partly I'm bored with it and partly because this is kind of a nerve-racking time. I'd like to get into an Ivy League school, so I'm kind of nervous. It's all anybody is talking about now. They say, Did you hear so-and-so didn't get into Stanford or this school or that school? People love to talk about where people have been rejected. It wouldn't be a surprise to hear that anybody was rejected anywhere. It's been hard at some schools. . . .

"There's the natural jealousy, too. Everybody was talking about this one girl who had just a B average, three-point-o, something like that. She's not really smart. She didn't have very good SATs, I heard, maybe somewhere around one thousand. But she got into this one school and a lot of people were saying it was because she applied to get into their community health service program and said she was going to major in health administration. And the school accepted her because health students are hard to get. It was a trick. That was the only way she could get in, some people said. They were putting her down, which was pretty unfair, but I guess I was bummed, too, because I have almost a four-point-o and good SATs and I didn't get in. My mom wanted me to call the school's admissions office and ask them why I got rejected. I didn't really want to, but I did. They said they had a formula to determine points — your g.p.a., SATs, and Achievement Tests are factored in — and that I came up just short. I wanted to be accepted, just because you want to get as many acceptances as possible, but I don't really care, because I don't want to go there. . . .

"I wasn't depressed by it. I'm kind of numb now, like you feel it but you don't. There's so much pressure, you get kind of used to it. I'll be glad when it's over. I had my Yale interview. It was in this office with a guy. He was nerdy. His phone kept ringing while we were doing it. He'd ask me about extracurricular things and you could tell he really wasn't listening. After five minutes he said, 'I'm sorry to rush you out of here but this is a crazy day for me. Don't worry. This interview will be the least important part of your application. . . .'

"I hope he was telling the truth. I can't wait until this is over. I want to go to an Ivy League school so much, but if I don't get in, I'll be satisfied with U.C. San Diego, I think. I could be happy in San Diego. It's close to my family and friends. I just want this over with. . . ."

APRIL

It may reveal something about the transcendent importance of the first week in April and the aberrant behavior it engenders to learn that Paul's father, Kelly's mother, Andy's father, and Hillary's mother have, for the first time all year, talked to their children each of the last five school days. "Dad, I still don't have anything to tell you," Andy says on the fifth day, a Friday, not even bothering to wait for his father to ask the question any longer, tired of these three-a-day phone calls that swiftly end after he has mumbled that nothing new has arrived from the colleges.

"Why do you think it is taking so long?" his father asks.

"It's taking a while for everybody, Dad. I don't know."

"Why do I detect a note of disinterest here?"

"Oh, shit, Dad. Don't do this to me. I'm not going to get all hyper about this. It's enough of a freak going through it on my own. I don't want to be worrying about you."

"Okay, take it easy. *Take it easy.*"

"I wish you'd show this much interest the rest of the time."

His father snorts. "What is it that you want to say, Andy?"

"About what?"

"You say that I don't show enough interest," his father says. "Well, now I'm giving you an opportunity to show me where I don't show enough interest."

"Oh, shit, Dad, I don't know."

"I think you do or you wouldn't have said it, my friend."

"It's just an expression."

"Well, I'm listening now, so what is it that you wanted to ask me?"

Andy says nothing.

"If you don't know, then don't be so quick to criticize me next time."

"Don't get so bummed, Dad."

"And let me know the second the next acceptance or rejection comes in."

"Mom is here, she wants me to do something," he says. "Hold on."

His mother, standing there in a white gown that he has not seen since the days his father took her to Chasen's, motions for him to put his hand over the phone. She looks nicer tonight, her face less fleshy. Perhaps she has dropped a few pounds. "I need you to drive me to a hotel downtown," she whispers. "I have to meet some people there and I can't take the car."

Ordinarily he would have hit her with a barrage of indignant questions: Why can't you take a cab? Why are you coming to me on such short notice? But, today, he sees her as his escape from the telephone. "Dad, I gotta drive Mom somewhere right now, so I have to get off."

"Keep me informed."

His mom has a blind date. "Turn up the air conditioning," she says, in the car. "If I get hot, my hair gets frizzy, I look like a mess, and it's seventy-five dollars' worth of perm down the drain."

He turns the air to Max.

"A blind date sounds so strange to me," he says, then, in the next instant, wishes he had kept quiet. He doesn't want to make his mother any more nervous than she must already be.

"We're not hopping into bed with each other and going to Las Vegas," she says, so casually that he feels a blush running across his face. Since when did his mom get so gross? He likes ribald and coarse adults actually; just doesn't need to see these qualities in his parents, who, if he had his way, would be asexual. The cooking class has loosened her up, he's noticed. The old widower, whom she often invites home for a friendly drink, is a fairly raunchy guy with a lot of funny stories from his days overseeing work on the Alaskan pipeline by day and watching his workers blow their dough on imported Anchorage hookers at night. One night, his mom asked for more details about a group of guys who spied through peepholes on a *ménage à trois* of one of their co-workers. She is checking her makeup and playing with the silver choker around her neck, taking it off and putting it back on. "Do you like it on or off?" she asks.

"On."

She puts it back on, leaves it there. "Lower the air conditioning now. I'm freezing."

"Okay." He points half the vents away from her. "Better?"

She nods. "Slow it down just a little, okay? I get nervous when you drive so fast."

"Why am I driving you at all?"

"I just don't like to drive home if I've had a couple of drinks."

"So this guy will take you home?"

She shrugs. "I imagine so, yes."

He doesn't want to know any more. Dropping her off in front of the hotel, he parks the car around the corner and strolls through the hotel lobby into a glass elevator. He rides it to the top, looking through the glass into rooms where unsuspecting guests, their curtains open, watch TV, recline on sofas, sip drinks, walk around shirtless. Feeling like a peeping Tom, he gets off the elevator at the top, then gets back on again for twenty minutes more, too fascinated not to look when he glimpses a blonde woman in a bra standing against the window of her room, somewhere around the twentieth floor. So many secret lives, he thinks, so much cover and illusion and success and misery. Where amid all the glass, all those rooms, is his mother?

The next morning he awakens to see her sitting at their breakfast table, sipping coffee. He's relieved to find her here. "How did it go?" he asks.

"I was about to ask you the same thing."

"Sorry. I came home late. I was at Jason's."

She opens a newspaper. "Have something to eat."

"Was the guy nice, Mom?"

"Nothing to write home about."

———

On Monday, in Steven's history class, a discussion on the causes of World War II has lagged, and everyone begins going off on tangents. A boy says Dwight Eisenhower was elected president because "he was the guy who decided to drop the bomb on Japan."

"No, that's not quite right," the teacher advises the kid.

A girl raises her hand. "Eisenhower wiped out Europe," she says. "Somebody else wiped out Japan. *Then*, the bomb was pretty cool because you could just destroy one country and you wouldn't have radiation going all over the world."

"I still think Eisenhower was the dude who dropped the bomb," insists the first boy.

"I wouldn't mind developing a medium bomb, like we had for Japan, so that we could do something to the Arabs, if they keep dumping on us," says the girl.

"*Whatever*," says another boy. "That'd be cool. It'd be a lot easier. We'd have to give it to the Russians, too, just so they would stay cool, and wouldn't screw up and drop a bomb on us."

"*Really*," says the girl.

"What do you think of that, Steven?" asks the teacher.

Steven flips his hand to indicate they are needlessly complicating this discussion. "We can kick their butts with what we already have."

"But I don't want to get in a nuclear war," says the girl.

"You can't wimp out," says the first boy.

"Maybe we should have some of these thoughts put on paper," says the teacher, "for future discussion."

A chorus of voices indicates that no one wants to write anything.

"Okay, well, let's get back to what we were originally talking about," says the teacher. He asks them to turn to a page in their text.

"Will anything from what we just talked about be on the final?" asks a boy sitting in the front row.

"No," says the teacher. "But I hope you were paying attention, Carl." The boy shrugs.

A blonde girl in the rear of the room raises her hand. "*Then you're definitely saying that nothing about nuclear war will be on the final. You promise.*"

The teacher nods.

"You can't play tricks with us about the final," says the girl.

On Wednesday, another class conversation is going nowhere, and somehow they're off talking about college admissions, particularly how the admissions of minorities with lower test scores might affect their own chances. "I don't see how that is fair," says the blonde girl in the back of the room. "I want everybody to have equal rights, but I don't want to be screwed just because some black kid lives in a poor area."

"I don't know why everybody is so down on blacks," says a red-haired girl. "They don't have it as good, and things should be better for them. I'm not saying that they should get every college spot, but you have to give them some because they don't get the same kind of good education. It is bizarre what black people had to go through in the 'forties and 'fifties. They couldn't even eat in the same restaurants in some places."

"Bullshit," says the boy in the back. "That was just a few places in the South. They did some marches, and John F. Kennedy and Lyndon Johnson gave them their equal rights. They didn't have to go to war or anything. They got what they wanted. It didn't take them so long."

"I don't know about that," says the redhead.

"It just took a few years after Martin Luther King started marching," says the boy. "Nobody fought them real hard about it. I saw this television thing where they went to Washington and spoke and then they got their rights. It was pretty easy. And now they want a lot more. They have everything already. I don't see why they have to get better advantage than white people in going to colleges and stuff. I don't think that is fair."

"When did Mexicans get equal rights?" someone asked.

"Same time as blacks," someone else answers, "or maybe just a little after."

"I just don't think that is very smart," says the redhead. "Since everybody is American, I think everybody should have more feelings for people who haven't had it easy. We can't always be thinking about ourselves."

"Well, *you* give up your spot at UCLA," says the blonde girl in the rear of the room.

Steven is ambivalent about the issue of special minority admissions. Nonetheless, he's disgusted. "You guys are so bogus," he says. "You don't know anything that went on in the 'sixties, do you?"

"You're so sarcastic," says the blonde girl in the back.

"*Lighten up*, Steven," says a boy.

"Okay, hold it down," shouts the teacher.

"How much of this will be on the test?" demands the blonde girl.

A half-hour later, out of class and back home, he has started making calls for Bobbi Fiedler when he hears a knock on the door. Laura has come over with some news: She has broken up with Aaron. The news does not come as a surprise and yet he can't think of anything to say, sensing that this break-up might be the catalyst for change in their own relationship.

"He was kind of an asshole," she says. "He shook me when I let him know. I should never have told him face-to-face. I got these bruises on my wrist."

She pulls up the sleeves of her sweater to reveal red and gray bumps upon her olive skin. He lets his thumbs and index fingers light only a second on the bumps before pulling them off, furrowing his brow, trying to demonstrate that his concern here is nothing more than clinical. "Shouldn't you put a bandage on those?" he says. He touches the bruises once, twice more. Her arm is as taut as ever.

"They'll be fine," she says. "But I gotta change the number on my phone because I know he'll bother the shit out of me if I don't. Why was I so stupid? That's what I wonder. He was such an ass."

"I didn't expect to see you," he says. "I have to go over to Vickie's to take some wallpaper off her bathroom walls."

"Sounds *happening*," she laughs.

He shrugs. She pulls down the sleeves of her sweater, kisses him on the forehead. "I know you have to go. I'll be fine. Don't worry."

Within twenty minutes, he is knee-deep in torn, gluey wallpaper that has ducks swimming on something that looks like a swamp in the Florida Everglades. "This shit is awful," he says. "How could anybody have put this up in your bathroom?"

"Wait until you see the new wallpaper," says Vickie. "It's just like the paper we have in the bathrooms at our beach house, a lime green, but not *loud, loud lime*, just an interesting green. You'll love it. I almost forgot to tell you. My mom said we could use the house after the prom if we want to."

He keeps his eyes fixed on the torn ducks. "Let's not make any definite plans until we know what we're doing, okay?"

"We're going to the prom, aren't we?"

There it is. The Question. They have been doomed from the beginning, he realizes. Only the grinds and scents of sweet sex have held them together this long. A simple no from him, and it could be over in five minutes. He could be over at Laura's in another ten.

"Well, aren't we?" Vickie demands.

"Sure," he says.

"God, the way you said that I wasn't sure for a sec," she admits.

"I just want to keep the after-prom stuff open, okay?"

"Okay," she says cheerfully, then shouts down the hall from her room. "Hey, Mom, we're going to the prom, but can we let you know about the house?"

"Certainly," says the voice from down the hall.

Now there is a witness to his capitulation. Within fifteen minutes of his indecision he has signed and sealed himself over to her for prom night and, in effect, for the rest of his senior year. She squeals, hugs him. "Oh, I want to go to bed with you," she whispers in his ear.

He laughs to suggest that he likes this idea but that they better stay riveted to the task of scraping off these ducks. She peels the paper alongside him, in a ratty pair of shorts, her hair scraggly and greasy, Steven thinking, for a moment, that he can see himself trapped with her in middle age, he with a beer belly that falls over wide jeans, she, a greasy, slowly graying matron, in these same ratty shorts that will someday reveal a forty-five-year-old woman's chunky thighs. He wears a condom each time they make love now, is taking no chances, doesn't think he can count on her to take the pill every day, though she insists she does. He tells her simply, when she protests that she has already taken precautions, that he likes the condom for its double-protection. She accepts this, which only makes matters worse for him, strengthening his conviction that she is hopelessly dumb, the knowledge leaving him guilty for living this charade so long. Gluey ducks pile around his ankles, sticking to his socks. Vickie is asking him what color he would like for the towel racks. A clean white? Maybe gold? He smiles, says white. "But white is so *ordinary*," she counters, less as a protest, he senses, than as a means to get a discussion going between them, even a disagreement, anything to fill the dead time. They don't talk much, he's noticed. Still, despite all his affection for Laura, he has come to care about Vickie, who may be a bit slow and shallow but still has a good heart. Less shallow than insecure, actually. He thinks all the talk about wallpaper and clothes covers some crying need in her to be recognized. There is no turf for her at Beverly to stand upon, really, no circle besides the one that she has to share with scores of other babes. These four years couldn't have been easy. He'll stick it out with her. In another year he might have a hard time remembering this moment. Where will he be next April? Shit, the colleges keep you hanging.

The next afternoon, he skips his economics class to go surfing with a few buddies. It is his first time out since last October. His timing has altogether left him, but just falling off his board and thrashing about in the water renews him. Driving home he feels serene for the first time in a couple of weeks. It is a good mood in which to confront the day's mail, filled with news from four of the colleges to which he has applied. *If these are rejections*, he tells himself, *I can live with that. I have an acceptance to Berkeley. I can do well there. I have a good life. I've done my best. I wish Laura were here. Or Vickie or anybody else who could assure me that bad news will not be the end of the world. Stay calm. I can surf tomorrow if I want to.* His mother, waiting next to him, finally tells him to stop staring into space and open the damn things. His father, hearing her order, has come rushing out of his study. One by one, Steven opens the thick envelopes filled with papers and forms, and reads the first couple sentences of each letter. The four envelopes contain three acceptances and one wait-list, the wait-list coming from a school that he doesn't care about. His mother's eyes are brimming. His dad hugs him. "I'm in," says Steven. "It's over."

Within a couple of hours, the thrill has worn off. Will he be able to compete in an elite university? He has told Laura, Vickie, and most of his buddies about the news, then suggested they all get together to party. He picks up Vickie, and everyone meets at the house of a surfing buddy whose parents have gone out of town for the weekend. The group chips in to buy two bottles of Chablis, four six-packs of Heineken, two bags of potato chips, and three hundred dollars' worth of coke. "If you're going to have a party, you have to have the kinds of things that people party with," Steven explains later. "If my parents had a party they wouldn't buy eight cases of soft drinks and one little pint of Scotch. They'd get a lot of Scotch. So we get some coke: so what? We're not kids anymore. These are *parties*. You get what people like."

Midway through the party, Laura arrives. Vickie, who has been talking to some of Steven's surfing buddies from Pali High, quickly returns and puts a proprietary arm around his waist. Laura strolls over.

"Hi, Vickie," Laura says. "I like your shoes."

Vickie smiles, looks to the side. "Hi, thanks. There's stuff to drink in the kitchen."

Laura moves on to the kitchen to get a glass of wine. Vickie excuses herself and goes back to talking with a guy from Pali. Someone proposes a toast: "Here's to either the future governor of California or the next surf bum." The kid raises his beer mug. "This Heinie's for you, Steven."

———

Hillary's mother, stretched out on the den floor, looks disconsolate when she arrives home.

"What's wrong?" Hillary asks.

"Nothing," her mother answers. "Just my back. An envelope arrived for you from UCLA. A thin one." Hillary begins walking to her bedroom.

"Aren't you going to open it?" her mother demands. "*You haven't?*"

Her mother rolls over and stands. "Do you really think I'd do that? Please, bring it here and open it."

Hillary gets the envelope and rips it open. She flushes out the rejection letter and hands it over to her mother. "We knew I didn't have much chance at UCLA," Hillary says. "Don't be too disappointed."

"Where were you last night?"

"At Karen's. I'm sorry that I didn't call. It got late, and so I just decided to sleep there."

Her mother doesn't respond immediately, raises her chin so that she can look authoritatively down at Hillary, pausing to give her daughter a last chance to back out of the lie. "We both know you weren't at Karen's. She called here last night."

"Well, I didn't want to tell you the truth."

"Where were you?"

"With Jeremy."

"I thought you'd stopped dating him?"

"I have. I just *saw* him, Mom."

"And you *just* slept at his apartment?"

"Oh, God, Mom, we didn't sleep together."

"A girl and boy spend the night and they're not sleeping together? I don't believe it."

"I didn't expect you'd be able to."

"What is that supposed to mean?"

"Nothing."

"Is he going to the prom with you at least?"

"Why do you ask that?"

Her mother, in a fury, tears up the UCLA envelope and letter. "*He probably won't. He's probably using you, isn't he? Isn't he?*"

"Mom, get a *head*."

The prom: Talk about it begins in earnest on the Third-Floor Patio, where a few classmates ask Hillary whom she is planning to bring.

"I don't know if I'm even going," she tells them. She doesn't want to ask Jeremy, afraid that he might interpret a prom date as a signal she wants to resume their romance. To go with him to a dance filled with couples holding hands and whispering about where they were sleeping that night would be, at the very least, cruel to him; he would know they wouldn't be spending the night together. Later, she calls him. "If I tell you that I'm confused and I need to talk to you as a friend about whether I should ask you to the prom, could you deal with that?"

"Oh, shit. I wouldn't be caught dead at a high school prom."

"Really?"

"*Really.*"

"So you won't be hurt if I go with someone else?"

His voice becomes lower, reasoned, the adult talking to the child.

"I don't think you have much choice. I want you to have a lot of fun. Of course I think you should ask someone else."

"Want to go out and have a pizza somewhere tonight anyway?"

"God, you really want to have it both ways, don't you?"

"I get confused," she says.

He clucks his tongue. "Do you know anyone who doesn't?"

———

It would have been unsafe to have told them earlier, Kelly keeps repeating to herself. *Unsafe.* Eyes closed, her stereo headphones on, she lies on the floor of her bedroom listening to her Wang Chung tape for the eighth time. She has not moved for three hours now, pressing a damp washcloth against her temples, telling herself that the world has not ended. She can still see her mother's mouth opening, knew at the moment it happened that she was in store for a large dose of humiliation. Tina and Shelly had been watching "Two on the Town" with her and discussing what great legs the show's hostess had, when her mom popped in and said congrats to Tina on having been accepted to UCLA. "What about you, Shelly?" her mom asked then, and Shelly, smiling with that self-effacing blush that she always pulls out for adults, said coyly that she was trying to decide between Berkeley and a couple of private colleges in the East. "I'm sure that Kelly wishes she could join you at any of those schools," said her mom. "But Kelly is going to try to work on her studies at Santa Monica City and then the sky is the limit, right, sweetheart?"

Kelly's mind's eye can see her own face growing red, her voice cracking, "Mom, we're *trying* to watch something here."

"Okay, all I was doing was saying congrats to Tina and Shelly," her mom said.

Tina, perhaps sensitive to the fact that Kelly had been excluded from praise here, added softly, "I'm sure we'll be saying congratulations to Kelly when her acceptance from San Diego State comes."

Her mom's eyes squinted in confusion. "San Diego State? *Isn't that where you got the rejection from, dear? Or was that somewhere else? Wasn't that San Diego State?*" Everyone's eyes turned upon Kelly, who had been exposed as a fraud. Tina, open-mouthed and leaning forward, seemed to realize the truth immediately, and looked down at the den floor. But a confused Shelly looked for clarification against a month's worth of misinformation: "I thought it was San Diego State that you wanted to go to?" She asked three times, as Kelly stared at her mom in misery. How many times had she told them about San Diego State during those lunches at Chin Chin's? Ten, twenty times at least. Ten, twenty lies at least. On the bedroom floor, Wang Chung pulsating through the headphones, she takes deep breaths. *This is not the end of the world. This is not the end of the world.* Wang Chung helps. If she has a serious dilemma, nothing aside from drugs soothes her like an hour under the headphones. "I think we should talk," her mom said after Tina and Shelly left, but Kelly, with the headphones already on, shook her head. Wang Chung is singing "Dance Hall Days." Press the washcloth harder against the temples. *This is not the end of the world.*

By the next evening, her mom is somewhere in southern Oregon, negotiating a shopping mall transaction. Usually that would mean another dinner alone for her, but, tonight, she is baby-sitting Timmy. Kurt comes over. A TV magazine show comes on. News: Maria Shriver has married Arnold Schwarzenegger. Kelly finds herself fascinated with stories about successful, happy women. At Beverly, the prettiest girl in the senior class, in Kelly's mind, is also the most successful, Jenny Hochman, who produces and co-anchors the Norman News Service on Beverly's television station, plays varsity tennis, and dates a cute junior boy whom Kelly had a slight crush on before she realized that Jenny was in the picture.

Looks aside, maybe she could have been like Jenny Hochman, she tells herself, with a little practice and courage. It pisses her off that she didn't wake up to the cost of bad grades earlier. She'll just have to try harder at Santa Monica City. If she fails there, then what?

She kisses Timmy, puts him to bed, and heads for Kurt. They make love in five minutes, and, afterwards, he is a lovey-dovey teddy bear, cuddling and kidding her about how she'll make a great mother for six rug-rats someday. She has ruled out taking him to the prom, if she goes at all. Her mom would freak at the news that a fifteen-year-old boy was going with her, though her reaction to the news that she had gone with Kurt into Westwood had been surprisingly mild. They had been standing in the master bedroom, and her mom had been putting on her makeup. "Are you *very close* to this boy?" she asked simply, and when Kelly said yes, she murmured, "Just be very careful." She began working on herself with an eyeliner pencil. "Are we understanding each other, Kelly? If there is anything that you need to talk about, or anything you need, *anything*, like in the way of a doctor, you let me know." Most of her friends' moms were equally businesslike about the subject of contraception. If some girl had not taken the appropriate precautions, her parents generally reminded her of what needed to be done. No one was going to let a pregnancy get in the way of the climb. Kelly, after listening to her mom, had herself fitted for a diaphragm. Kurt is still talking about jeeps. Thank God for the diaphragm. She arises from the bed, puts on a robe, and watches him try to arrange the collar of his shirt so that it falls stylishly over his sweater. He doesn't get it quite right. A bit slow, her muscular fifteen-year-old hunk, but a sweet boy. The first of presumably many guys younger than she. A friend, a visitor floating through her life for a few months. A cuddly bear. It's been fun.

———

Paul drives over to Tony's. Randy is in the den watching "The Flintstones." Paul finds Tony in the backyard lifting weights in just his jockey briefs. Tony looks preoccupied. "What's happening, dude?" Paul asks. Tony shrugs. The sphinx is silent. Fuck him. Randy comes outside saying Barney Rubble is a freak. Paul and Tony say nothing. "You missed some intense partying in Palm Springs," he says to Paul.

Paul snickers. "Tell me it was *hard-core*, Randy."

"You're just jealous. You wish you'd been there."

"And you're so fucking bogus."

"Yeah, like the chicks we met were *bogus*, too. Tony, tell him about the chicks."

"You tell him."

Randy sticks out his tongue. "These chicks were just so hot. Freshmen at Cal State Dominguez Hills. Partyers supreme. Tora, tora, tora. I had this one who didn't know how to say quit. Randy's brother had some seventh-grader, no bullshit."

"We *understand*," says Tony.

Paul stares at a barbell. "Who was everybody else with?"

"Adam was with this blonde with legs up to her neck. Tony could have had her, but he didn't want her."

"Whatever you say," mumbles Tony, working on his triceps.

"You weren't into them, dude?" Paul asks him.

"Not really," says Tony, groaning as he brings a dumbbell behind his neck and then back in front of him again, stealing glances at the triceps to see if he is getting any added definition. "Let me just work out here, will you?"

After an hour's worth of aerobics with Roxanne, Paul eats dinner with her family. Her father has rushed home after a shift at the auto repair shop to barbecue hamburgers on the grill in their yard. The hamburgers aren't bad, though he wishes he hadn't eaten that third one; he doesn't want to jump on any scale now. Roxanne's father has gone down into their basement to work on his model ships. Paul's own father doesn't have a hobby, though his mother likes to say his father's avocation is collecting people's asses in a glass jar. She always laughs when she says it. Does his father know how to whittle or use a lathe? Should ask him. He remembers: His father is in Barcelona.

He has cut back his drug use by a half, he guesses. There are still moments, away from Roxanne, when he'll do a few lines with Tony and Adam, but he stops now long before they do: The sense of euphoria that the drug gives him has slackened a little lately. Roxanne persuades him to stay away from the shit on some nights when Tony calls and pleads with him to come over for *just a while, just a while, we can just do a little, and then you can bail, guy.* So why does he feel like dealing? The risks attract him. Even thinking of making an illicit delivery shoots him full of adrenaline. He loves listening to Adam's stories about deliveries, felt a chill when Adam talked of a cop car that pulled around the corner after a deal was complete, he and the buyer freezing, the cop car finally passing. Before he leaves with Roxanne's family for a movie, he calls Adam again. Get me a chance to meet this dude you keep talking about, Paul insists.

Sometime, next week maybe, Adam says.

After dinner, he goes home to check the mail. There is a sheaf of envelopes lying on a small table in the foyer. Nothing, just junk mail, a couple of music magazines telling him that his subscriptions have lapsed. There have been three college rejections in the last three weeks but not a word from the remaining eight schools. To compound his headache, he has a one-thousand-word book report to write, due tomorrow, on *Catch-22*, which he hasn't read. The teacher has said that the reports needn't deal necessarily with the book's plot or themes, or Joseph Heller's prose, just so long as the reports touch on the book in some way. Paul knows leeway when he hears it. He gets out his father's *Encyclopaedia Britannica* and paraphrases three pages about the Battle of the Bulge. "It was an ugly war that we won in WWII, and Heller wouldn't want to fight in it and I wouldn't either," he writes. "Heller is writing about war's stupidity."

He calls Tony to ask how he has made out with the paper. Tony's machine answers. Paul hangs up. He watches a little of David Letterman

and calls back at one A.M. Tony answers, but before Paul can say anything, he hears another voice, male and deep, laughing loudly and telling
Tony to hang up. Tony giggles and says, "Wait, I'll be off in a *sec.*" Paul
hangs up.

"How did your paper turn out?" he asks Tony the next day
at school.

"Fine. I finished it at least."

"What did you do last night?"

Tony groans. "I thought I was getting a cold, so I just turned on
the machine and crashed. I didn't even watch 'Moonlighting.' "

"I called you at one," Paul says. "You answered. Who was that
with you?"

Tony hesitates only a second. "Oh, yeah? That was you who
hung up? I was talking to my dad. Why did you hang up? You know you
can call late."

"That wasn't your dad," Paul says. "That was some guy, but it
wasn't your dad. What was the guy doing over there?"

"You're being so weird, guy. Who could it be besides my dad? It
was one o'clock. Get real."

Paul feels himself chickening out. "Forget about it."

"You need to lighten up a little."

"All right. Just leave me alone."

"You were the one who got weird."

"Let's drop it."

"Okay, but in the future stop being such a prick."

Something in Paul goes off. It was inevitable; his psyche has been
on overload too long. He jabs his finger in Tony's chest. *"Don't ever call
me a prick again. You've been the prick. You've been the liar. I know you
were fooling around with that guy. You're gay, Tony. Why don't you at
least admit it to me? No one else, just me. Why can't you do that?"* He
feels himself shaking, realizes he has not stopped jabbing Tony's chest,
pulls the finger away. *"Why can't you just tell me?"*

"Go fuck yourself."

"I don't want to see your lying, weird ass around again, Tony.
Don't even call. I'm warning you."

He drives for two hours along the Pacific Coast Highway before going
home. His mom hands him three envelopes — two thin ones with
rejections from the University of California at San Diego and the Univer-

sity of California at Santa Barbara, and an acceptance from a local private college. She kisses him. He feels nothing so much as relief. "Great, Mom, this is great. I'm going to lie down on my bed for a while. I've got a headache."

"Just tension, dear, over this whole college thing, I'm sure," she says.

"Probably."

"Congratulations, sweetheart."

"Okay."

Coming home, still fuming about Tony, he saw Adam, who said that he had gotten him a meeting with his connection tomorrow night. Paul writes, "CP, 6 P.M.," in his little address book. He's never been to Canoga Park. Valley tract houses. A mall in the next town over, if he remembers right. He thinks he went there once with his mom and his grandmother. What will this dealer want to ask him? *Think about college*, he tells himself. There could have been better days for a celebration.

———

April 14. Melinda drops her five college rejection letters on the floor. "Don't pick them up, *don't touch them, I don't want them*," she says to Pam. Harvard, Yale, Columbia, Stanford, and a private college in the East have all said no. The house feels cold. "I want to build a fire," she says. Pam arranges logs in the fireplace while Melinda places old newspapers under them. "Light it up," she commands, and Pam takes a cigarette lighter from her purse and sets fire to the newspapers. In a minute, they have a warm, raging fire. Melinda, in one swift motion, sweeps up the rejections and tosses them into the blaze.

They eat their dinner in front of the fire — salad, fish, and white wine. The girls can talk about little but their remaining college prospects. Pam, who has been rejected at Berkeley and U.C. San Diego, still counts upon UCLA to say yes to her 3.6 g.p.a. Melinda holds out hope that one of the Ivy League schools to which she has applied will at least wait-list her. "What should we do tomorrow?" asks Pam, and Melinda answers with what has become an almost daily refrain — "Go to the beach." They'll just forge their mothers' names on sick notes again. The next few weeks may be their last rest for another four years, and they intend to make the most of it.

The following day, Melinda receives two more letters — an acceptance from a lower-echelon Ivy League school and a letter from a more prestigious Ivy informing her that she has been placed on the university's wait-list. In addition, the University of California at San Diego has accepted her. A happy Pam has been admitted to UCLA.

The girls celebrate in their own ways. Pam goes to dinner with another friend. Melinda sees a guy from one of her classes with whom she has been going out, a popular, handsome boy named Barry. Melinda's mom, hearing of the boy's entrance into her daughter's life while sitting in a London hotel room, says excitedly that Barry "is a dream date." Melinda likes the boy's attention. "I guess it makes me feel attractive, but I'm doing it partly because we do some fun things," she says. Last week, Barry took her horseback riding and later on an afternoon to Redondo Beach with a group of his close soshe friends, and, though she didn't find him funny or scintillating, he was sweet to her, bringing her to a nice restaurant and constantly asking if she wanted anything. Tonight, with his parents having gone out, he has asked her over to his house, to watch a rented movie. They sit on a couch, making out, as the movie rolls in front of them, unwatched. Barry is breathing heavily. She feels un-aroused.

Roger, the boy with whom she wants to be on a couch, is at his fifteen-year-old girlfriend's house, a couple of miles away, up for the weekend from his fraternity at U.C. San Diego. She had never regarded Roger as a possible boyfriend until the last month or so, when she began thinking about him constantly. She hoped that by going out with Barry, she might spur Roger into realizing what he was missing. It may have worked, for Roger started asking her the insistent questions that she had wanted to hear: "Are you going out tonight? Who's taking you?" And then came the night when he told her how much he cared and started making out with her in his car. He told her that when he heard "Missing You" on the radio while at school, he thought of her. They fell asleep on his bed with their clothes on.

But, aside from his promise to go to the prom with her, nothing has changed really. He still has his fifteen-year-old girlfriend, who slept with him on their first date. At the time Melinda heard the story, she laughed, Roger being nothing more than a close friend, but now she feels an awful jealousy thinking of that girl *under her boy.* She does not precisely understand why her thinking about Roger has changed so radically, wonders if this is simply a case of wanting something that has been denied her. She understands herself well enough to know that she is attracted to the impossible-to-get, only to dispose of such things and people the moment they've entered her possession — toys, boys; it is a trait she does not like about herself. But Roger is not just another thing, another boy; this is her good friend, and she knows she wants to be with him and not this sweet, earnest, geeky boy grabbing at her on the couch. At the end of the evening, Barry breaks open a bottle of champagne and hands her an envelope. Inside is a card with an inscription asking her to the prom. She wanted this invitation, weeks ago, if for no other reason than that it would make her feel good. "I'm sorry," she tells Barry. "This is so sweet of you, but I'm already going with somebody."

"Oh, this is *really good* for my ego," he responds.

His slumping head reminds her of the dangers of dating, of putting your neck out there on the block for someone to chop off, of ever allowing yourself to be vulnerable. Although she regrets having done the axing, far better that his ego be felled than hers. One of the attractive features of pursuing a relationship with Roger has been in knowing they understand each other well enough to dispense with the typical games and ritualistic ego battles that usually precede the moment when most boys and girls come together. There has always been so much about him that she liked, especially his laugh and irreverence, and even if one day soon she stopped feeling sexually drawn by his green eyes and nice body, her funny maverick would still be there as a buddy. They've talked of his fifteen-year-old girlfriend, whom he said he cared for, though not in the same way as he did for Melinda, who asked if he was still sleeping with the younger girl since their own night, in the car. He nodded. This didn't surprise her. She knew his sexual history. "She's good in bed," Roger had told her about another girl, a couple of years before, the way a football announcer might say that a quarterback throws a nice long pass. For the time being, she can cope with the thought of Roger lying in bed with the fifteen-year-old. It sounds, she told him, "just physical." More troublesome are Roger's daily lapses in good judgment. This weekend, his car is in the shop, and he didn't bring enough money up from San Diego to pay for the repairs or take her to dinner. His parents will help him with the car, but dinner is out. "He's a fuck-up a lot of the time," Melinda says. "He never seems to have any money or be organized. I know I'll have to pay for the prom. A hundred and ten bucks for the two of us and then there'll be the limo. I don't know how much that will be yet. He's *such* a fuck-up, but he's a real good friend. I don't know what's going to happen. I'll have to wait and see."

She will have to wait for quite a while. He undoubtedly will be spending the night with his girlfriend, and she must still extricate herself from the determined Barry. "I had a real good time," she says to him when the champagne is finished. "Maybe we can go to dinner some-time." But her cool, polite tone has made it clear: She will not be sleeping with him tonight or any other night. She will not be going to any major senior functions with him. She clasps his arm warmly and hugs him. Another sign: The evening is over.

"I had a good time, too," he says, keeping his dignity. "It's real late. I'm burnt. I guess you are, too."

"Uh-huh."

They kiss goodnight and she is gone, driving herself home. In her bedroom, she calls Roger to leave a message on his machine. Surpris-ingly, he answers the phone. "I thought you'd be out," she says.

"I thought you were doing something with Barry," he shoots back.

"Well, I'm not," she mumbles. "I just called to say hi."

"Want me to come over?"

"Okay."

Roger is there in fifteen minutes. They watch a late movie and talk about his girlfriend.

"Sometimes I think this is crazy," Roger says to her.

"Well, what isn't?"

———

April 17. Citing "indisputable evidence" linking Libya and Muammar Qaddafi to a string of terrorist attacks, including a West Berlin disco bombing that leaves an American soldier dead, the United States strikes back. Several military and civilian installations are bombed, including Qaddafi's residence in Tripoli. Extremist elements in the Middle East vow revenge. Melinda gets worried. At that moment, her parents are climbing aboard a jumbo jet to fly home. How tight is airport security in London? How tight will security be at the international terminal at LAX when she drives there to pick them up?

At school, reaction varies. Doug Chu, the senior class president during fall semester, confesses, "When I heard about the bombing, I said to myself, 'You might as well drink, Doug, and lose your brain cells because you won't be getting out of college alive.' I wouldn't be surprised if it happens, a nuclear war. When I heard, I thought that the bombing put us a step closer to war. But I'd just let Reagan handle it anyway. There's so much he knows that we don't. I think you have to keep those kinds of discussions outside the populace. So I'd let him do what he wants to do, but the consequences are scary. I just thought that first night, 'Drink up, Doug.' "

In Melinda's economics class, one boy suggests that Reagan should "waste Libya this week so nobody has to fight there, and none of us have to be drafted."

"Could we be drafted?" someone demands of the teacher.

In Steven's European history class, a girl asks whether Libya has nuclear weapons. The teacher says no, no, he doesn't think so. "What do you mean you *don't think so?*" demands the girl. She looks slightly unnerved. *Anything could happen,* says the teacher, and Steven can see how much that disturbs some of his classmates, who, staring blankly through this adult, are tapping teeth with pens or sucking on polished fingernails, their doodling temporarily halted, brains frozen. They're not used to uncertainty. The pretty blonde who sits next to Steven says, "You mean, nobody knows if something bad might happen? Our State Department doesn't? Don't they have that CIA stuff? Doesn't somebody know?"

――――――

More news from the colleges arrives within the next week. Andy does little these days but rush home after school to grab the mail. Holding waiting-list notifications from two respectable colleges, he feels cautiously optimistic about his chances, realizing that many of the kids already accepted at these schools will be opting to go to more prominent universities. His mom, usually so tense and pessimistic about such things, has been giddy about the wait-list news. "You're in like Flynn," she says to him. Who is Flynn? He shakes his head, grinning at her unfounded but infectious confidence. "You're in, Andy-wandy," she beams.

She has not called him this since he was a pitcher in Little League, striking out hitter after hitter. She tickles his neck. *"You're in, Andy-wandy."* He has become a little weary. He doesn't want to be let down. "I don't know, Mom," he says. "Maybe. Yeah. Okay, Mom. We'll see."

――――――

There are no miracles for Kelly. A last state college rejects her. She will definitely be going to a junior college now, probably Santa Monica City. "No *prob,*" she says. "I've accepted it. I'm trying not to think about it."

――――――

For Steven, Hillary, Melinda, and Paul, all of whom have been accepted by at least one desirable college, the ecstasy of admission news fades with the realization that a new test will soon begin. Steven sums up their sentiment: "I'm just glad the fucker is over — SATs, application essays, Achievement Tests, interviews, high school tests, Beverly, the whole goddamn thing. I've made it. I'm gone. But I know it's going to start again soon. Besides, I got lots of other shit on my mind."

Each is once more engrossed in personal matters. Steven has been trying to work up the nerve to tell Vickie about his feelings for Laura. Hillary's brother has dropped out of college without warning and come home to live with their mother and Harry. Melinda, tanning on the beach every afternoon, wonders whether becoming lovers with Roger might ruin their friendship.

A sweating Paul, anxious over his meeting with Adam's connection, lies on a chaise longue in Roxanne's backyard, drinking a Coke and watching Roxanne's father work on repairing a backyard fence that borders their alley. Roxanne, leaning out of a window, shouts to him that Randy is at the front door.

"Tell him to come back here," he yells.

"He says that he just wants to say *hi.*"

He trudges into the house. Randy is sitting on the front steps, chewing a slice of beef jerky. "We're going to Carney's," he says. "You and Roxanne want to come? This shit is nasty." He flings the beef jerky at a palm tree. "We're bailin'. You coming?"

"Who's *we?*"

"Tony, Adam, my brother, and a couple of other people."

"I've got something to do."

"Adam says that you don't have anything to do now. It's been canceled."

So Adam told the whole world about the meeting. What an asshole. He notices Randy's car across the street, sees Tony sitting in the rear. "I don't know, guy. I was helping Roxanne's father with something and . . ."

"Nobody gives a shit if you're pissed off at Tony."

"He said *that?*"

"He just said that he'd been kind of an asshole to you, that he'd yelled at you when you called his house late, and then that you'd got pissed and yelled at him and told him to fuck off."

Paul says nothing.

"Man, let's just get a fucking hamburger," says Randy. "It's not like it's ultra-serious or anything. So you yelled at him. Big fucking deal."

"I can't. C'mon, I'll walk down to the car with you."

He can see Tony trying to read his expression as they get close. Fuck him. Adam, rolling a joint in the front seat, lifts a finger, mumbles, "What's happening?"

Randy's little brother shouts, "Let's cruise."

"Well, you coming or not?" Adam asks him, arranging his joints in a fresh-lock sandwich bag.

"He's gotta help Roxanne's old man," Randy answers for him.

Adam looks up, grins. "Well, we'll come get you later, dude."

"Later on," Tony pipes in from the back seat.

Paul looks at him. "Yeah." He thinks of saying something else, changes his mind. This is high school, he realizes, watching the car speed away. No one breaks away from anything in high school. Adults could say fuck off and never see each other again, but in high school, when you got in an argument, a group of guys rolled up in a car the next day, trying to humor you as if you were some fourteen-year-old moron who'd respond to that bullshit. *Goddamn.* College is still five months away. He wonders what he'll say to Tony during the summer. Maybe he'll just give him the silent treatment. He walks inside, opens a Lite beer, hugs Roxanne, and says, "I've got to have an aspirin." She gives him the bottle. He grabs two aspirin, closes the bottle, opens it. He needs one more.

MAY

Everything in the high school looks so much smaller to them these days, like a dimly remembered hometown to old-timers who have not carefully examined it since their days as awed toddlers, leaving them at once embarrassed that they were ever unnerved by the place and proud, even vain, for having grown bigger than it. They have arrived at the point where they feel contemptuous of its small-town ways. The lush green tiered lawn and the auditorium, so forebodingly immense during their freshman year, look intimate, even dinky, now that they have roamed colleges that stretch like small cities. The athletic fields and bleachers are tattered compared to the enormous multisport complexes that will be theirs next year in intramural competitions. The cafeterias and the halls which, during the mad rush between classes, once seemed teeming with cooler, prettier, and older people, now appear dull, its inhabitants diminished, administrators, teachers, office personnel, and younger students all part of the Smallness they want out from. Hillary is stunned to hear how hungry and desperate freshman girls sound in her cooking class, gabbing about what juniors and seniors they'd like to sleep with, which ones are richer, more popular. Once, Hillary would have been fascinated to join in, but now she regards the talk as an invasion, tells the girls to shut up or move their things to another burner: She doesn't need any fourteen-year-old geeks taking up her space.

Andy feels squeezed now, too, a lame duck, two months from freedom, staring at the same assigned heads in front of him that were there eight months ago, surrounded by the same paraphernalia that he remembers from freshman year, the banners emblazoned with motivational slogans and the charts of the elements and the sun-faded maps to which the teachers never referred. Everybody in his classes, even the teachers, are playing out the game, he's convinced. *Education for a senior in spring semester is a joke*: He says it aloud in a class, and everyone laughs, except the teacher, which doesn't bother Andy, who couldn't care less if teachers yell at him anymore. He has a college acceptance. They can't touch him. Neither can those attendance office assholes who have hassled him for three and a half years, who regularly pointed with relish to the parental signatures that he forged on his absentee notes and mockingly demanded to know how he thought he could get away with such a thing — *forging a note like that with a child's scrawl* — to which he would reply that he had done no such thing. "I can assure you, we'll be getting in touch with your mom or dad," one of the clerks would call out to him, a parting shot that unnerved him enough that he would race home after school to tell his mother in his most earnest tone that, incidentally, he had gone by the drugstore the other day to pick up some aspirin and *he had missed a class.*

"This forgery job isn't up to your usual standards, Andrew," one of the clerks tells him on the first Monday in May. "*Crayon.* Now, I don't suppose you expect us to believe that your father used a red crayon to write you a note, to get you out of school early."

"Call him," Andy says.

Something tells him they won't. Something tells him they have stopped worrying, too. In truth, his father did sign the note in red crayon because, a couple of nights before, he had failed to retrieve his favorite pen with the genuine silver casing from a girl whose number he'd asked for at Nate 'n Al's. Worse, the phone number she had left him on the napkin was a phony. His father had pulled out the red crayon from a drawer full of other forgotten crayons, pencils, and cheap ball-point pens.

At eleven fifteen, his father is standing at the curb, next to Andy's uncle. The two men are eyeing a group of kids lying on the school lawn. "How do you get any work done here?" his uncle asks him. "You must be *boffing* them all the time."

"What do you mean?"

His uncle elbows his father. "Your son asks, 'What do you mean?' " The two men laugh. His father elbows his uncle back. "That's pretty good: '*What do you mean?*' "

"I mean, the sun and the smog, what do you think I mean?" his uncle shouts at him.

"Girls, Andy," his father says. "Your Uncle Phil means the *girls* here . . ."

"No, dummy," his uncle shouts at his father. "*Their legs,* I mean. *Boffing,* I *mean.*"

The two older men guffaw. Andy smiles politely. It is a little embarrassing, having such lechers as role models. Then again, his uncle talks much more about boffing these days than his father, who, Andy worries, has sunk into a mild depression since his twenty-two-year-old girlfriend left him a month ago for a younger guy. His uncle won't say so, but Andy thinks that his father's problems are what brought him to Los Angeles. He heard the two brothers talking in his father's condo den last night, the doors closed behind them, their words muffled by the walls so that Andy could discern only tones, his father's voice surprisingly high, soft, and fragile, Phil's baritone resonating assurance and authority, once more the older brother giving counsel to the runt in trouble, alternately barking and cajoling. Andy felt relieved that he couldn't make out their words.

He grins at his uncle, who's watching some jean-clad girls plop down on the grass. He tries to get in on the ribald humor. "Remember, Uncle Phil, no *boffing* in this city without a permit," he says. "And there's a limit of four to a catch."

His father frowns.

His uncle laughs.

They go to the Polo Lounge at the Beverly Hills Hotel, Andy's father strolling inside in his khakis and a polo shirt open at the chest, Uncle Phil, looking around wide-eyed, in jeans and blue Oxford shirt. The maître d' scrutinizes them. They are dispatched to a small table on the side, too far away from the action to glimpse anyone famous, but Uncle Phil does not seem to notice, excitedly craning his neck. "*Look, look,*" he gushes. "Linda Gray. There she is. Over *there.*" He stands and gestures. Andy studies the tablecloth, afraid that Uncle Phil might actually stand and shout at the actress. His father pulls Phil down into his seat.

A red-faced waiter rushes up, hurriedly asks them what they want to drink. Andy searches for his fake ID.

"A double scotch," says his father.

"*Linda Gray, unbelievable,*" says his uncle.

"Ah, yes," says the waiter. "May I bring you something to drink?"

"Is she here often?" his uncle persists.

"I don't know, sir."

"*You work here, don't you?*"

"Phil," interrupts his father, "just tell him what you goddamn want to drink."

"A mineral water," says Phil.

"What kind?"

"Bring him a Perrier or anything else that bubbles."

"Yes, sir."

"And for you?" The waiter looks at Andy.

"A Heineken."

"May I see some ID?"

"He'll have a Coke," his father says.

"Ah, let the kid have a beer," his uncle pipes in.

"May I see an ID?"

"I have one right here," Andy begins.

"Give the kid a goddamn Coke."

Uncle Phil resumes ogling Linda Gray. His father asks the waiter to bring over some matches. They drink and smoke in quiet. After a few minutes his father asks him if he'd like to walk around the hotel.

"Sure," he says.

"Okay, we'll see you back here in a half-hour."

"I thought you were coming."

"I have some things I have to talk to Phil about."

"Like what?"

"Like they're private. Anything else?"

"Can I have ten?"

His father reaches into his wallet, doesn't ask him why he needs the dough, just hands it over. Andy walks out of the Polo Lounge, through the hotel, into the pool area, orders a beer, and falls asleep.

An hour and a half later, he strolls back into the lounge, dark and near-empty. His uncle and father have not moved, his uncle sipping another Perrier while his father jiggles some ice in a glass. His presence startles them. They look up quickly at the sound of their intruder, clone-faces with narrow-set eyes, receding blond hair, and crooked smiles that turn from consternation to relief with the realization that it is only him. His uncle shakes his head, laughs, turns back to his father. "See, you got a super kid, you got a super life, what's the point of worrying about another bimbo."

"Why don't we continue this later," says his father. "I'm a little tired. I feel like getting some rest."

His father and uncle take him home. He says goodbye to them in the driveway; his uncle doesn't have any desire to see his mother either.

"Who was that?" she asks airily as he walks inside.

"Dad and Uncle Phil."

"Oh, how are they?" she wonders casually, the same way that she might have asked how he liked his lunch. It is a new tone.

"Fine. How was your little trip?"

"Delightful. Such nice people. Palm Springs is wonderful. We went hot-air ballooning. Did I tell you?"

"No. Which guy do you like?"

"What?"

"Robert or Ted? Which guy do you like more? You went with a group, didn't you? I'm just asking which one you like the best."

"It's not like that, sweetheart. I'm just having a nice time. They're new friends."

"Did you each have your own room?"

Peals of laughter. "Aren't we getting *aggressive* here. Sweetheart, believe me, I'm happy to be with nice people again. That's all. Yes, dear, each of us had our own room. *Really*."

He knows by her smirk when she is simply laying out the bare facts, believes her now. "And how are Phil's kids?" she asks in a cheery tone that seems not to take into account the ridicule Uncle Phil heaped upon her before the divorce.

"He didn't say anything about them."

She nods, smiles. Some part of her that he has not seen in a long while has been rekindled. "Give Phil my best if you see him again," she says happily.

"It's such a freak," he says to Jason that night in his bedroom. "My mom is real stoked, because she's seeing these new friends of hers all the time now, but my dad is kind of bummed about some chick who he went out with for a couple of months. It's like, things are all turned around. I can't even remember the chick's name. He doesn't talk about it with me."

"Dude, he's getting older now," observes Jason, looking through Andy's cassette collection. "You got Run DMC. They're intense, huh? One of my grandfathers had an impotency problem once. It must be fucked when you start getting gray hair and shit and you can't get young, tasty chicks. My grandfather was a wild man until his problem. He *burned*. He used to fool around with women all the time, my mom says. I'd be so pissed if I couldn't scam chicks."

"Yeah."

Jason walks over to the television, sees Andy's video games on top of the VCR. "You didn't tell me you had Donkey Kong. I'm gonna play some."

It is Jason's first time here. Andy doesn't know why he hasn't had him over before, except maybe he worried, in the kid's excitement with all his high-tech gadgetry in the bedroom, Jason might fuck something up, ruin his VCR or CD player or spill beer all over a speaker or make off with some of his video games. He wouldn't blame him really. He pulls a cellophane bag out from beneath some underwear. "I think my mom's gone for a while," he says. "Let's split a joint. Then we'll get something to eat."

"Does your mom hate your dad?"

"Sometimes. Not now. It's fairly bizarre." He lights the joint with his Polo Lounge matches, his lips drawing on the joint until the flame takes. "She's happy now, which is good, because my father totally screwed her over. She deserves to be happy. He doesn't, but I shouldn't say that just because he was an asshole once." He hands the joint to Jason.

"Why do you even care?"

"Because he's my father, asshole."

Jason takes a hit. "No," he says, holding the smoke in so long that Andy thinks of Lloyd Bridges in "Sea Hunt." "No, I mean, why do you get so bummed?"

"I'm not."

"You're acting like it."

Andy waves the joint like a baton. "I just worry that I'm gonna have to look after them someday."

"Bullshit. They have money."

"I mean, seeing if they're happy and shit."

"Oh, right. Are you going to visit them much after college starts?"

Andy thinks about this. "Yeah, I guess. Probably my mom. She's said that she kinda needs me around. She gets bummed out sometimes. God, I'm never getting married. You get divorced and your whole life gets so weird. I don't want kids ever having to check on me."

Andy hears a door opening and closing. "*Hear that?* Open the window."

Jason opens three windows.

Andy reaches behind them, extinguishes the roach, and turns on a fan. He flicks the roach through one of the open windows. "You never can be too safe," he says.

The bedroom door opens.

It is the housekeeper.

Andy tells her they would like some tamales.

Jason, reaching under Andy's bed, pulls out a toy robot which one of Andy's younger cousins forgot to take home after a sleep-over last summer. "How many times does your maid come to your house each week?"

"She lives here."

"*Really?*" In his wonderment, he starts laughing. "That is *so* cool. What are you going to do with your dorm room at college when she's not around to clean it?"

"I'm not a dildo, dude. I can do it."

Jason guides the toy robot along Andy's bedspread, making clucking sounds in cadence with the robot's walk. "Hey, I'm just kidding, man. I think it's cool you have somebody to make your bed. I hate it. I tell my mom that, once college starts, you might as well close my door twenty-four hours a day, because my room is going to look like a garbage can. I'm going to have a lot of studying to do at UCLA. They say to me that I'm naturally smart, but there are a lot of smart people at UCLA. At least, you'll have some fun in college, partying and all."

"Just so I don't fuck up," Andy says.

Jason shrugs, walks the robot up and down one of the bed legs. "You're gonna drive yourself crazy if you keep thinking about it like that."

"I'm halfway there."

Jason says that he has to leave. Later Andy goes to a party in Encino with some Beverly acquaintances. He doesn't know why he is there other than that he was at Carney's and some people mentioned a party and he thought that he might want to score with some Valley girl. They seem so much more desperate than Westside girls to him, stuck as they are in those tract neighborhoods where smog settles like a blanket. Maybe they think a Beverly guy is their ticket to cool breezes. Who cares about their motives? The whole world is scamming.

Sitting in a corner, guzzling a beer, he looks up to see a girl approaching, long-legged in black fishnet stockings, with bleached-blonde hair and black mascara lashes that hang over brown eyes like hoods. He feels flattered that she is smiling, guesses her to be nineteen or twenty, a college sophomore or junior. "Hi, Andy," says the girl, her voice considerably higher than he expected.

He smiles back, tries to place the face.

"At Patti's, remember? Last summer."

Patti's. His mind shuffles through names. . . . No, this isn't the junior high kid — what was her name? Ann? Annie? — who lied that she went to Cleveland High. This is someone else, dimly remembered. The girl giggles. "We were downstairs and your friend and Patti were upstairs and . . ."

He cuts her off. "Oh yeah." He suddenly sees himself with her on some couch. He must have been destroyed on margaritas.

"You graduate soon, right?" the girl asks him.

He is surprised that she remembers so much. It was just one night, after all, back in July. Or August? September? Whenever. "I graduate June twenty-fifth," he says. "And you're . . ."

"I get out on June twentieth."

"Out of where?"

"Ninth grade."

Jesus. "You look different," he says tactfully.

"Want to party tonight?"

He doesn't have the stomach for it. There's already been enough weirdness for one year, but he tries to be nice, offers to drive her home.

"But do you want to party?" she persists.

"I don't think so."

"Do your friends like to party?"

He says nothing.

"That friend of yours with the wavy hair told my friend that he had a half gram still."

He says nothing.

"Do you think he'd let me have some, or would I have to pay?"

He says nothing.

"Okay, I think he is real cute, but do you think he likes to party? My parents are away on a trip. You sure *you* don't want to party? We could have some fun."

"Sorry, I don't think so," he says, feeling suddenly that he has to get out of here.

"I got my ears pierced last week. What do you think of these earrings?"

"Nice."

"For my semisweet fourteenth. That's what my mom called it. She was being sarcastic."

He gets a bad picture in his mind of the two of them on a couch. "It was a lot of fun that night," she says, *"if you remember."*

"Good."

"I wish I had my own car. I'd love to come to Beverly Hills more. What kind of car does your friend have? Do you think you could introduce me to him? My parents aren't coming home."

"I feel burnt. Sorry, I gotta go."

On the way home, he takes a familiar detour, getting off the San Diego Freeway at Mulholland and speeding toward Benedict Canyon. Fog thick as soup rolls in. Some people get scared driving winding Mulholland in the fog, but he doesn't mind, kind of likes it actually, being able to see nothing ahead or behind him, rocketing along in a mystical cocoon illuminated only by his car's headlights, feeling at once on the edge and at peace, however briefly. One night in the fog he had been cruising up here at about forty with a couple of excited girls, just acquaintances, and without any warning, he stepped the car up to sixty and then seventy, barely able to see turns twenty feet in front of him, this being the way he wanted it, the girls suddenly panicking, screaming *Slow down, slow down . . . Are you fucking crazy? . . . Don't you know some Beverly guy killed himself driving off a cliff?* In fact, he did know, but the poor kid had done it intentionally, people had told him, just drove his Volkswagen right off the road after letting a friend in on his plan, and Andy told the girls he wouldn't ever do anything that stupid. *Retarded asshole,* one of the girls shouted at him when he finally stopped to let her out at a corner. The other girl made him bring her straight to the Bagel Nosh and hasn't spoken to him since.

Since then, whenever he gets caught in the fog, he can't help but see that moment — the car sliding, he wrestling with the wheel, the girls screaming, that instant when he wondered, quite calmly, whether he could ever possibly get so screwed up that he'd drop himself and his car over a cliff. He's never found out as much about the dead kid as he would have liked. Once he heard the guy was very straight, that he'd had no drugs or alcohol in his system when they found him, that he was nice and a tennis player and popular and all that, but all kids who offed themselves got described as nice and popular, so that didn't mean much. What did was that he wore braces and that some kind of report, a cop's report or doctor's report or something on the crash, had said he was sixty-nine inches tall. That really got him. Sixty-nine *inches*, like death had to have its own bizarre scale of measurements. Or like they'd taken out a tape measure and just didn't have the time to put the number in feet, so that people would understand. It took him a few seconds to convert the number — five feet, nine inches. A measly inch taller than himself. Just another little kid with braces, like his former self, too, though, thank God, he'd gotten rid of his steel factory of a mouth, even the retainers, before junior year.

The fog has enveloped the car. *Oh, yeah. . . .* He cranks up an old Doors tape that Jason gave him and cruises through the blind turns, seeing nothing but soup in front and behind through the rearview mirror, all alone here, hitting the accelerator a little harder, a little harder. The harrowing ride at seventy takes two minutes. He stops at Benedict Canyon, breathes deeply. It's not quite enough tonight. He wheels around to drive his slalom course again. Why? Why not? He's asleep by five.

The next afternoon, he sees Sandra. They eat at the Cheesecake Factory and walk through some stores. He drinks bottled water everywhere they go, a hangover from last night lingering. In Saks, he finally gets to the purpose of this stroll. "Would you like to go to the prom with me?"

She surprises him. "Do you really want to go?"

"Yeah, sure."

"Why?"

He thinks about this. "Everybody goes. Aren't you going to your own prom next year?"

"I don't know."

"Well, I don't want to *not* go. It's kind of embarrassing in a way if you don't go."

"But do you really want to go?"

"No," he admits. "But I feel like I have to."

"Let's do something real fun instead," she suggests. "It'll probably be the first time all year we did something that we totally want to do."

"I'll think about it," he says.

———

Nearly every Beverly senior attending will be going to the prom in a limousine. Not any limousine will do. Most kids want the long stretch limo. Preferably black. Those whose after-prom party location will be far from the Beverly Hilton Hotel, the site of the prom, have made arrangements to stock their limos with everything from Perrier to tequila. Weeks ago, while considering holding a post-prom party with his closest friends in a hotel suite near the Mexican border, Steven made inquiries into having a helicopter whisk everyone from the Hilton to San Diego. "You get these big plans, because you want it to be so hot," he says.

Steven will be going to the prom with Vickie, of course. There is no way out. Not that he hasn't looked for one the last few days. If Vickie's father hadn't put a security and cleaning deposit on a rented downtown hotel suite, and his own father hadn't already arranged for the limo, he would have told her to take a hike by now. *Bitch.* He suddenly can't stand the sight of her. A few days ago, three of his friends saw Vickie making out with his surfing buddy from Pali in full view of people along the bar at Cutter's. It had been a near-fatal blow to his ego, so much so that he immediately called a precinct organizer for Bobbi Fiedler and told him he couldn't help with pamphlet distribution that day. He lay on his bed. He wondered how many of his friends knew he had been played for a sucker. Had he been the secret butt of gossip on the Third-Floor Patio? Oh, *shit. After all he had done for her.* How long had it been going on? He remembered Vickie spending a lot of time talking to Rick, the Pali dude, at his party. The realization struck:

This was very bad.

He had been made a fool of.

Totally.

He felt like a *geek.* And yet the word put his humiliation into perspective for him. *Heartbroken,* for instance, was not a word that came to mind. He did not love this girl: At its best, their relationship had always been based upon mutual lust and her desperation. He picked up the phone, got Vickie's answering machine. "Hi, it's me," he said casually to the machine. "When you get in, why don't you give me a call."

That was Sunday night. He skips school on Monday to go surfing, not quite ready to face Vickie. The surf is lousy, one- to two-footers, with no shape. He gets a Michelob, takes it into the water, and drinks it while sitting on his board. Four hours and five Michelobs later he calls Laura from a pay phone.

"Have you already made your prom plans?" As his words come out he realizes the hot sun and five beers have made him speak too soon.

"I'm about to, why?"

"I don't know. I'll call you later."

When he gets home, Vickie is waiting in her car by his driveway.

"You didn't even come by school today," she says. "I thought you might be avoiding me." A grin to suggest that she is not being serious here, testing, probing to see how much he knows.

He just wants to get this over with, he decides. "I really couldn't have faced you today. It would have been too hard."

"You don't understand," she says.

He gets angry. "What's there to understand? You're into him. You were making out with him on some bar stool at Cutter's. You slept with him, right?"

"You've been listening to stories."

"Well, are they bullshit?"

A sob. "No."

"You're such a bitch for doing this and not telling me."

She runs at him. He puts out his hand, stops her, pushes her away. Hard. She flies into the garage wall, and topples onto the floor. "Sorry," he says immediately, and sticks out a hand to help her up. She slaps it away. "Fucking bastard," she wails, refusing to move from the cold and dirty floor, her white pants being stained by a tiny puddle of oil that has collected in the garage's corner. He touches her shoulder gently. She begins crying. "You just wanted me gone as soon as Laura got back in the picture," she shouts, between sobs. "It's . . . your . . . fa . . . fault."

"*My fault?* How do you get that? *My* fault?"

"You wanted to be with Laura. How do you think that made me feel? I wanted to be with *you*."

"You have bizarre ways of showing it."

The truth, or as much of it as she will reveal, comes slowly. She brings her knees to her chest on the garage floor. She bawls that she first met Rick at the party a few weeks ago. She let herself be persuaded by Rick to have a couple of rum and Cokes with him in the backyard. At some point, he suggested that they should get together sometime. "It went from there," she says, mascara running beneath her eyes, "because you just seemed so hot about being around Laura the whole time at the party. It's like you're in space whenever anybody mentions her name. You totally ignored my feelings. You were just dumping on me."

"I never did anything except talk to Laura. I never *slept* with her, that's for fucking sure."

"But you wanted to, *didn't you?* She's all you talk about half the time. *Get real.* I'm not a total idiot, Steven. You've wanted to sleep with her, so what's the difference? Tell me."

"You don't know how I feel."

"I don't. I never know exactly how you feel, because you're so secret about it. But you have all those long talks with Laura. How do you think that makes me feel? I wanted to be with somebody who wanted to be with me and Rick was just there, you know? At least he listens to me. The thing with Laura *hurts*. You've been such a fucking asshole. It's like I'm not worth shit. I'm pathetic: That's what you think. My life is a joke, right? I hate it, talking about all of this, but you've been such an asshole . . ."

She has cried herself out. She presses her face against her pants. He bends down to help her up. "*Don't*," she warns, but she is too spent to shake his hand off, does not resist when he puts a second hand under her armpit and brings her to her feet. "I just don't want you to ruin your pants," he says softly. She moves a few feet backwards along the garage wall to get away from him and bumps dumbly into his surfboard, sending it toppling. "I'll get it," he says, watching her lean wearily against a new place on the wall, eyes closed, her smeared mascara giving her a raccoon's look — two black eyes; she is beaten. He feels not the pleasant revenge that he expected but guilt, embarrassed that she read his passion for Laura so easily. "Why didn't you ever talk to me?" the limp figure asks him, her voice suddenly flat, simply curious now to understand her deficiencies. "Am I just too stupid for you? Something like that?" She wipes at a damp cheek, stares at bits of mascara on her fingers. "I've been too boring, right? Or something?" She closes her eyes and leans her head back against the wall as if trying to sleep.

"What are we going to do?" he asks, putting his surfboard back in place.

"Well, you probably want to go with Laura, right?"

"To the prom, you mean?"

She does not open her eyes. "Yeah."

"No. I think we should still go together, unless you want to go with Rick." He doesn't need any more guilt at this moment. Let her make the decision. "It would be okay if you really want to go with him. I'll understand."

"I could still go with you, if you want to go."

"Okay."

"Okay," she says, not opening her eyes.

"Can I ask you something?" His voice is high and curious, the way it sounded in his freshman-geek days. "Did you really sleep with him?"

She opens her eyes. A faint smile. "Not really. Close, but we didn't."

"Are you into him at all?"

"Kind of, I guess. He's real nice. I care about you, but I care about him a lot, too."

"Uh-huh."

"Are you into Laura?"

"Kind of."

"I wonder where I'm going to find pants like these."

One great thing about Laura, he reasons on the way over to her house later, is that no one better understands his capacity for bumbling with girls, for completely misreading a smile, pout, or tear, and reacting like a geek, or not reacting at all. During his freshman year, when a sophomore girl smiled and thanked him for grabbing some of her papers that had blown away in a stiff wind, he took it to mean that she had the hots for him. "You think with your dick, Steven," Laura irritably told him on that occasion. And when he had failed to notice, during his sophomore year, that a shy girl in his biology class liked him, Laura pulled him aside and shook sense into him before shoving him into the direction of the girl. She will understand, he tells himself, when he explains that he has bumbled again, that he feels guilty for having given Vickie so little attention these past few weeks. She will understand when he says that he still must take Vickie to the prom.

"I don't know why you have to go with her," Laura protests.

"It's just that I *think* I should. I've been kind of a shit, I guess."

"What about *her?*"

"She's been, too."

"Oh," Laura says, "this is so screwed, isn't it?"

"Yeah."

"Sometimes I think we're supposed to be together, you know."

"Uh-huh," he says, shrugging.

"And sometimes I don't know."

"Uh-huh."

She sighs. "It's weird."

He does not arrive home until one thirty A.M. Never before this semester would Steven have allowed anything, besides studying, to keep him from getting a minimum of eight hours sleep on a school night, but no one, not even Steven, is thinking much of school these days. He does not awaken until nine thirty, long after his first class has ended. He has no incentives to study or, more aptly, no disincentives to keep him from taking it easy.

He wonders what he'll need to do to stay ahead of the pack in college, realizes, in the same instant, that he'll do anything. A kid from UCLA told him of a grad student who writes English and history papers for undergraduates for anywhere from fifty to fifteen hundred dollars, depending on the length of the paper and whether the grad student has ever researched the topic before. Interest in the specially tailored papers ran so high that, a few months earlier, the grad student took on another writer to meet student demand. Steven resolves to discover whether such a service can be found in the Berkeley or Palo Alto area. A degree from

Stanford or Berkeley without a high g.p.a. and a ticket into a prestigious professional or graduate school probably means goddamn nothing. *Do whatever it takes.*

In the last few days, he has talked a great deal about Harvard, as well as one other school that rejected him. The initial sweetness of acceptances from schools like Berkeley and Stanford has turned sour with the understanding that not every institution in the nation wanted him. "I kind of assumed in tenth grade that I'd be accepted everywhere, including Harvard, and that I'd then have to decide between the East Coast and the West Coast," he says. "My parents kind of assumed it, too, plus my friends, my parents' friends, and some of my teachers. Part of the thing is that you feel you have to live up to an image. But the bigger part is that you worked so hard proving yourself, getting every good grade that counts, and then you fail in a way; a couple of schools don't think that you're good enough for them. That's a little *disheartening* — that's the best word I can think of for it — and you gotta tell yourself that if Harvard didn't want you, at least another good place did. I still can't figure out what I was missing, why Harvard didn't want me. It bothers you, you know? . . ."

———

With Hillary's brother Matt back home, on indefinite "leave of absence" from college, Harry is unhappy. He has not been able to abide the boy, since the first night, when Matt usurped his favorite chair in the den and moved his golf clubs out of their anointed corner in the guest room so that Matt could install his telescope there.

"I don't want to come home every day and find that kid of yours plopped in front of the television munching potato chips and drinking our soft drinks and beers," Harry shouted at her mother one afternoon. "He clearly doesn't like me. He never talks to me. Around the rest of the world the kid is Howdy Doody. Around me, he's the deaf-mute. What the hell have I done?"

"Harry, I'm surprised I have to say this to you, but this is his house, too. I think that both of you have to make an effort to understand each other better. *Both* of you."

"Jesus Christ, don't lecture me like *I'm* the flunky on academic probation."

"*He didn't flunk out, Harry.* He isn't on academic probation. He came home because he needed a rest from it. And I don't need you to speak in that tone to me again."

It got so bad one night that Harry took off. Just upped and left with a small duffel bag, a sandwich, and his golf clubs. Hillary's mother conjured up an excuse that Harry had to go out of town on business. Hillary didn't press her for the truth but when Harry didn't come back the next day she asked her mom if everything was okay.

"Harry's feeling a little strain, that's all," replied her mom.

"When is he coming back?"

"I don't know. But it's very nice of you, dear, to show concern."

Was it concern or merely curiosity, a desire to be informed when their boarder officially gave notice of his intent to vacate? She didn't trust him. He remained, in her eyes, an oafish, officious presence, parading bare-chested around the house and dispensing banal advice. "You should try some bran, sweetheart," he had said to her one morning, before adding, "and some vitamin E might help that tiny bit of sunburn you've got on your nose." Sitting at breakfast, he asked her sweetly if she had been "studying enough lately." Averting her eyes from his chest, she curtly reminded him that he was neither her teacher nor parent. He apologized immediately, and that evening gave her a Cross pen to replace a similar one she had lost. She couldn't help but feel a grudging respect for his unflappable kindness and the tenacity with which he tried to woo them all. She wanted her mom to be happy, and maybe happiness necessitated Harry, she thought, the night he left. Glimpsing her mom, who was staring blankly through a window in the den, she saw not a parent but merely an older woman fearing that time might be running out. *Get home, Harry.*

It would be two more days before he did. Something about Hillary's feelings changed in his absence. Hillary encourages her older brother to meet Harry halfway, and Matt always replies that she should stop speaking in clichés. The older and younger man co-exist during the evenings now, the burgundy leather chair in front of the den television, once Harry's exclusive domain, now tacitly understood to be the dominion of whoever arrives there first each night. The arrangement gives a decided advantage to the vacationing Matt, who usually settles into it at six thirty P.M., about a half-hour before Harry arrives home and in enough time to set up his tray of potato chips, dip, and soft drinks. After Harry walks through the door and changes into his sweats, the two men sit together in stony silence. *"Talk to him,"* Hillary will urge her brother when Harry has left the room. Matt might later ask the older man if he wants a potato chip, but not much else. Peace seems to be prevailing anyway. Hillary communicates the news to her father, who worries about the possibility of discord in the new household. "Good," he tells her on the phone one night. "I get worried about your brother and mother sometimes. They're very similar, both shaky personalities. You're very solid, whether you know it or not. I'm counting upon you to keep everything together."

She thinks it's sweet that he would be concerned about keeping together a family of which he is no longer a day-to-day member, then realizes her perspective is silly, archaic; that her father is a daily member whether he lives with them or not, that what he has been talking about all along is keeping the different pieces of the family together, wherever they are. She thought, in the beginning, that the family had perished with the appearance of Harry, but begins to believe now that it has simply changed shape. One afternoon, Harry strolls into her bedroom and says he's had a sudden inspiration that involves her. "*You*," he says slowly, grinning to suggest that what he is about to say is momentous, "should take a speed-reading course before college, so you can go from a B student who doesn't have enough time to read all the things she wants, to an A student who has all the time in the world. What do you think?" She manages a smile, says she'll think about it.

The day for Paul's meeting with the dealer in Canoga Park has arrived. He has a snack over at Roxanne's house and tells her he has to go with Adam into the Valley to pick up some water-skis. When Adam pulls up in front of her house, Paul is furious to see Tony and Randy sitting in the back seat. "I thought we were seeing this guy alone," he says to Adam, not bothering to look at Tony.

"The meeting is only going to take a few minutes so I thought we'd cruise somewhere afterwards," says Adam.

"You should have told me."

"Don't get hard-core about it," groans Randy.

Normally, Paul would have turned around to the back seat and told Randy to fuck off, but he doesn't want to look at Tony. He opens the car window instead and stays quiet as they race on to the freeway, trying to relax, to think only of being cool and laid-back when they arrive at the dealer's house. He tells himself that he should smile a lot, and practices a tight, quick smile in the car. Smile. Stop. Smile. Stop. Smile. Okay. Okay. Relax.

The house is not a house at all but a faded yellow shack on the edge of Canoga Park. A grove of orange and lemon trees stands nearby, and the lot on which the shack sits has a half-dozen fruit trees that have yet to be harvested. Overripe fruit lies fallen everywhere. The dealer, a skinny balding guy, wearing a straw hat and cut-off jeans, sits on his porch, sucking on an orange, waving at them with long stick-arms. He has a thin jet-black ponytail, and a shimmering jewel of some sort stuck in his earlobe. *"That's the dude?"* Paul asks, in the car, unable to stifle a smile.

"Uh-huh." Adam, looking a little nervous, slams his car's wheels into the curb.

"He kind of looks like a wimp."

"Keep that to yourself."

"He kind of reminds me of one of those scarecrow dudes."

Adam grabs his shoulder. "You're not understanding, Paul. You don't want to fuck with this guy. Randy and Tony, you guys stay here until we're done. Just don't fuck up, Paul. Believe me, you'd regret it. *You get it? You understand?*"

Paul removes Adam's hand from his shoulder. *"Whatever. Hey, take it easy, Adam."*

The two get out of the car, walk across the lawn, and sit down on the porch with the dealer, who offers them oranges. He gestures at the trees to indicate that they should pick the fruit themselves.

"Thanks," says Paul, remembering to smile, coolly tilting his sunglasses upon the top of his head.

"Vitamin C is real important," says the dealer. "I read everything I can about health. You can't get enough C."

Paul grabs two small oranges off a tree, sits back down on the porch, and puts the oranges between his feet.

"You don't want to eat too much of the pulp," the dealer cautions, "and always stay away from the seeds. Hey, aren't you going to eat them? *Eat.* It's a lot better than beer for the gut, I'll tell you. It's *Paul,* right? Adam tells me you exercise a lot. Listen, you drink orange juice instead of Budweisers and you'll see pounds fly off. Better for your skin coloring, too. What kind of vitamins do you take?"

"I don't know," Paul says slowly. "Whatever my mom's got in the house. She has good vitamins, I guess."

"Make sure you take a B-complex, but don't exceed the RDAs for A. It can hurt you."

"Yeah, okay. You're probably right."

"And if you really want to be smart — and I'm only saying this because Adam says how hard you're working out at your gym — if you want to be real smart you should stay away from red meat and concentrate on the fish and fowl. *Listen* to me: And do a lot of light weights to get toned. Concentrate on *tone*. Weights that give you a lot of bulk only slow you down and make you age faster. Get some wheat germ, too."

"Okay."

"So you want to sell some blow?"

He hadn't been ready. He tells himself to smile. "I don't know, yeah, I'd like to."

"How much?"

"I don't know. But I'd go for whatever you think is right."

"Uh-huh. Who are those people, Adam, in the back seat of your car?"

Adam grins. "Just some buddies. They're pussies. They're okay."

The dealer peels an orange. "They make me nervous sitting there, staring like that. Get them out of there. Tell them they can get some oranges if they want."

Adam shouts to Tony and Randy to get out of the car.

"The amount I could give would have to be very small at this point, you understand," the dealer says to Paul.

"Sure."

"And you'd have to handle it exactly as I said."

"Okay."

"And times and places would have to be at my convenience."

"Whatever. Sure."

"You're an awfully agreeable guy."

Paul, unsure how to respond to this, smiles.

"You damn well smile a lot."

Paul stops smiling.

"Paul, you're not stupid, are you?"

"No."

"Because I get annoyed at stupid people."

"Uh-huh."

"Paul, do you get annoyed at stupid people?"

"Yeah."

"Not as much as me. Believe me. I get very annoyed."

Forty feet away, Randy, pulling hard upon a tree branch to get his orange, stumbles, falls, and loses grip of the branch, which whips into Tony's face. Tony swears and grabs his nose. From out of the shack come three giants in tight T-shirts, looking at the dealer for some signal. The dealer motions for them to sit down.

"Oh, fuck, you're bleeding, man," says Randy. "I'm sorry. Jesus Christ, I slipped."

Tony rips a piece of peel off an orange, sticking it against his nostrils.

"Did I already ask you if you were a fuck-up?" the dealer asks Paul, glancing over at his friends.

"Kind of."

"And what?"

"I'm not," says Paul, softly. "I mean, I'm not a screw-up." Out of the corner of his right eye, he sees Tony leaning against an orange tree, putting his head back in an effort to stop the flow of blood. An embarrassed Randy helps Tony hold the peel against his face. Could you get AIDS from touching someone's blood during a nosebleed? Paul wants to shout, *Get away, get away.* The dealer is studying his expression. He should say something to assure this man that he can do the job. "I'm a hard worker when I want to be," he boasts, in his coolest voice.

"And what about when you don't want to be?"

"Well, that wouldn't be with this, because this wouldn't bore me."

"*Now* it doesn't. But what if it did later?"

"Well, I don't think it would. But if it did, I'd tell you and quit."

"And go to work at your daddy's?"

The dealer is grinning. The three giants laugh.

"No. I don't know what I want to do for a job."

"Yeah, you seem *not to know* a lot. But what *do* you know?"

"I know enough," Paul protests.

"Hey, you don't even know where your mommy keeps your vitamins."

The dealer and his arm-breakers chuckle. Paul feels stumped, like he did in second grade when the teacher berated him for not being able to subtract single numbers, asking him how *he could not know that. You have to answer this by yourself, Paulie,* the teacher would say. *I can't help you. And your mommy can't help you.* The dealer puts an orange slice in Paul's hand. "Eat it. Why haven't you lost a lot of weight if you're trying so hard?"

"I *have* lost some."

"Did your mommy make you go to the gym?"

"No, like, I'm sure. Why do you keep asking about my mother?"

"Listen, you're not going to pay for this stuff I give you with your parents' Visa. And you're not going to be able to have your maid put the stuff in nice little baggies for your friends if you don't want to be around one day. And you can't go rushing to Mommy if you need money. I don't want any of your mommy's *steenking* checks. No *steenking* Beverly Hills shit, do you get that?"

He tries to stay cool. "I know that, dude."

"What did you call me?"

"Huh?"

"Don't call him dude, asshole," Adam snaps at him.

"Sorry."

"Don't ever, *ever* call me dude."

"I won't."

"Just take off. I gotta do some business. Adam will be in touch if we're interested."

"Okay."

"Split. Go."

"Sure." He stands to leave with his oranges.

"And take your friends. I don't want that guy bleeding any more on my tree."

Tony has overheard him. "Fuck your tree."

The dealer stands very slowly. "What did you say?"

"I *said*," Tony repeats, moving the peel away from his nose, *"go fuck your tree."*

The three giants stand. "You got a big mouth," says the dealer.

"And you're an asshole," says Tony.

The dealer looks at Adam. "Your friend has a bad habit of talking when he shouldn't. You better get him in the car right now, man."

"Get in the car, Tony," Adam commands.

"I could probably sue you," says Tony to the dealer. "This tree branch I got hit with is dangerous."

"There are fuckin' bigger dangers," the dealer says.

Paul sees three of the dangers taking tiny, almost imperceptible steps in Tony's direction; it occurs to him that all trained killers — pit bulls, coyotes, mercenaries, and homicidal enforcers for little pushers — move with tiny steps. To stop the tattooed giants, to interrupt this staredown between his erstwhile friend and the dealer, he shouts, "Hey, when am I going to hear from you?"

The dealer wheels around to face him. "Shut up."

"Shut up, Paul," says Adam.

Bravado has never been one of his strong suits. "I just want to go," he says weakly.

The dealer shakes his head at his enforcers, puts up his hand like a stop sign.

"Get out of here," orders the dealer.

The boys walk to the curb.

"One more thing," shouts Tony, looking back. "You can have your *steenking* oranges."

"You should have shut your mouth, Tony," Adam sneers as they get on the freeway. "You got lucky that somebody didn't rip you a new asshole. You're such a dick sometimes. What makes you think you can get away with that shit?"

"Adam," says Tony, "at least once in your life you should listen to how your asshole drug buddies treat people."

"You could have made things bad for all of us," Adam screams. "You never know when to shut up. Paul and I are trying to do something and you and Randy are being dicks."

"*Dicks?* Hey, we *had* to get out of the car because that paranoid pencil-neck geek thought we were narcs or something."

"You don't know what you're talking about. He's cool. Didn't you think he was okay, Paul?"

"I don't know."

"Well, you better know, if you feel like doing anything with him."

"That's what I mean," says Tony. "You're like the full-on wimp around the guy. He says, 'Jump,' and you jump like a dog, Adam. I can't believe you even hang with him. The guy is a total asshole."

"Oh, yeah? So why didn't you say that to him?"

Tony laughs. "I did."

"Yeah, he did," says Randy.

Adam looks over at Paul, who nods.

"It still doesn't make it cool what you did," says Adam.

"And you were gonna be a pussy and say nothing?" asks Tony. "Just sit there and let the guy talk all this shit? He's calling one of your friends a fuck-up and a Mommy's boy and you're saying, 'Yes, yes.' "

"His name is Paul," Randy says.

Tony says nothing.

Paul says nothing.

Randy shakes his head. "Are we going to have to listen to this one-of-your-friends shit until you guys apologize to each other? Are we, dude? Tony? Paul? Say something, okay?"

"Okay, Randy, I'll say something," says Tony. "Shut up."

Randy shrugs. "Don't freak about it, dude."

Tony grimaces, blood suddenly gushing from his nose down onto his pants. He throws his head back. Adam hands him a box of tissues from the glove compartment. Paul still sees Tony, in his mind's eye, bleeding upon that orange peel and telling the dealer, *"Fuck your tree."* No doubt about it: The guy has balls.

He arrives home to find his father, who's just returned from another business trip that took him through Lima, Quito, and Mexico City. Paul doesn't know where Lima and Quito are.

"I understand congratulations are in order, college man," his father says, carrying a drink and his briefcase into the den. Paul nods, lying on the floor, propping his head on a pillow to watch "Leave It to Beaver." He hopes his old man won't choose the middle of "Beaver" for a talk. Bones waddles in and curls at his feet. His father sticks in his ear plugs.

After "Beaver," Paul wanders into the kitchen, looking for a beer. His mom and the housekeeper are making a clam dip for his father.

"Sweetheart," she says to him, "Tony came by earlier and dropped off some tickets for a Laker game he said you gave him but that he can't use. I put them on top of the refrigerator."

"Okay."

"Why can't he use them?"

"Probably has to do something."

"Are you going to the game?"

"Probably."

"Is anything wrong?"

"Mom don't interrogate me, okay?" *Interrogate:* He likes the word. He heard it on an old "Highway Patrol" that he had managed to find on his father's satellite dish the other day. The fat cop had used it: "Interrogate them and see what you can find out." Paul puts up his hand. "No more interrogation, Mom."

"I'm just interested, dear," his mom says. "I know Tony is a good friend."

"Don't try and help me with everything, okay?"

He tells her that he's getting dinner at Jack-in-the-Box and drives over to Roxanne's. "Tony just dumped these Laker tickets back on me," he tells her. "I wouldn't have minded him going with us. Adam and Randy or some other guys could have come along. I didn't ask for the tickets back or anything."

"You could say that to him."

"No way."

"Why are you so full-on angry at him?"

"I don't know. He's pissed at me, too. It's hard to explain."

"What *is* it?"

"It's kind of personal — not for me. For him. It's one thing I can't really talk about. Don't ask me."

"All right."

"Because I *really* can't."

"Okay, okay. Is he going to the prom?"

"I don't know," he says, reminding himself to ask Randy what the latest is on this.

"Who are you taking?"

Paul smiles. This has become a joke between them now. A couple of weeks ago, he invited her, but she has to fly East with her mom and dad to visit an ailing grandmother on the same weekend as the prom. "*You know* who I'm taking," he says.

When they were in bed together last night, he told her: He's invited an old friend. It is important to him that he be at the prom. Roxanne understood.

"I'm just giving you shit." She laughs. "Were you relieved at all that I couldn't go? Not being a Beverly girl and all?"

"No." He is stunned that she senses this. "I wanted *you* to go with me. Nobody else."

She smiles. "You weren't even thinking about it a little?"

"Maybe in the beginning. Just a little."

"You're cute." She kisses him.

"I get weirded by things sometimes. I don't know why."

"Who would Tony go with if he went?"

"I'm not sure. Do we have to keep talking about Tony?"

"I don't know, Paul. He's your friend, or your old friend, but you should at least talk to him if you don't want to be buddies anymore. You could be kind or *something*. Talk to him."

"What do I say?"

———

"No prom?" Kelly's father asks in amazement.

He has taken her to dinner; but she really doesn't want to discuss anything about school. "There's no one to go with," she says brusquely, studying a menu, anxious to finish this discussion so that she can order and eat. She needs something in her stomach. For breakfast, she only had a pear; for lunch, nothing; and, as usual since she went on her "kamikaze" diet, she feels light-headed. In two months, she has shed only five of the twenty pounds projected by the nutritionist her mom hired for her at fifty dollars per half-hour, despite consuming five hundred calories fewer per day than what the nutritionist declared to be necessary for good health. She's having too many pear slices at breakfast, she thinks. "Maybe I'm too overweight, Dad. Or not cool enough. I don't have a lot of friends, you know."

"What about that boy?"

"He's fifteen, Dad. I'd feel embarrassed in a way taking him to the prom."

"Your mom doesn't feel embarrassed about younger guys, does she?"

"Let's drop that."

"How old was the last guy — twenty-three, if that?"

"I don't remember, Dad. Can we talk about me? Can we get some appetizers first?"

"Sure, sweetheart. But I just can't imagine there isn't some nice, attractive guy in your class who can't use a date. Can't you put out the word — however it's done — that you're free that night, that maybe you haven't been asked by the right guy."

"Everybody knows who's free. That's part of the problem. You don't want to go out with a loser. Everybody who isn't going already is looked at like they're losers. Probably me, too."

"No, sweetheart, people wouldn't think like that."

"You're wrong, Dad. Why do you and Mom tell me how people think? A lot of 'em think that way." She pauses, feels her eyes stinging, takes a deep breath. *Do not cry here.* "I don't even care so much about going, you know. I just feel like such a geek not being invited." She closes her eyes, but a few tears come down her cheeks anyway. "I'm sorry, I don't usually freak like this."

"No problem, darling. Everything is fine."

She shields her eyes with her hand. "Don't always say that, okay?"

"Okay, sweetheart."

"Everything is not all right."

"That's okay, sweetheart. That's why I'm here. There are boys at other schools. We'll figure something out."

"Why don't you listen to me? *I don't want you to figure out anything, Dad.* I don't want to talk about the prom. Can we please get something to eat? *Now?* My head hurts so much. Just give me a piece of bread, okay?"

"Okay, sweetheart."

"I'd just like it to be quiet for a second so I can think."

"Okay."

"I wish this would go away."

"What?"

"My head. Everything."

They eat in silence. "Does it ever help to talk to a close friend — Tina or Andrea or that boy you see — someone like that?" her father asks on the way home.

"No," she says, "I wouldn't do that." Kurt, at fifteen, has yet to grasp her anxieties about college and the future, her feelings of failure and low self-worth. Her friends, even Tina, gossip so much about other people, including each other, that it has come to worry her. "They might use it against me sometime," she says, "if I said something weird. I get tired of worrying about what they think about me. It's hard. There's no one really to talk to. Have you ever been on a diet, Dad? You get so tired. God, really tired. Why am I telling you? You've never been on a diet. See, there's no one for me to talk to about any of this."

———

Melinda, sitting in a coffee shop, is angry. "I guess I'm just worrying about things right now," she says. "Things" means Roger, her friend with whom she will be going to the prom, with whom she may or may not be in love, with whom she is furious at this moment because he called her the other night to say, "I'm kind of like in jail."

He was clutching a pay phone in a holding tank of the San Diego jail. On the other end of the line, Melinda could hear bars slamming. He had been charged with aiding and abetting a girl, a college classmate, who had tried to shoplift a dress at a department store. Melinda asked him if he was all right. Roger said coolly, *Yeah, fine.* He had been searched and fingerprinted, and, finally, they had taken his mug shot, but everything would be fine, since the cops indicated they were releasing him on his own recognizance. She thought she heard a chuckle from him. She asked him if he had cried, and he said *no* so casually that she became livid. He was treating the affair as just another joke in his life, another fuck-up that would be swept under the rug as easily as all the others. "What *happened?*" she demanded.

He had been waiting for the girl outside the store, unaware of what was happening inside, he said, when the girl suddenly appeared and said they needed to go. "It was a felony for the girl," he said softly into the phone. "She would have been in big trouble. I had to help her out." The girl jumped into his car but the bust happened too quickly for them. Melinda could hear gruff shouts and more bars clanging in the background.

"You *sure* you're all right?" she asked.

"Oh, yeah."

There didn't seem to be anything more worth saying. He said that he'd call her later. She could not resist the urge to remind him that he needn't do anything stupid for a while, then hung up. She immediately thought that it'd be nice if he made it home that weekend. She'd been off the phone only ten seconds and already missed him. She found herself forgiving a great deal. "He gets involved in things he can't control," she says, rapping her plate with a fork. A waitress surveys her, smiles, moves on. "I don't know, I'm kind of less annoyed about it now. Sometimes I'm annoyed, sometimes I'm not. I can be a pain to him, too. I can be real harsh, and then I can sometimes be nice. I don't know. Roger will say to me, 'Stop acting like yourself,' and I'll know he means for me to calm down. I get emotional, up and down, especially about *her*. Mostly, that's what we talk about — the little girl."

The Little Girl: It is her moniker for Roger's fifteen-year-old girlfriend. "The fact that he sleeps with her doesn't bother me as much as it used to," Melinda says. "Maybe she's real good in bed. I don't care. It doesn't mean much to him, so it doesn't bother me much. I guess what bothers me is that he spends time with her when I want to be with him, too. Maybe I have a selfish attitude, but I think he belongs to me. I saw him first, and I've known him a lot, lot longer. . . .

"We're kind of playing games with each other for the first time. We never did it when we were just friends, so I don't like it. It's like he wants to see how high I'll jump for him, and I'll tell him on the phone, when he's in San Diego, that I'm going out somewhere and he'll start up with, 'Who are you going out with? Who?' I'll evade the question. He tells me he's confused about his feelings. He has to get his tuxedo picked out tomorrow. He promises not to come in a 'Dynasty' tuxedo or looking like 'Miami Vice,' so I think he'll be all right. And I told him, 'You better not go to jail anymore.' He knows I want him to go to the prom, but he knows I won't accept him fucking up anymore, so he better be on good behavior. . . .

"I'm handling the prom arrangements for everything. I've got the limo rented. We're going with two other couples, but I'm the one stuck with everything to do, naturally. I don't want to go to the after-prom party at the Palace with everybody there. I want to do something private and fun. I don't want to be somewhere that just has school kids. We could go to a condo in the Marina, but I think we're going to Vertigo instead. You stand there at the door, and this doorman for the club picks people to go inside. Whatever you do when the prom is over is so important because they're real strict at the prom. You can't do much. . . .

"I heard that at the Beverly Hilton they're going to have narcs dressed like these bathroom maids. If you stay in the bathroom stall too long, they knock on the door. That's what I heard. And they only allow fruit juices and soft drinks in the limos. That's so lame. The idea of a prom is geeky, I think. Nearly everybody does coke at a prom. It kind of goes together, coke and prom. . . .

"I wouldn't do it before the prom because I'd be afraid I'd get nervous and hyper. I wouldn't do it in the bathrooms there because I wouldn't want to get busted and sent home. I'd do it in the limousine. Well, not there, because no one is doing it in our limo. Oh, Cecilia will. Her boyfriend is twenty-seven. Like I'm sure, he shouldn't be able to do what he wants to. He's *twenty-seven*. I'll do it in the limo, too, I guess. Cathy and Greg are bringing two grams, probably. That's another expense. Maybe we'll get it free from Cathy and Greg. Or maybe Roger will get us some, too. . . .

"The plan right now is to get my nails and toes done the day before the prom, right after I go to the beach. I need a little more of a tan. The day of the prom I'll get my hair done at four forty-five, then Cecilia will come by at six and we'll do our makeup together. Everybody else will meet at my house at seven thirty, and that is when the limo will arrive. We should be at the Beverly Hilton when it starts, like around eight thirty. They say that they are closing the doors at nine. I have to do all the arrangements because I'm the only one I really trust. I'm talking so much about it it must seem like it's the only thing on my mind. . . .

"I want to look right. I'm just so perfect-conscious these days, maybe. I don't know, maybe I'm trying to be perfect because of Roger. Maybe I should relax a little more about it, but it is hard because sometimes I think it can work and sometimes I don't. I just wouldn't want a fuck-up, but I'm glad he's not totally straight and his mind isn't made up about everything, because mine isn't. Barry, that other guy from

Beverly, was so set in his views; that is partly why I thought he was so boring. Roger isn't. Roger isn't a perfect kid, but I know he has a good heart."

A young man in a business suit at a nearby table glances at her, elbowing a couple of his friends to indicate that the unsuspecting pretty girl should be scrutinized. The three young men murmur something to each other. Most of the words are inaudible but two — "All-American" — somehow jump the gap between the two tables. "All-American girl," or "All-American looking": They are unmistakably speaking of Melinda.

All-American: She would not have liked that. "All-American people are just so fixed in everything they think and do, you know?" she says. She will never see herself that way, indeed takes a somewhat perverse pride in having experimented with drugs. Yet seldom, even during the period when she aroused her parents' concern by hanging out with a group of rakish girls, did her routine change a great deal at home. Usually, she took her accustomed position on the couch, between her mom, who read the newspaper, and her father, who alternately looked at the TV and his legal briefs. "I think being around them and talking about stuff probably made it easier to get my mind back on doing ordinary things in school again, when I decided to do that," Melinda says. "It was a weird time because I was totally unintellectual, even though I was doing pretty well — it wasn't like I was failing, I was getting mostly A's — but I kind of thought, being around them, that when I was ready to get back into really working hard, it would be all right. I didn't talk to them about anything special. They were just really good parents, understanding most of the time. I was never hating them, which, I think, was real important. By the ninth grade or so, I did really well. I started hearing about colleges a lot, and I thought, 'I better do something if I want to go anywhere good.' My parents were fine when they saw that my grades were good and I was studying more."

It is the same way she blithely sums up seventeen years of life with them: "I think they've been cool most of the time and, you know, smart, and always around." She knows, she says, parents who have not been cool, not been smart, not been around, mentions households where the "priorities are all screwed up." She vows to be an involved mother. All the while, a voice tells her that she must guard against being detoured by pedestrian notions of creating the conventional family. "I tell myself once in a while that I'm not going to become another silly housewife who throws away a career just to shuttle her kids and make perfectly balanced meals. The key is kind of running my own life. That's why I don't want some guy running my life either."

When families in Beverly Hills disintegrate, she notices that more often than not, working women receive the blame. "Women get it bad all ways," she says. "They take a lot of grief for working too much and then in their jobs, they are screwed, too. I read somewhere that women doctors only make half as much as men. There are still so many double standards. I don't know why guys aren't expected to do more at home with kids and things; why it is just the woman. I'm afraid that basic, traditional things will need to change before attitudes will change. I've kind of decided to do my best to make it, to do whatever it takes, but — and this might sound like a contradiction — I don't want a screwed-up family. I'm going to make sure my family is all right, so if I have to cut back a little in my job, I've decided that I will. . . . I think some of these working couples I see are going to have a lot of problems. So I have to figure out how I'll do it. Those working couples haven't thought it out. I'm going to try. Maybe I'll take some time off and then go back. I don't know. . . . I just don't want to have a husband and kids who are like strangers after a while because there wasn't enough time spent with them. You see too much of that."

Melinda's family is one of the exceptions, a model unit led by parents who nurtured her through difficult growing pains, parents whom she can call "geeks" one evening and sit with for hours the next. She sees herself as a "normal" teenager with "normal problems," but there are few lives more idyllic at Beverly. "The only thing I worry about," Melinda says now, biting a nail, whispering conspiratorially, "is that I've got to make sure I get a good enough tan before the prom or I'll look grossly pale in that gown."

———

The prom is the predominant topic now. Hillary, Kelly, and Andy will not be going. Hillary thinks she'll have a better time just hanging out with Jeremy. Kelly says, "It would have been too uncomfortable with Kurt. The hardest thing was telling my mom. I felt like enough of a geek already." Andy considered his friend Sandra's advice, and decided she was right: He really doesn't want to be at the Beverly Hilton dancing in a tuxedo with one eye on everyone else to decide whether he and Sandra look hot enough.

"I'm real surprised to hear you're not going to your own prom," his mother says.

"I'll have a lot better time not going, Mom, believe me."

"I guess you will if you think so, but missing your prom like that, I don't know. I was counting on it, I guess — seeing you all dressed up and taking your picture."

"Mom, Sandra and I could still have wine with you that night. Then you could take pictures of us just like we were going to the prom."

"Okay."

"You won't be going out on the twenty-fourth?"

She laughs. "Have I been going out that much that you need to check my social calendar?"

He shrugs. "I think it's good. Don't take this in a bad way, but you seem a lot happier."

"It's that obvious, huh?"

He nods.

"I have to tell you, I was a little scared at the beginning of the year with you applying to colleges. I didn't want to lose you and be all alone. I'm still going to miss you more than you can imagine, but I'm feeling much more secure about things. Do you understand what I mean?"

"Sure, Mom."

"Do you hate hearing that?"

"No, Mom."

"Does it embarrass you, hearing your mom talk like that?"

"No."

"I love you. I'm still going to miss you terribly. You know that, right?"

"I know, Mom." When he told her last week that he had decided upon attending a state college in Northern California, she turned her head away for the briefest of moments before wheeling back to him with that practiced shimmering smile from her debutante days. He had to remind her that it could have been worse if he had decided to go to the small private college, three thousand miles away, where his father and uncle had successfully managed to get him an acceptance. "Mom, I'm going to be home a lot, you know."

"Wonderful." She gives him her cheery smile, changes the subject. "Has your senior year been everything you thought it'd be?"

He does not know how to answer or even where to begin. "It seems like it took a long time to be over," he says simply.

———

Paul tells Roxanne that night about his meeting with the dealer in the Valley.

"*I can't believe you'd ever want to sell even a little coke,*" she shrieks. "That's hard-core. How could you?"

"I don't know," he mumbles. "I've been thinking crazy things, I guess. I thought it might be exciting. I don't know. I'm not going to do it. I'm a little scared."

"Why?"

He tells her about the dealer and his three enforcers. "Well, you shouldn't even go see that guy again," she tells him. "Just tell Adam you're *totally* not interested. And what you should be really scared of is that one of those guys could be a narc or something."

He hasn't thought of this. "No way narcs would go all the way to Canoga Park," he says.

"*Who are you?*" she wails. " *'Miami Vice'? What do you know?*"

He calls Adam to tell him he's no longer interested in dealing. They hang up on each other. The break comes at an especially bad time, because he must see Adam, Randy, and Tony that afternoon. The four have tickets to go to an Angels game in Anaheim. They meet at Randy's. When Paul arrives, Randy and Tony are lobbing a Whiffle Ball back and forth.

"Where's Adam?" he asks. "We should get going if we don't want to miss the first three innings."

Randy whips the Whiffle Ball at him. "He'll be here in a couple of minutes."

Thirty minutes later, Adam pulls up in a Corvette that Paul has never seen before. One of the dealer's giants is sitting next to him. "Sorry I'm late, dudes," Adam says. "Had something to take care of. I just got to do one more thing. It will take us five minutes. We can do it on the way."

"We're late already," Randy says. "I don't think we have time to do anything else."

"I have to do this, dude," Adam says in a flat tone that suggests there's to be no argument. "So we *have* to."

"Just give Adam his ticket," Tony says to Randy. "He can meet us there."

"Good idea," says Randy.

"This car isn't mine," says Adam. "Manny has to take it back. How do I get to Anaheim?"

"You figure that out. We're cruising. Later on."

"Don't be an asshole, Tony," Adam says.

Paul feels the giant staring at him. "Hey, man, why don't you lighten up?" he says to the giant.

The giant steps out of the car.

Tony laughs. "Randy," he says, his eyes never leaving the giant, "go inside your house and call both the police and the security patrol and tell them there is an emergency. Tell them there is a burglar and a drug dealer on your premises. Tell them the piece of shit is driving a tacky white Corvette. Tell them he is also wearing a smelly white T-shirt."

Randy starts running toward his house.

"*Dumb*, Tony," says Adam. "*Dumb.*"

"Adam, you're a stupid motherfucker," says Tony. "So you stay the fuck out of this." He turns toward the giant. "Now what the hell are you going to do, asshole? In a couple of minutes, you're going to be handcuffed and have the shit kicked out of you. Take a swing at me. Make it worse for yourself."

Randy appears at his front door.

"Did you call?" shouts Paul.

Randy, looking a little shaken, nods.

"I'd say Manny here has about two minutes before they deep-fry his ass," Tony says, taking a step closer to the giant. He glances at Paul. "What would you say?"

"I wouldn't give him that long."

"I think I'll kick your ass anyway," says the giant.

Adam tugs at the giant's wrist. "Let's go, Manny. We better go."

The giant angrily shakes off Adam's hand.

"*We gotta go, Manny.*"

The giant gets in the Corvette.

"What is the rush, guys?" says Tony. "The caterer's bringing over a nice fondue. . . ."

Adam starts the car, guns the engine.

". . . And I could make everyone a tasty wine spritzer."

The giant gives him the finger.

"So good to see you," says Tony. "Maybe, for dessert, we could have a few of your oranges. Hurry back."

The car races away.

Randy says, "I didn't call."

"Of course not," says Tony.

They decide not to go to the game and instead sit on chaise longues in Randy's backyard, Randy falling asleep, Tony and Paul flicking pebbles from the cactus garden into the pool.

"Your father is right," says Paul. "You have more balls than brains."

Tony says nothing.

"Not that that is always bad."

"Well, I didn't see you getting ready to do anything," says Tony.

Paul shrugs. "Didn't you think that guy was going to punch you out?"

"Yeah."

"It didn't bother you?"

"I knew you would have jumped on top of him at some point. Two on one, we would have had a chance."

Paul nods. "Yeah, with a tire iron." He takes a swig of beer. "Do you ever think that, like, we'll be able to talk about shit again?"

"Wasn't me who stopped talking," Tony reminds him.

"I know."

"I kind of thought, you know, that if I couldn't say something," Tony mumbles, "that you'd understand why and not hassle me. . . ."

"Maybe you're right," says Paul. "I don't know. It's bizarre for me."

"I guess what bothered me the most is that you thought I turned into some freak."

How far does Tony want to pursue this? "I didn't know what to think," he admits.

"You might not understand this but I'm still trying to work it out for myself. Because it's not going to change."

"I'm not trying to hassle you."

Tony flicks a pebble at Randy's cat.

"It's just a little weird for me," says Paul. He looks to see if Tony is grimacing. "Does that make me sound like a total asshole?"

Tony shrugs.

"Well, what do you think?"

"I just can't talk about it yet, okay?" Tony says softly.

"Okay."

———

Seven P.M. Saturday, May 24. *Prom Night.*

For Melinda, everything has been on schedule. Yesterday, she ditched school to get a tan at the beach, and, late in the afternoon, went to a beauty salon for a manicure and pedicure. Today, she had her hair done, and, an hour ago, put on her makeup with Cecilia. Nothing left to

do but go to the dance. Roger and Cecilia's boyfriend are making themselves a drink. The other couple with whom they will be sharing the limo
has just arrived. Melinda gives everyone a glass of wine. Her parents are
excited. They want to take pictures. Melinda, feeling squeezed by their
presence, suggests to her friends that they take the couple of bottles of
wine out to the pool house and drink in peace until the limo comes. The
six teenagers walk outside, past the pool, and come to the little house,
about the size of her garage, which has a bar and a long couch. "I totally
thought they'd never leave," Melinda says to her friends, who laugh. Two
of the boys have brought enough coke for eight, but everyone voices fear
about snorting in the limo. "We'll be able to do it in the bathrooms at the
prom," one of the boys says, but Melinda and the other girls aren't so
sure, Melinda relating her narcs-in-the-bathroom stories to the group,
the boys thinking hard about this while going through a bottle of wine in
twenty minutes. They're all drinking quite a bit, Melinda notices, on a
third glass herself, looking out a window toward the house for some sign
from her parents that the limo has arrived. By the time it does, at eight
thirty, an hour late, she feels drunk. "I got a good buzz on," says Cecilia's
date. They all have good buzzes. "No one goes to the prom sober," says
Melinda cheerfully, as they stream out of the pool house.

Her parents bid them goodbye and Melinda and the others rush
into the privacy of the stretch limousine's big back seats, only to have
their giddiness interrupted by the solemn expression of their driver.
"There will be no drugs and no alcohol in my limo," he announces.
"There are decanters in the back with water, Cokes, and fruit juices if you
want that."

They make it to the prom fifteen minutes before the doors of the
Beverly Hilton's banquet room close. Dinner has already begun — salad,
chicken with mozzarella cheese, and a dessert of chocolate strawberries.
Melinda and Roger, the wine having stripped them of all inhibitions,
begin talking about the problems in their relationship. Likewise, each of
the other couples seems lost in private conversation. "I have hope for us,"
Roger says to Melinda, but it becomes clear as they talk that there is no
hope; he still has feelings for his fifteen-year-old girlfriend, and Melinda
has a strong suspicion that a romantic relationship between them, even
without the presence of this other girl, would not work, could not work;
he is simply too flaky to be a steady boyfriend. "We'll always be great
friends," he says, reading her mind, and she smiles, holding his hand. He
doesn't ask her to dance, knows that she gets self-conscious dancing to fast
tunes. They just sit there, returning to old roles, Roger confiding some-

thing about his girlfriend, Melinda gossiping about several couples on the dance floor. They talk so long they lose track of time. Nearly three hours have passed. Melinda needs to use the bathroom. Beverly teachers are acting as monitors inside, seeing to it that kids don't use drugs in the stalls. Still, people are finding ways to get coke and booze into the banquet hall. A little less than half the kids whom she sees have brought blow. Others have flasks and small bottles. One girl, visibly drunk, throws up inside the bathroom, and a couple of teachers help her outside the prom doors. She will not be allowed back inside. At twelve thirty, Melinda, Roger, and the two other couples leave. They tell the limo driver that they want him to stop at 7-Eleven. The driver stonily nods his head. With the driver's back turned, Melinda and Cecilia make funny faces at him. Someone says, "Knock it off, Melinda."

"Fuck the driver," snarls Melinda. "He's not our mother."

At 7-Eleven, Cecilia's boyfriend buys a large bottle of rum for everyone and a few six-packs of Cola. If the driver notices the liquor he does not say so. Going to Vertigo is definitely out now. It is one A.M., too late for any serious clubbing to begin. They have the driver bring them instead to Cecilia's sister's apartment in Santa Monica and tell him that he can leave. "I'm glad that geek is gone," says Cecilia, watching the limo pull away.

"*Totally,*" says Melinda.

Freed, they go inside and have their party. Cecilia's sister is out of town. The boys take a full-length dressing mirror off the wall, and spread their coke upon it. All told, they have four grams to do. No one has seen this much blow for a long while. Melinda wants to get some Polaroids. She snaps pictures of Cecilia holding a straw in her hand, and Roger positioning himself over the mirror that lies on the floor. Nothing that Melinda can show her parents, so she'll put the Polaroids into her private collection. Everyone talks and dances for a while. At some point, Melinda gets a straw, bends down to the mirror, and does a few lines herself, wiggling her nose. By three A.M., she feels shredded. It's been a long night, but a good night, she tells Roger. They don't stop until five A.M. Then the boys put the dressing mirror back onto the wall and everyone goes home.

———

Andy takes his friend Sandra to dinner in Brentwood as the prom goes on at the Beverly Hilton.

"Missing it?" she asks as they work on their third margarita.

"Blowing the fucking prom off was the best thing I ever did," he says, licking the salt from the glass's edge. "I've got to get myself a new ID. I screwed up my age on this. It says I'm twenty-three. No way I look twenty-three. Good thing this guy went for it."

"Let's have one more," she suggests.

After dinner, he takes her on a drive across town, along the beach, finally ending up at the Santa Monica airport.

"What are we doing?" she demands.

"You'll see."

In a minute, they've come to a small plane, already warming up, his father in the pilot seat.

"I can't believe it," she says. "We're going on it?"

In five minutes, they're flying over the ocean, looking down on the lights of the coastline from the back seat of the Piper that his father has rented. "I didn't know your father could fly," she says.

"I didn't either until a couple weeks ago. He's been taking lessons for three years. He just got his license six months ago."

"You'll have one of these planes when you become a big rock star."

"Nah, we kind of broke up the band. It wasn't any good. We weren't practicing, we were all flaking. It was fun, but I don't think I need it. I've kind of decided I'm gonna try to burn in college, and do real hot. *Look at that.*" He points at the glistening Los Angeles downtown area, behind them.

"So hot," she says.

"I should have done more surprise stuff in school, you know?" he says. "It's a lot more fun doing surprise things. Beverly was just too intense."

Hillary goes to a play in Westwood with Jeremy on prom night. Kelly and Kurt stay at her house to watch a rented movie. Steven and Vickie sit in a mild funk at the prom, aware that their relationship is over at the end of the evening, Steven furtively glancing at Laura, who is slow-dancing cheek to cheek with her date, a chunky football player who, Steven remembers, talked lustfully about her at one of the Beer-Bong Madness parties. Will she let this guy have a little fun afterwards? No, no, no; can't think those kind of things; it'll just drive him crazy.

At midnight, he leaves with Vickie for the hotel suite that her father booked for them weeks ago. Their friends arrive about one. Three couples sit on the bed, watching the hotel's cable television and doing some coke that someone's brother gave him as an early graduation present. "Having a good time?" Vickie asks him.

He feels so sorry for her. She looks pathetic, so anxious to please, so heartbroken. He suggests they take a walk. "What about everybody else?" she asks.

"They'll still be here when we get back, believe me," he says. "They still have a couple of grams left. They won't be leaving until they do them."

They walk out of the room, and take the elevator down to the pool. They sit on the diving board. "I've been an asshole," he says. "I should have told you earlier about a lot of things."

"I *knew*," she says, "but I was feeling so good being with you that I just pretended to myself that everything would be perfect, even though I knew it wasn't. Do you know what I mean?"

"Uh-huh."

"Are you going to start going out with Laura?"

"I think so."

"Do you love her?"

"In a way, but I don't really know. Do you like Rick?"

"Yeah." She looks away, sounds uncomfortable admitting this. "His high school is an awesome place. Have you seen it?"

He nods. "You can see the beach right from the school."

"I didn't know that," she murmurs, "until he showed me. It's so cool."

"You want to just sit here for a while and have drinks?"

"That'd be nice."

"We never talked enough."

"I know."

They talk for an hour and then go back to the room. Everyone is gone.

———

Paul calls Roxanne at her grandparents' in New York, then picks up his date and goes to the prom. He spends a large portion of the evening talking to Tony, who has come with one of the class beauties. "Hey, dudes, we got to do some serious partying after this," Tony tells a group of people.

His friend will always be a star, Paul realizes. He lets his eyes dance upon Gregg Silver and Leslie Paul. To whom do they turn in bad times? What would they say to him if they knew of his real life? Of Tony's? His date asks him about getting another glass of punch. He says, "Sure," in a voice so nervous and constricted that he needs to clear his throat once, twice, to get the words out. *"Sure, I'll get it."* He always feels conscious of sucking in his breath at class functions, as if his entire body were on guard against moving a wrong muscle, or making a stupid gesture. His tuxedo shirt is soaked with sweat. What is *Roxanne* doing? When the night ends at two thirty A.M., he goes to a pay phone and calls her.

JUNE

Monday, June 2. A hiker found the body, a young male Caucasian, in the brush alongside a remote water plant, in Malibu. Nearby lay a gun with one bullet expended. The sheriff's office called it a "self-inflicted gunshot wound." Then an officer informed the parents of eighteen-year-old Keith Van Leeuwen, a Beverly Hills High School senior and a straight-A student, of their son's death.

The news travels slowly tonight. Greg Seton, one of Keith Van Leeuwen's close friends and a teammate on Beverly's Academic Decathlon squad, gets a phone call. His girlfriend, Nazy Zargarpour, tells him that he should come over to her house immediately: Something bad has happened; she doesn't know what; she just wants him to get over there. He thinks that he knows what has happened. Minutes before her call, the thought crossed his mind that Keith was dead. If you were to die at all, Keith had once philosophized, best that it happened while you were in your prime so that you didn't need to watch yourself go downhill the rest of your life. "There is no reason to put up with a life if you don't like it," he told Greg. When Greg arrives at Nazy's house, they call a kid who says that the police found Keith's body at the beach. Nazy cries. "I kind of think there was a little cowardice in what he did," Greg says later. "A little spite and sadness in that kind of act. That made me disappointed and mad. But another part of me thinks of all the pain he must have been feeling. . . .

"He might have been a bit lonely. He held a lot in. He was, at the same time, very comforting to others. He would talk and help anyone who came to him. And he was very proud. His father told me that he never made noise when he cried."

At the senior assembly that week, school officials spend forty-five minutes talking about Keith's death. Melinda still doesn't know how it happened. The latest false rumor to go around is that Keith said goodbye to his best friend, overdosed, and drowned himself. Melinda has heard nothing about a gun. On the stage, school officials carefully avoid any discussion of the suicide's particulars. A vice-principal calls for a moment of silence. The principal stands and says, ". . . We're very saddened by this. . . ." A psychologist comes to the rostrum and urges the students to "listen when unhappy people say something to you," adding that counseling will be available for those students needing to discuss their grief and confusion. The hum of the bored rises in the auditorium. "They always say the same thing," Melinda complains. She wants to hear this psychologist anyway. She never had more than a couple of words with Keith, always regarded him as a quiet, tall, skinny loner. She thinks it was dumb what he did. Straight A's or not, he hadn't seen the big picture. If he hated school or his life, he should have realized that everything would be changing in three months when he enrolled at Stanford. The psychologist says something more about remaining alert to a friend's warning signals. Melinda can almost mouth the words coming from the speakers. Around her, people have stopped listening. One kid listens to music on his headphones. Somebody else is giggling loudly and swatting one of his buddies. Melinda turns around and tells him to shut up. The kid pays no attention. "We must listen to each other . . . ," the psychologist is saying.

Randy doodles as the psychologist talks. "*Babble, babble, babble,*" he says to Paul, who would just as soon have the principal and this psychologist wrap it up. All this talk about future precautions cheapens Keith's memory, he thinks, institutionalizing the suicide as if it were another unfortunate health problem, like the Asian flu. Tony, looking shaken, has his eyes fixed on a *Los Angeles Times* sports section. He doesn't even want to glance at the psychologist. "Some people just seem doomed, you know?" Tony whispers.

"Nobody is doomed," Paul says to his friend. Paul doesn't want Tony talking about being doomed. He feels like he should say something else. "Being doomed is a bunch of shit," he tells him.

Andy, Kelly, and Hillary wish they had spoken to the dead boy a couple of times. They ask their friends what he was like. Their friends don't know. One of Kelly's friends remembers Keith always having the right answers to math problems in fifth grade, then says she isn't sure if that was Keith or another Brain.

It is surprising to see how quickly the town and school put The Incident, as many people around here have taken to calling it, behind them. The *Beverly Hills Courier* keeps The Incident off its front page. After the senior assembly, the high school administration does not mention the suicide again. The Beverly officials are doing the prudent thing, authorities around here contend. Perhaps . . . but there also seems to be a collective amnesia at work. "Everyone wants to forget about it, so it doesn't ruin the school year," Paul says.

———

Paul, Roxanne, Tony, Randy, and some freshman girl whom Randy has asked along, go to a Dodger game. Randy and his date spend most of the time making out. Roxanne makes paper airplanes out of pages from a Dodger souvenir book, and Paul and Tony flick the planes in the direction of the field. One lands on the dugout. Roxanne applauds. There seems nothing better to do. The Dodgers are losing again.

"You think you'll ever marry her or anything?" Tony asks him when they are alone in a hot dog line.

"She's just a friend, dude. I don't know what will happen. What makes you ask me that?"

"I don't know. You seem into her."

"Whatever."

"Do you sleep with her?"

"Yeah."

"What does she use?"

"Dude, *why* are you asking all this?"

Tony shrugs. "Okay, don't tell me."

"Oh, fuck. She uses the pill, okay?"

Slopping mustard and relish on some dogs, Paul sees an opportunity. "I'd like to ask you *one* thing now," he says.

"Yeah?"

"*You* protected?"

Tony does not take his eyes off the mustard jar.

"I'm not trying to hassle you, Tony. I just think about it. Okay?"

"No questions," says Tony. "All right? I thought we talked about this."

"Okay."

"I know you're just being a friend. But it's impossible right now."

"All right. Hey, the Dodgers suck, huh?"

———

Andy has dinner with his father, who called earlier that day to ask if he might like to come over to his condo to shoot some pool and have a little barbecue. The last time his father invited him over for dinner was three years ago, when his mother and housekeeper had both been ill. Father and son cooked Stouffer's Welsh Rarebit in the microwave that night, washed it down with root beer, and Andy went home after a game of eight-ball. "Thanks for the plane ride again," Andy says. "Sandra loved it. It blew the prom right away."

His father, standing over the barbecue, moves some charcoal with a fork. He says hoarsely, "Terrific."

"So what's been going on, Dad?"

"SOS. Same old shit. Just trying to survive out there. Same thing everybody's trying to do."

"You okay, Dad?"

"Sure."

Andy finds himself staring at his father's receding hairline. When will his own hair go? He has lost a few strands in the shower lately. Growing old must be a bummer. "When Uncle Phil was out here, you seemed a little upset."

"Not really."

"That girl didn't upset you, did she?"

"Which one?"

He has to stop himself from saying, The One Who Dumped You. "The one you're not seeing anymore."

"Pal, women aren't the easiest thing to talk about with your own son." His father sprinkles some tenderizer on the sizzling steaks. "Somebody told me they say this shit has carcinogens in it, but I think it makes steak taste good." He sprinkles on a little more. "Hell, I'm not going to be around forever. I'll enjoy my steak while I can."

"Uncle Phil was right, Dad. She was just a bimbo."

His father waves a hand to indicate that he should be quiet. "I'm not wounded, pal. It just threw your old man for a loop for a while. There are other fish out there."

"You're right, Dad."

"Those things come and go anyway. *Women.* They are in and out. Don't worry about me."

"Dad, I'm not. We're just talking."

"Okay. Get the Lo-Cal dressing out of the fridge, will you?"

"Dad, the *meat.*"

The steaks are caught in an inferno.

His father turns over the steaks. "Is it strange for you?"

"What?"

"I don't know. Everything."

"Dad, you better get those steaks."

His father tosses the black meat onto a platter.

"Those steaks look *shredded*, Dad. You need a housekeeper or something."

"Stacey could really cook."

"Who's that?"

His father twists his fork. "The bimbo."

"You'll meet somebody, Dad. Everything changes back and forth. Things get bad, then they get good again. You shouldn't think like you made some big mistake. Nothing goes forever."

Nothing goes forever. Andy's father never replies to that. There seems to be some shared resignation between father and son: Nothing has worked; nothing goes forever.

———

June 18. A school year, like life, seldom ends in crescendos. The final week for the Beverly class of 1986 begins amid the familiar, even monotonous rhythms of day-to-day life unabated. For the most part, June is like May, which was like April and March.

Kelly continues baby-sitting Timmy, sleeping with young Kurt, ingesting hallucinogenic mushrooms, lunching with friends at Chin Chin's, and, afterwards, wondering if they think less of her because she will be going to a junior college. She calls her mother's hotel in Salt Lake City and leaves messages with the desk clerk.

Day-to-day routines.

Unabated.

"My senior year has been the same as my junior year," she says.

No crescendos.

"I thought it might be different, but I don't know why I thought that — it hasn't been."

———

Hillary has felt her life in flux every day for the last month. On some evenings, her brother, trapped in the den with nowhere to go, gets so morose and foul that everyone else vacates the room. Inexplicably, on other evenings, he will cheerfully announce that he has made dinner for everyone — a superb spaghetti one night, a rib roast the next. Hillary worries he might be schizoid. Occasionally, his good mood will be interrupted by questions from Hillary's mother — "I don't mean to press you on this, sweetheart, but what were you thinking of doing with your time? Maybe a job?" — and, in the time it takes a light switch to work, his smile will go off, his eyes will cloud over once more, and Hillary will know that they are all in for trouble; know that her brother will be swearing at them in a few seconds, that her mother will tell him to be quiet, that Harry's hand will knot with tension around his fork. She keeps an eye on Harry in these moments, gauging each of the smoldering, lip-curled glances that he flashes at her mom as if she were somehow responsible for her son's obnoxiousness. They have had more arguments in their bedroom, behind closed doors, Harry screaming, "I can't take him much longer like this," pounding his fists so hard against the wall that Hillary ran to the door to listen. Her mother answered in a soothing voice, said something that Hillary couldn't quite make out but which must have assuaged Harry's anger, for he apologized immediately and said, yes, he'd try to get through this thing; yes, she was right about needing patience, but, god-dammit, *the kid gets on his nerves.*

As much as possible during the weekends now, Harry and her mom steer clear of the den where Hillary's brother has set up camp. Harry has taken up gardening and listening to ball games on a transistor that he leaves in the dirt as he weeds and sprays his plot of azaleas, her mom alongside him, the two adults on their haunches, digging into the soil and teasingly bumping into each other, sprinkling dirt on each other's grubby sweatshirts, laughing, finally plopping onto the grass to talk, her mom's legs propped upon his. They are a good pair, Hillary realizes. With time, she has begun to understand Harry's appeal — a warm and reasonably secure, attractive, and stable man with no serious hang-ups. There aren't many of them around, as her mom always says. She sees the two of them together for the long haul — if not marriage, then some indefinite live-in arrangement. The only thing that could stop it, she senses, would be unbearable problems from her brother, a distinct possibility given the regularity with which he has been flipping out at the dinner table lately. Outside, she sees her mother, squealing and flipping dirt on Harry's jeans. No doubt about it, Mom's in love. Weird. She never quite imagined it happening. Someone must speak to her brother.

Sunday morning. The digital clock-radio by her bed reads 5:12. Noise. Noise is waking her up. Loud shouts coming from . . . somewhere. Where? Groggily, instinctively, she reaches to flick off her stereo. It's not on. A television. The television is on. Downstairs. *Fuck.* Her brother. Who else could it be but the asshole? She manages to roll out of bed, and trips over her tennis shoes. She can hear the television getting louder. One symptom of her brother's problems has been the odd hours at which he has been arising, one day at noon, another at three in the morning, the next at two in the afternoon. Swearing loudly, she throws on a robe and stumbles downstairs to find him drinking a glass of orange juice in the dark, a bag of Doritos at his feet. "What the fuck are you doing, Matt?"

He looks at her and turns back to the TV. "Want a chip? I already finished the dip or I'd offer you some."

She shuts off the television.

"*Why did you do that?*" he demands.

"Because you're waking up everyone."

"I'll lower it. Is that okay, princess?" He angrily flicks it back on. A Western with John Wayne. He munches on a tortilla chip. "Go back to bed, Hillary, if you're going to give me that too-disgusted-for-words look."

"I think that you really want to believe everyone is against you."

"Bullshit."

"I'm pissed off you're acting like such an asshole. But I'm not against you."

"Good for you, Joan of Arc. Nighty-night. Run off to wet dream land."

"Why are you acting like such a prick?"

He hides his head. Is he crying? She hasn't seen him cry since he was twelve or thirteen and he ran smack into a car door on the street while playing touch football and lost a tooth. He won't look up. "Things are fucked. Did I tell you I got an F in my American lit course? I'm on probation."

"No."

"I'm not any good at school."

"You will be. You'll work at it."

"Mom must think I'm a complete asshole. And Harry, too. Fuck him. He's not Dad."

"Harry isn't so bad, Matt. And this might sound weird, but I think Mom loves him. We gotta stick by Mom."

"What does that got to do with anything?"

"She's happy with him. You have to start seeing stuff like that, Matt. You're too sunk into yourself right now. I know things are bad for you, but they won't always be, and Mom and him are trying to make it work. Don't always be screaming at them."

"And you think I'm some evil thing that is hurting them?"

"It doesn't help. That's all I'm saying."

He lifts his head, stares at John Wayne. "And like I'm scuz?"

"Stop it, Matt. I'm just kind of concerned for Mom."

"Just say it: You think I'm an asshole."

"Yeah, a little." She tries to buffer this. "I know it's been hard. But, yeah, a little. If you could, just lighten up."

He takes a deep breath, looks at John Wayne punching out some guy in a bar. "The dude is unreal, huh? Look at that other chump falling all over the place."

"Matt, did you hear me?"

Her brother smiles as John Wayne and the other guy go sailing through barroom doors into the street. "John Wayne looks like he needed a good aerobics program," her brother says. "He must of liked malt liquor." Standing, he pantomimes Wayne's walk, his eyes never leaving the television, "Yup, ma'am, I heard you," he drawls.

In the morning, Harry finds her in the kitchen. "I don't know how to ask you this, but do you think you and your brother might come to dinner with us tonight?" he asks. "Maybe it is a silly idea, but I'd like to try. What do you think?"

She feels sorry for him. "No, no, it's not a bad idea. Matt will be fine. He isn't freaking anymore, I don't think. It has just been a bizarre time for him, with school being so hard this year. He's a fun person. Really. You'll see. He'll be fine."

But if they're going to dinner, she wants to bring someone so that she won't have to watch her mom and Harry cooing all night. She makes a call, and, afterwards, tells her mom that Jeremy will be going with them.

"I thought you weren't going out with him?"

"I'm not, he's just coming to dinner with us."

"I never understand this."

"Mom, I don't always understand you either, so let's get off that, okay?"

"I still don't know."

A husky voice from the den interrupts them. "Hey, I think it's fine he's coming," Harry shouts. "I want to meet this guy. The more, the merrier. It'll be more fun for Hillary. She doesn't want to stare at us smooching all night."

"Right," laughs Hillary, a little surprised that Harry has become so attuned to her thoughts.

"Okay," says her mom. And then in a whisper: "But I'm counting upon you to keep an eye on your brother."

Jeremy arrives at seven, resplendent in a blue sports coat and tan slacks. Her mom introduces him to everyone. Matt sighs theatrically, rolls his eyes. Is her brother going into a funk? Hillary's mother flashes her look. If her brother goes wacky and the evening is a disaster, she'll be the one blamed. Yet, an hour and two drinks later at the restaurant, Hillary and Matt having been permitted to use their fake IDs, everyone is chummy. Jeremy and Harry talk about sports photography. Matt muses to Hillary that he might want to be a roadie for a rock band. Hillary's smiling mom orders appetizers for everyone. "I think," she whispers to her daughter, "that everything is working out nicely."

Even Matt's spirits are high. "Sometimes," he whispers to his sister, "I think this deal with Mom and the golfer might work."

"His name is Harry."

"Okay, let me detox slowly."

———

Melinda has felt restless with all this time to kill in spring semester. At school, liberated from worries about grades, the future Ivy Leaguer has become assertive to the point of rebelliousness during class discussions, deriding her physiology teacher's fundamentalist opposition to abortion so relentlessly that he finally stops calling on her to participate. She doesn't care. She is finished trying to impress him, embarrassed that she compromised her beliefs earlier in the year for the sake of an A in his class. On a fall semester test about reproduction, one of his true-or-false questions had read, "Life begins at conception." Melinda, having heard the teacher rail for weeks that life could begin at *no time but conception*, marked true on her SCAN-TRON computer answer sheet, then false to an accompanying query: "True or False: Life begins at birth." She thought that the answers were nonsense, but she wanted an A on the exam and so, as usual, she had given the teacher what he wanted, held back her disgust even when one question took on a stridently ideological slant: "True or False: If your mother had an abortion while she was pregnant with you, you would be here today." In fall discussions about abortion and birth control, she muted her opposition to his viewpoint, the deception wearing upon her as much as studying. Now, with a vengeance, she is doing what she wants. She doesn't study for her final exam in physiology or any other class, spends the night before the physiology final at a party her mom is hosting. It will be fine, she tells herself. Most of the questions will doubtless have been asked on earlier tests. She awakens the next morning with a stomachache and arrives at the exam to discover that most of the two hundred questions are about digestion, a study unit that she missed while touring Eastern colleges in the fall. She gets a D. Her physiology teacher will be able to give her, at best, a B for the course. "Maybe I should have studied," she says. "But the only reason to do it was to keep my grade point average high enough to get honors at graduation, and I said, 'Fuck it.' I didn't want to do it. And I don't feel bad now, because I'm *glad* I didn't do it. I'm glad I didn't study for *any* of the exams. Maybe I'll do all right on the rest of them. Maybe I won't. It doesn't matter. I'm into college. I'll still be close for honors. I may get them. Whatever, I'm tired of the bullshit . . . and now that nothing counts really — not grades or what the teachers think of you — I can do what I want. And what I want to do is relax. I'm totally burnt on Beverly."

The lack of importance of grades now means that she has virtually no interest in learning. Melinda admits to having trouble functioning without the incentive of grades. "I don't read as much as I should," she says. "I know I don't. I will when it counts." It will count in college, when there will be vital A's to earn again.

———

While Melinda sees friends and watches television on the nights before her meaningless finals, Andy labors over books and review problems. His hard work yields three A's and one B, his finest report card ever, including an A on a final exam in a history course that he views as his toughest class of the semester. The exam grades, though meaningless insofar as they do not impact on his college admissions, encourage him. A couple of kids, a few rows over, brag that they didn't study and don't care about receiving B's. "I have my college, this is all crap," says one of them, then looks at Andy and laughs. "That A isn't changing *your* destination, dude."

Andy gives him the finger. *Adios.*

———

Paul gets his copy of *The Watchtower*, the school yearbook. There seem to be more yearbook advertisements than ever before, ads for everything — tutors, fitness instructors, bikini shops, and a facial surgery office. Paul's old friend Joey pats him on the back and shouts, "I want you to sign mine, dude," thrusting his yearbook into Paul's hands, opened to a page with Paul's senior picture. Paul writes, "It's been great knowing you, dude, since we were little kids. . . . Let's do some serious partying this summer. I'm sure you're stoked to think of three months of vacation before college. I know I am. Thanks for being such a good bud . . . — Paul." He thinks of adding a P.S. to apologize for avoiding him most of the year, then decides against it; a yearbook isn't the place to bare your soul. People read these stupid inscriptions forever. He knows that everybody passes around the yearbooks to get a few affectionate remembrances and a lot of jokes, so he writes, "P.S.," in Joey's book, and sketches their old math teacher, a guy with a potbelly whose shirt was always coming out of his pants, exposing his belly button and the top of his boxer shorts. Next to the sketch, Paul writes, "Aren't you glad this dude is history? *We're outta here.* See you this summer." He looks over his work admiringly, and draws the belly button a little bigger. *Yeah.* In truth, when he thinks about it, he doesn't feel very guilty about anything; he had some of his own problems to work out this year and if Joey fell between the cracks, well — it might sound harsh — but everybody has to make it on his own. It's been a hard year for everyone. No sense in rolling around in guilt. He'll do his best to be a good friend now, has decided to take Joey to a few Dodger games with Roxanne and Tony and try to make up for time lost. Focus on the hot times ahead, he tells himself. He rounds out the belly button a little more.

At lunch, on the Third-Floor Patio, he gives his book to Tony. The inscription that comes back says, "To a great friend, with hopes for your great future. . . . Have fun this summer. Thanks for all your help and friendship throughout the years — Tony."

Kind of formal, Paul thinks. Typical of Tony, though, to play it safe, slightly above it all; no "dudes" in any of his inscriptions. On the other hand, Paul has written a lengthy and gushing tribute in Tony's book. Chagrined, he hands Tony his book back and says, "I never know what kind of shit to write. I'm not very good at it."

Tony smiles. "Pretty good yearbook," he says. "I think there are a lot of funny pictures in it."

Paul nods, flipping through the pages, stopping at a shot of a smiling boy on a skateboard. "Did you see this picture of Keith Van Leeuwen?"

Tony shakes his head. Paul can see that he doesn't want to talk about the picture. But no one, Paul notices through the rest of the day, can keep his eyes off it. There it is, on page fifty-four, not a small senior photo but a large candid shot, prominently displayed, of Keith, dark hair matted down, on his skateboard in a classroom, flashing a broad smile, wearing a T-shirt with an alligator on it, one hand holding what looks to be a bagel or donut, the other giving a mock salute. Then Paul stumbles upon another picture, on page eighty-five, of Keith with two girls, one of whom has a friendly arm around him. Keith has given the camera a small smile. His dark eyes are opened wide. Paul likes the way Keith looks, happy and impish, feels glad that the yearbook went into production before the suicide, since it gave the school administration no chance to consider yanking the photos. He knows that no one wants to talk about them, but he can't help himself. "I think these are pretty cool pictures of Keith," he says to one of the dead boy's friends. "Maybe I shouldn't have said that, but I'm glad they're in here."

"Yeah," says the other boy, surprising Paul. "It's good to remember him that way. I like that salute. That was hot."

Paul wanders around, getting more yearbook inscriptions. The popular kids write the most brazen things, he thinks, the stars knowing, as they've known all along, that they can say or write anything at Beverly with impunity. Most of the Senior Wills, printed in the special Senior Edition of the yearbook, are cryptic and coded messages of affection meant to be understood by a private few; but the stars do not hide behind initials and incomprehensibly abbreviated phrases, proudly detailing dreams, achievements, and loves. Gregg Silver, en route to Pitzer College, leaves his girlfriend, Leslie Paul, "all the happiness and love in the world, always and forever." Silver has been named Beverly's Athlete of the Year. Paul feels glad to be getting out of here with a diploma. When will he next see the studs? In a mall? At the ten-year reunion? Will they remember him? In ten years, will they hope that he remembers them? He'd like to turn the tables on them, be the stud when that time rolls around, knows he shouldn't be so competitive, can't help it.

Steven daydreams during the senior assembly, an event mostly geared toward providing students with early instructions for Wednesday's graduation ceremony. Laura, sitting next to him, writes a letter to her cousin in New York, trying to persuade her to come to Beverly Hills this summer. "I'm telling her that you'll introduce her to all your cute friends," she says to him, rubbing his knee. In the last few days, less aware of Vickie's shadow, they have begun holding hands and kissing in public.

"If she is too cute, maybe I'll introduce her to me," he jokes.

"Kinky," she laughs, shifting in her seat to get closer to him, squeezing his arm.

They're squirming to get comfortable in these new girlfriend and boyfriend personas, he senses, trying to find the right rhythms for a romance, alternately fondling and teasing each other, all the while struggling to keep the old spontaneity and irreverence alive. It has not been as easy as he had imagined when he climbed into her bed. Whoever said you could not go back had it only half-right: Sometimes, bound by the past, you couldn't go forward. He loves her, but he feels them straining to make this work — the jokes between them suddenly a tad flat, the conversation a note off. He recognizes, for the first time, the possibility of failure. He tells himself that he must play it out, that, even if it fails, he will be richer for the experience. Isn't that what you're supposed to say? He will always have her as a friend. His fingers stroke her palm. She squeezes them gently.

He awakens Tuesday morning to news on his clock-radio: Three people died yesterday at Van Cleef & Arpels on Rodeo during a bungled robbery and subsequent siege. The robber, a twenty-two-year-old fugitive from Nevada, murdered a security guard and a saleswoman, execution style, and then the police mistakenly killed Van Cleef's store manager when the gunman brought him and two other hostages out of the store, late at night, in an escape attempt. The siege lasted a total of thirteen and a half hours, the drama unfolding along the same street that Steven has driven for months. He feels shaken, doesn't understand why. He tells Laura over the phone, "I went in there with my mom a few times. It is scary when you think about it. It *really* happened here. It's so bizarre. I don't think I want to drive by it, if that's okay."

He could stand a dose of amusement. He gets off the phone and watches a tape of one of the school's cable television shows. It is a spoof of a drug bust. A suspected drug dealer, played by Gregg Silver, has been arrested, and a cop is yelling at him, "*You're a cancer on our society.*" Steven laughs. Everyone who sees this, he realizes, will know that the inspiration for the line came from the principal. Maybe the guy will find himself a new line now. *High school:* He can't describe how happy he feels to be getting out.

———

Melinda watches the drug bust comedy, too. She has to rush this morning to get to graduation rehearsal. Her grades have come in for the meaningless spring term: five A's and the one B, in physiology. She will receive honors at graduation. On the TV, the cop snarls at Gregg Silver, *"You're a cancer on our society."* Silver, feigning puzzlement, shakes his head and says, "No, I'm a *Gemini.*" Melinda laughs and races for her car. She hopes they'll be spared the antidrug clichés at graduation, wants an upbeat ceremony. Some wine or booze during the speeches would be nice. Must remember to check if somebody can sneak some in. In twenty-four hours, it will all be over.

———

At graduation rehearsal, the principal lays down the law to the assemblage of seniors. "We don't want random cheering or noise during the ceremony . . . ," he says. "You will be given a chance to show your exuberance at the appropriate point." That point will come, he adds, when he formally introduces the class to the audience. There will even be a cue. "I will say," the principal tells them, " *'And now I present to you the graduating class of 1986,'* and you can all then stand and cheer and demonstrate your enthusiasm." The principal looks over his notes. "And you should know that to ensure an orderly graduation, there will be teachers seated in the middle of all your rows." There will be no wine, Melinda thinks to herself. The principal remembers one last thing. "And no wild displays when you are handed your diplomas."

———

On the night before graduation, Paul sits in his bedroom, with Tony and Randy, watching a tape of an old "Twilight Zone" in which a guy wants to die but can't because he took a witch's potion five thousand years ago, when he thought that he wanted to live forever. *"Bummer,"* says Randy. The Five-Thousand-Year-Old Man doesn't get diseases and never looks a day older than a handsome and distinguishedly graying forty-five. The guy has known Plato personally and Julius Caesar and Jesus Christ and Genghis Khan and Bach and Alexander the Great and Napoleon, and he commanded battalions in the Revolutionary War and the Civil War, and he has had about a thousand mortal wives, each of whom, of course, died at some point along the way, leaving him no choice but to find a new woman. Randy brightens at this last piece of information. "Very cool," he says, petting Bones, who laps up Randy's beer from a mug. " 'Cause that means he's always getting that young wool. Like even if he was married to some fifty-year-old bitch, he knows that he is going to get one of those hot college babes sometime again, right?" He looks for confirmation of this to Tony, who shrugs and drinks his Heineken. *I'm not sure,* says Tony. *Maybe. Let me watch the show.* Tony has dropped the macho act when the subject of babes comes up, Paul notices; wonders in the next instant if this is some kind of concession from his friend not to be a phony in his presence. Must make Tony a little nervous to drop the act, he thinks, to have his defenses down like that, especially around Randy, who's always trying to figure out who at Beverly is gay or bisexual. Hell, Randy lives in awe of Tony, would never be able to guess in a thousand years. *Would he?* Paul has to tell himself to stop being so paranoid. If the incident with the drug dealer should have taught him anything, it's that he gets unnerved too easily.

"Wouldn't you want a twenty-year-old chick if you were forty-five?" Randy persists. "*C'mon*, Tony, you *know* you would."

Tony stares at the screen.

"*C'mon.*"

Paul can't take Tony's silence. "Yeah, of course," he shouts at Randy. "Anybody would, dude. That is a fucking stupid question."

Bones finishes lapping up Randy's Heineken. Tony pets him, and then yanks away his hand, grimacing. "Burrs," explains Paul apologetically. He pulls Bones over to him, wipes some beer off the dog's nose, and tries burying his head in the sparse fur, closing his eyes and rubbing Bones's throat, which is the only place, the vet says, where the dog doesn't feel pain. He rubs as hard as he can, has always done this when feeling nervous, wonders whether he has made his best friend's position more precarious by having confronted him. How many Randys were walking around, ready to spill their guts if they ever suspected?

"I think the dude should definitely give her the beef injection," says Randy. The Five-Thousand-Year-Old Man, now a university professor, wants to marry a college coed. The girl's frantic father objects, having seen the Five-Thousand-Year-Old Man's face in an 1861 Civil War photograph of Union soldiers. Randy laughs. "Five thousand years old and the guy still gets a vitamin-fortified hard-on. *Classic.* Look at that chick, Paul. *Tasty,* huh, Tony?"

"Yeah," says Tony, not looking away from the screen. "Tasty."

Paul glances at him. You can't always be rattling people's cages, he's begun to feel. Randy won't shut up about the college coed on the screen. Paul punches him gently in the arm and says, laughing, "I wouldn't push her out of the sack either."

The Five-Thousand-Year-Old Man gets shot and dies. Randy stands, says he has to split. "Are we going to the beach Saturday?" he asks. "You gonna let us see you in a bathing suit this summer, Paul?"

"If you stop being such a prick, maybe."

"Hey, I was just asking if you can go," Randy protests, grinning.

Paul opens another Heineken, takes a swig. "Yeah, well, maybe. I don't know yet." Bones drools on his socks. Randy is blabbering about some hot group they should check out at the Roxy. The kid flips him a couple of bucks, his share of the six-dollar six-pack, and asks him if he might want to go to a movie on Friday. Paul says, yeah, probably. Loyalty counts. He might not like hanging around Randy all the time, but he can't escape the feeling that Randy is meant to be around them, that, for all the sniping they do at each other, they're a threesome. The world is a bad-ass place. A guy better hold on to whatever real friends he's got. Let 'em have their fucking masks.

Randy walks out the door, humming the "Twilight Zone" theme song. Tony listens to his car pull away, then stands, too. "This gets a little bizarre sometimes," he says.

"What?"

"You know."

Paul rubs Bones's throat. "No. It'll be fine. Really."

"I don't know."

"Don't worry."

Tony strokes Bones's head. The dog yelps. Too much pain there. "What a bizarre year," Tony says softly. "I don't even feel like we're in high school anymore."

"We're not," says Paul. "Not come tomorrow." He reaches down and hugs Bones. "We're free. Aren't we Bones? *Aren't we?*"

Bones stares at a rerun of "The Brady Bunch."

Tony gives the dog his beer mug.

———

Hillary helps Harry make a chef's salad. Her mom has gone to a charity auxiliary meeting, so Harry is on his own for dinner.

"I should have learned how to do this stuff years ago," he moans, feebly trying to slice egg yolks, cutting his index finger.

"Let me do this," she insists.

"No, no. You've got homework."

"Harry, it's graduation tomorrow. I'm finished. Put a Band-Aid on your finger. Go in the den and turn on the TV or something."

Harry obeys, leaving the room just like her father would. *Men:* They have so much to learn. Women's liberation hasn't changed a goddamn thing. She sure as hell won't be slicing eggs for any man twenty years from now, she tells herself. Harry shouts from the den: Can he help her with anything? He's sweet enough. Mom has what she wants.

"No thanks, you just watch TV," she says. She brings in his salad on a tray, with a tall glass of iced tea. He smiles and opens his hand to reveal a heart-shaped diamond necklace.

"For you," he says tentatively. "For graduation."

She kisses him primly on the cheek. She never knows what to say these days.

Andy goes over to Jason's house. He wasn't supposed to go anywhere on graduation eve, but his mom has a date, and besides, there weren't any beers in the house. Jason takes a couple of Buds out of his tiny bedroom refrigerator and locks his door.

"What kind of job do you have for the summer?" Jason asks him.

"Nothing yet. I don't know if I'm gonna work."

"You stoked about graduation?"

Andy shrugs. "I don't know. I'm gonna go to Hawaii with my dad for a couple of weeks."

"That's cool."

"Whatever. I figure it's two months until the college ball-busting starts. I wanna party for at least a few weeks."

"I gotta get a job," says Jason.

"I think I need a little rest," says Andy. "I'm gonna have to get my energy up again. I don't know, maybe if I get bored I'll work somewhere. Probably not. I'm burnt."

Wednesday, June 25. Graduation Day. *The Eighty-First Commencement*, reads the grand embossing on the graduation program handed out by ushers. Parents and friends of the graduates are seated on folding chairs on the school's front lawn. Above them, on the lawn's upper tier, sit the graduates. Melinda is hot and irritable. She has worn a long-sleeved dress beneath her black graduation gown and, though it is only nine forty-five A.M., the temperature must already be eighty degrees. She can feel sweat beneath her dress. Let's get this thing going, she thinks. To pass the time, she looks for her parents and two sisters in the audience. God, she's thirsty. Let's get this damn thing over with and get out of here.

The last spectators are arriving. A couple of limousines stop, chauffeurs open doors, and contingents spill out, scrambling for seats. Some parents have brought along professional photographers and small film crews to record the occasion. The band plays "Pomp and Circumstance." A couple of the photographers block the view of spectators who scream at them to get the hell out of the way. One photographer turns around and barks, "Hey, pal, I'm working here. Cool it." A spectator orders him to move or else. The photographer says fuck off, finally moves. Everybody is sweating, squirming, looking toward the rostrum for something to happen. In the back, near the street, a few kids unfurl a professionally made banner, with block letters, two feet high, that says: "DAVID — CONGRATULATIONS. LET'S PARTY, DUDE — THE GANG."

"When is this show gonna move?" one parent wonders aloud. "When will somebody up there say something?" In the next instant, someone does. The music ends, and Doug Chu, senior class president of the fall semester, leads everyone in the Pledge of Allegiance. "Welcome to the graduation of the Beverly Hills High School class of nineteen eighty-six," he says. ". . . The end has arrived." Some of his classmates, not heeding the principal's warning, applaud and squeal. The student speeches begin. A girl proclaims, ". . . One path is to despair and hopelessness and the other to extinction. . . . We are growing up in a fearful and chaotic world. . . . We are reminded that we are living in a dangerous world with dangerous crime in our city. . . ." The last phrase seems to be a reference to the killings at Van Cleef's, and Melinda rolls her eyes. The speech, which follows with allusions to nuclear war, child abuse, Nazi death camp mercy abortions, and Auschwitz New Year's Eve parties, strikes her as inappropriate and sensationalistic. She looks around to gauge the reaction of classmates in her section, many of whom are laughing. Most pay no attention. Paul chews a wad of smokeless tobacco, a graduation gift from Roxanne's younger brother. Hillary works on a broken ruby-red fingernail. Andy sneaks sips of rum out of a miniature bottle, hidden under his robe. Kelly draws hearts and flowers on a graduation card from little Timmy. Steven, who has liked what he has heard of this speech, gives up trying to listen after some kid asks him if he brought any "doobies."

After telling the gathering that "We've laughed, applauded, and mourned together . . . ," the principal formally presents the graduating class of 1986. On his cue, the senior class cheers, and workers release several hundred balloons. The president of the board of education comes to the rostrum, declares that diplomas should be awarded, and, twenty minutes later, graduation has ended. "Dick," a woman in the audience says to her husband, "get the car. *Hurry.*"

Andy feels a slight buzz from the rum. His parents and a few friends stand with him for pictures. "How does it feel?" one of his father's friends keeps shouting at him. "Do you feel any different, hotshot?"

"I feel good," Andy says, grinning wackily. "Are we out of here, or what?" He looks over at the Swim-Gym. "*Sayonara.*"

Hillary's dad has been with Harry and her mom all morning. The three appear to be getting along fine. Hillary's brother has been searching for old friends who can't be found.

"I imagine we should get some pictures," says Hillary's mom.

"Wonderful," says her dad.

"Maybe we should switch off taking them," suggests Harry gently, not looking at her father. Her mom nods. Her dad nods. Harry and her father alternate taking photos, with the other in the pictures. "You are a doll, Daddy," Hillary whispers to him, a few feet away from the others.

Her father kisses her forehead. "Harry seems fine."

Kelly's mother and father give her separate graduation gifts: a watch from her, a ring from him.

"It is actually a little weird leaving," she says to no one in particular. "I never thought I'd get out of this place."

Steven finds himself engulfed by friends who want to have their pictures taken with him. "I've been real fortunate," he tells his dad. "I'm gonna kind of miss Beverly. I have a lot of good memories — good friends and all. I feel like a big fish in a small pond, kind of. It's gonna be scary to lose that feeling."

Laura throws her arms around him from behind. They persuade his mother to take a few pictures of them kissing with their caps and gowns on.

"Let's do an open-mouth," whispers Laura, giggling.

Paul is laughing. His parents want his friends to do nothing more than
smile when they pose with him, but, just before each shot, his friends do
something bizarre — goose each other, stick out tongues, cross their eyes.

"You're going to have nothing to remember your graduation by,"
Paul's mother says sternly, "except a roll of pictures of kids goofing
around. I *hope* that is what you want."

"*Two more pictures,*" orders Paul's dad, hoisting the camera.

Paul and his friends put their arms around each other and smile
demurely for the camera. *Click.*

"That will be a very nice picture," says his mom.

"One more," says his dad.

They smile again. Just before the shot, Paul gooses some kid on
the end. They all goose each other in the next millisecond. One kid
laughs so hard that he drools. *Click.*

"*Dammit,*" says his father. "Oh, that is just *great.* Just *great.*"

"Hey, that one was *perfect,*" Paul says.

The kids untangle. Some run off to find parents. Paul's mom
shouts, "*Wait.*" She wants to get a few pictures of Paul and Tony alone
together. "I want to get the best friends in their caps and gowns," she says.
"You guys will be glad that you have these pictures someday."

Click, click, click.

Tony's parents join everyone.

"A very nice year, wasn't it?" Tony's mother asks Paul's.

"Delightful."

"No hang-ups. Couldn't have been more peaceful."

———

Quickly, after the ceremony ends, Melinda turns in her cap and gown. It
takes a half-hour to find her parents in the mob scene. The temperature
has risen another five degrees. She is sweltering.

"Where is your graduation gown?" her mom demands.

"I turned it in."

"We have no pictures. Go borrow one from someone."

Her father has brought along a Polaroid camera for the occasion.
Melinda doesn't care. She yells at them. "It's too hot and I got this dress
on. I don't *need* pictures with my graduation gown. I want to get going.
I've been looking around for you for a half-hour."

Her parents say, almost simultaneously, "You didn't try to
find us."

"I did so."

"Well, even if you're not going to borrow a robe," her mom says, "we still want some pictures, okay?"

After ten minutes of pictures with her sisters and parents, Melinda insists they leave. "It is just too hot. I want to get lunch. Let's go." Her father puts the camera in its case.

Later, she will try to recall those last moments on the Beverly lawn. "I wasn't really thinking of anything except being hot and hungry," she says. "I know some people are afraid to leave high school, because it is secure and you're living at home. I'm not *thrilled* with leaving home for college in the East, but it's what I was working for. And I'm glad to be gone from Beverly. . . .

"I wonder if high school would have been any different if I'd gone to a school in Ohio, where we moved from before I got in kindergarten. Maybe it is more close-knit there. Maybe not. But here it hasn't been a nice, caring, healthy environment, and I'm lucky that I've had a good home and that I worked hard when it counted. There is no school spirit here. Nobody cares about anyone. The only organized thing for a lot of people were beer-bong parties. So I'm not missing anything being out of high school. When you think of it that way, you're glad it's over. I'm going to the Ivies, and I like to think that I'm more mature and comfortable with myself than I used to be. I got out of here in one piece and I'm pretty secure and so I have a lot to be thankful for. I've got a great college. It will be fun."

Her mom pensively studies all of them, trying to figure out whether there are any possible permutations of siblings and parents that their pictures have missed. "Okay, I'd just like a couple more," she tells them.

"*Mom*." Melinda cannot take it a second longer. "*Dad*."

"All right, we're going to lunch," says her father. "Let's go."

Her mother capitulates, begins walking toward the car.

No crescendos.

"Thank God," says Melinda, who cannot get out of here soon enough. She heads quickly across the immense lawn, once lush everywhere, now sun-scorched in patches, the turf torn up in a few spots where sprinklers never reached. A group of students, still in graduation gowns, toss Frisbees back and forth. One of her classmates poses regally for a private photographer, atop the lawn's upper tier, surrounded by a few of his father's Hollywood friends. Sweat drips off her forehead. She can see the car. Almost there now. On the lawn, under a tree, a few of her classmates have taken asylum in a scarce spot of shade and kicked off their shoes. A boy chugs mineral water from a bottle, and wonders aloud where the party is tonight. She doesn't slow. Almost there now. Her classmates languidly lean back against the tree, their legs stretching over a small oval of grass as verdant and lush as ever, and laugh excitedly over the prospect of holding an impromptu picnic. A girl gets on a boy's shoulders. Parents scurry to take their pictures. The shaded piece of green looks so cool, so tranquil.